sane

Z961810

sane

How I shaped up my mind,
improved my mental strength and found calm

EMMA YOUNG

First published in Great Britain in 2015 by Yellow Kite
An imprint of Hodder & Stoughton
An Hachette UK company

1

A CIP catalogue record for this title
is available from the British Library

Hardback ISBN 978 1 473 61924 1
Trade Paperback ISBN 978 1 473 61925 8
eBook ISBN 978 1 473 61926 5

Typeset by Palimpsest Book Production Ltd, Falkirk, Stirlingshire

Printed and bound by
CPI Group (UK) Ltd, Croydon, CR0 4YY

Hodder & Stoughton policy is to use papers that are natural, renewable and
recyclable products and made from wood grown in sustainable forests.
The logging and manufacturing processes are expected to conform
to the environmental regulations of the country of origin.

Carmelite House
50 Victoria Embankment
London EC4Y 0DZ

www.hodder.co.uk

For everyone who thinks,
'I'm doing OK . . . but not great.'

CONTENTS

I KNEW I HAD A PROBLEM . . .

I knew I had a problem when my work became about me. Researching a feature on the upsides of anger for a science magazine, I found myself taking the opportunity to quiz academic experts on topics that were relevant not to the piece, but to my own life. One well-known researcher even got coaxed into doing an anger-exploration interview on the phone. (When presented with my life situation and the things that made me cross, his conclusion, essentially, was that I should put up and shut up.) After agreeing to be interviewed for another assignment, an American psychologist who has found that 'loving-kindness' meditation can improve relationships with other people and boost psychological wellbeing found herself so enthusiastically interrogated it came across as aggressive. (I winced repeatedly while transcribing the recording of our conversation.)

The thing is, I don't actually have a problem with anger.

And my relationships with my family and friends are pretty good. What I do have is a more general kind of mental weakness, for want of a better word, and a mid-life recognition that if I don't do something about it now, I probably never will.

This year, I turned forty. Over the past twelve months, I've celebrated the fifth anniversary of my happy marriage, and the second and fourth birthdays of my two healthy children. I have a relatively small but solid group of friends, a career I enjoy, as a journalist and writer, and, while I don't think of myself as anything like wealthy, a financial situation that puts me ahead of the vast majority of people on the planet. I have, in short, everything. Except – and here I hesitate, because I'm aware of where this would rank if placed on the spectrum of psychological suffering – except this: my mind is all over the place, and it always has been.

I don't have major depression, bipolar disorder or diagnosable anxiety. But my mental state is volatile, my equanimity faltering in response to sometimes the slightest of forces. I feel my stress levels rise – the tension in my chest, the rush in my blood, the seemingly unstoppable acceleration towards a loss of normal control. I lose my temper with the kids. I get irritable with my husband. I find it difficult to concentrate on work. Yet sometimes, nothing negative happens – *absolutely nothing*, it seems – but still I feel down, and I struggle to get myself back up.

My emotional lows and lack of regulation aren't the only problem. I make diet and exercise plans I don't stick to. I decide this will be the year I finally learn French. (Jakob, my four-year-old, started learning French three months ago.

Already, he knows far more than me.) And I regularly think back over past 'mistakes', and wonder if I'd feel much more positive about life if I'd made different decisions. There's one particular job I turned down when I was twenty-seven, and I *still* think, *why?* I left the *Guardian* to go travelling. What kind of journalist does that? Some time later, I went for a job on the *Observer*; the interviewer looked at my extensive CV and said, 'It seems you're something of a flibbertigibbet . . .' *Yeah*, I often think at 3am, *I've aban-doned so many great opportunities.* And while flibberti-gibbet is one term for me, impulsive would be another. Self-destructive might be a third.

And what about our move to Sheffield, two years ago? I often find myself thinking, *I wish we hadn't done it.* After twenty years in London and then Sydney, I've found it hard to get used to being out of a global city. Actually, I still haven't adapted. I know plenty of people who adore Sheffield, and I do understand why. I don't think they're crazy. It's *my* problem, my fit with the place, and I just can't seem to make it right, as much as I really would like to.

At this point, it would be great if I were able to give you a comprehensive example of my everyday 'mental weakness' to clarify some of the things I'd most like to change. But my life feels like one long example.

Take yesterday.

I'm encouraging (a euphemism if ever I've written one) Jakob to go and get dressed for school. Meanwhile, Lucas is sitting at the kitchen table, arms folded, refusing with all the absolute, immovable determination of a two-year-old to eat his cereal because I absent-mindedly stirred in the banana and yoghurt instead of leaving it on top, as he likes it . . . I'm throwing stuff all over the hall because I can't find their wellies, and it's raining, and it *never* rained in Sydney (not actually true) . . . and now James is saying he'll have to stay at his work flat over in Liverpool tonight, so the work I was planning to get done during bath- and bed-time won't get finished, leaving me likely to miss a deadline for the first time in my life . . . and maybe I should just do as my mother-in-law keeps saying and stop work to focus on my family (but that's just a *crazy* idea) . . . and in frustration with *everything*, I yell at Lucas, 'Eat your breakfast now or go to your room!' It's 7.32am, the day's barely begun and already I feel like I'm going to explode.

Everyday domestic problems – hardly a life-or-death scenario. And nobody benefited from my stressed-out state, least of all my kids, as of course I realise later, when I feel awful for shouting at my little boy and wish I could grab him back from the childminder to hug him.

I've talked all this over with friends. The consensus seems to be that a misbehaving mind is pretty normal. Over coffee recently with two other working mothers, one confided that she was having acupuncture to help with 'mental calmness'. She works four days a week in a high-level IT job, and has one daughter in her first year at school and another at pre-school. She says she feels that she isn't doing anything very well. She is not performing at work as she'd like, and doesn't feel successful as a mother. This is getting to her. A lot of the time, she feels anxious, on edge, worried, unable to relax. She isn't sleeping properly. Her sister had recommended the acupuncture.

The other friend, who in some ways has fewer pressures – she's a self-employed artist, who chooses when she works – revealed that she's been going to regular talks organised by a local Brahma Kumaris group (part of a world-wide organisation with origins in Hinduism), directed at reducing negative self-talk and enhancing self-esteem. She said she isn't depressed exactly, but lacking in positivity and enthusiasm for herself and for life, and was looking for explanations why. The talks were providing her with possibilities to think about.

When I brought up my 'problem' – my mental weakness – with a third friend, whom I'd always thought of as exceptionally mentally strong, she told me that at times she feels down, and has absolutely no idea what triggers it, or how to get out of it. During these periods, which can last hours or sometimes days, she finds herself focusing on negative thoughts about herself and her decisions, and worrying about her kids. When she feels like this, she just sits it out, and waits to feel better.

None of these people needs to see a psychiatrist. None would see a psychotherapist. But while having an out-of-control mind might be 'normal', it clearly isn't desirable. It isn't enough to just 'get by' – is it? It shouldn't be enough for me, I decide, or for my family.

The friends I'd talked to had taken steps to try to help themselves with what, following further conversation, seemed really, broadly speaking, to be the same problem that affects me. But their steps seemed slight, and erratic: hopeful shots in the dark, more than anything else. Perhaps, I thought, there was a book out there that could help.

I did find a few with tips on how to get through a major

trauma, like a death in the family. Then there was one that pointed out the difference between 'good stress' (the invigorating kind you feel when you go on a date with someone you really like or walk in to an interview for your dream job – assuming you're not immediately informed you're a flibbertigibbet) and 'bad stress' (the more chronic kind, which can be caused by conflict at home, tough expectations at work or a negative self-image). It's this bad stress that can put you into a potentially damaging state of ongoing alarm. That's worth noting, I think. I don't want to become unflappable. I still want important things to bother me, and to experience the useful and even enjoyable physical and psychological buzz of a challenge. I do, however, want to be less *dis*tressed . . . and more composed.

Next, I came across a book that argued that to be psychologically 'resilient', I should change my 'emotional style' (would that really cover all my issues?), and then I found business-type books with titles like *Executive Toughness*, packed with suggestions on how to get what you want from negotiations and colleagues (not really any help to me). There's no shortage, of course, of books on how to be 'happier', but that isn't what I'm after either. And let me note that, sadly, there's plenty of research finding that people who pursue happiness end up feeling *more* depressed, not less.

While interesting (to varying degrees,) none of these books addresses what I really want, or need. Which is?

Something fundamental. A comprehensive programme to build mental strength. A kind of boot camp for the mind.

And so, I decide, I'll have to construct it for myself.

I have a degree in psychology and twenty years' experience

as a science and health journalist on newspapers and magazines. I know how to go about scouring journal papers and conference presentations and questioning scientists to find what I need. And I know to be very careful about some of the claims that are made.

You don't have to search hard to find tips on how to 'keep calm', 'boost your energy levels', 'achieve your goals' or 'beat the blues'. But the recommendations from the experts can be contradictory – and frustratingly vague: 'Eat blueberries!' Really? How many? How often? And what real-world effect will that have on my mind? 'Take up mindfulness' – oh? Is it better than other styles of meditation – and, if so, how much better, and why? 'Make sure you allow time for mind-wandering!' I thought it was crucial to be mindful? 'Do more exercise!' How much more? And what type? And how *exactly* will I feel better – and for how long?

Vagueness isn't helpful, but it's probably the most benign of the faults of some of the health advice you read. In my experience, many doctors and psychiatrists are, yes, fair and conservative-minded, and acutely aware of the need to be measured in what they advocate because people, quite reasonably, believe and act on what they say. But some aren't. And unfortunately, it's the ones with the most extreme ideas who tend to be over-represented in the media, because they're saying something different – something new.

Journalists have to carry some of the blame. But not all of it. A study published in December 2014 in the *British Medical Journal* concluded that most of the hype in media health coverage originates not with journalists but with press releases cleared by the academics involved. As one experienced science journalist noted in an online discussion in the wake of this: 'One truth is that journals . . . tell authors to alter their conclusions, on the basis that the paper as it is to be published does not support them. So authors like to reinstate the conclusions when their university's press office puts out a release. It can take a very brave, experienced and confident press officer (and there are a few) to stand up to a professor in hot pursuit of a headline.'

A big advantage of creating a programme for myself is that I know I'm coming to the field with an entirely open mind. Unlike a professor 'in hot pursuit of a headline', or a doctor with a pet theory to protect, or even a journalist trying to satisfy an editor's demand for a quick, new take on an old complaint, I want what you want: to discover the 'truth', or as close as I can get to it, about what the balance of decent evidence reveals about how to build a stronger mind – because it matters to *me*. Because *I* need to know it.

Of course, I talk to academics. But I home in on those who, as far as I can tell, have a passion, but not an agenda.

After a little initial reading, it becomes clear that what I want should be possible. While psychologists once thought that a person's ability to cope with stressful circumstances, for instance, was largely innate or set early in life, there's plenty of research now showing that it isn't – and that just as physically healthy people can become fitter, psychologically 'normal' people (that is, without a disorder) *can* become stronger. In theory, as far as I can tell, we *all* could benefit from mind-boosting strategies – and this book investigates what they are and how well they work.

My plan is to start with the fundamentals: to ask, which

factors most influence the brain to improve psychological functioning – dietary supplements? Certain types of physical exercise? Meditation? Modifications to natural daily rhythms in the release of various hormones? I find out, I talk to people who use these strategies and try them for myself. Then I move on to thoughts themselves, and research on how to achieve goals.

It's important to me that whatever I come up with should be not only evidence-based, but practical. There's just no way I can end up telling James and the boys: 'We're moving to Queensland! I'll be running meditation marathons in the rainforest every morning! We'll be eating only wild fish and native berries!'

It'd never happen. And I could never do it, anyway. Yes, I want to 'realise my potential' (in the least get-ahead-in-business kind of way), but I want to be in my life, as *me* – only more able to deal with life's irritations and tribulations, more mentally balanced, tougher, more positive, more likely to set and achieve goals (and to welcome the process, not just the outcome), better able to deal calmly with my family, and to enjoy them more. Put simply: more sane. And I want to achieve all this through a programme that can be realisti-cally incorporated into my normal week of work, kids, time out and time in.

Will I be transformed? I don't know – but I'm excited to finally be doing something systematic instead of just snatching bits and pieces of advice from work interviews.

The truth is, *any* improvement will be worth it. James tells me with a smile that he agrees. But I know he's keen to discover what I learn. In fact, just about everyone I've told about my plans – from my mothers' group to Jakob's headmaster to other science and health journalists – has said something along the lines of, 'I'd love to hear what you find out'.

So, here goes.

CHAPTER ONE

CLEAR YOUR MIND

The voice that answers the phone is fragile with age, but warm.

'Thanks very much for sparing the time to talk,' I say. 'I—'

Herbert Benson, Professor of Medicine at Harvard Medical School, Boston, interrupts me gently. 'How are your two children? How old are they?' he asks.

I'd mentioned the kids in an introductory email, requesting an interview. I'd explained that I finish work relatively early to collect them from school and a childminder, but hoped we'd be able to find a time in our respective work days that overlapped. I hadn't expected him to remember, never mind to *ask* about them.

I tell him their ages, and there's a pause on the line.

Then, 'Mothers of young children are under enormous stress,' he says, with what sounds like real sympathy. 'Wouldn't it be nice if they could take advantage of the Relaxation Response? Would you like me to teach it to you?'

This is unexpected. *I* know, of course, that looking after young kids is so often stressful. But here's someone who can only be described as a legend in the field of meditation science not only acknowledging this, but offering to help. What else am I going to say in reply, but 'Yes, I'd love that.'

'Can you put the phone on loudspeaker?'

I do so.

'Close your eyes,' he says then. 'Relax your muscles – your feet, your calves, your thighs . . .'

Benson has adopted the tone of an old-school hypnotist, slow and reassuring.

'Shrug your shoulders . . .

'Roll your head and neck around . . .

'Sit at ease, without movement, and breathe slowly.'

My eyes are closed . . . My neck is loosened . . . I'm feeling decidedly calmer already, and this is just the preamble. The crucial bit – the technique that emerged from research that astonished other scientists, toppled medical dogma and was the subject of a series of landmark journal papers – is yet to come.

But not just yet.

Because I'm going to put Herbert Benson on hold for now. What he had to say in that phone conversation became pivotal for me, but I only got to him after a good month of research – talking to practitioners and scientists and witnessing meditation in action (or the tease of it) in places as diverse as a high-achieving grammar school in Altrincham, Greater Manchester and a sinisterly bland office suite in New York

City. And what came before that phone call to Boston still really matters. Not least, because you might find what you're looking for not in Benson's recommendations, but in other techniques.

So, I'll backtrack from that phone call to the beginning – to where I'm considering what I know about meditation and deciding: *very little.*

Meditation isn't something I've ever tried. Unless you count the one time in the garden of a shared house in Clapham, London, twenty years ago, when my boyfriend at the time banged a wooden spoon against a brass Tibetan bowl and suggested we sit quietly. I had no idea what I was meant to be doing. (I'm sure he didn't, either.)

Growing up, meditation wasn't something I even really heard about. I was vaguely aware that Buddhists did it. I think I knew the Beatles had been into it. My parents, who in the 1960s had grown their hair long, worn Cuban heels and cried when Bob Dylan went electric (at least, my mum did), had no interest in it whatsoever, which perhaps I might have found surprising – except that my father was a neuroscientist, and deeply cynical of anything 'mystic'. None of my friends meditated, either. At least, not in the 80s or the 90s or the noughties . . .

Then suddenly, mindfulness was *everywhere*. It *is* everywhere. I don't know many people who meditate regularly, but those who do almost all do mindfulness. And I wonder: do they seem calm *because* they do the meditations? Or is it that they're the kind of people who are more in control in all kinds of important ways – more likely to go to a yoga class on a Saturday morning, say, than out for a triple-shot flat white and a bacon-stacked breakfast bagel with a croissant on the side, like me?

Of course, I know now that Buddhist monks are meant to be the epitome of psychological calm. But do you have to meditate all day to really alter your mind? What difference does a bit of mindfulness really make, I wonder. And what relationship does it have with Herbert Benson's 'Relaxation Response', which I'd come across once or twice in academic papers? Or with Transcendental Meditation – TM? Or with Stoic meditation? Or Jewish Kabbalah meditation?

An Internet search quickly reveals there to be all kinds of styles of meditation. Should I investigate *all* of them?

In the end, I decide to focus on the types most evaluated by scientists because if I'm asking about impacts on psychological strength and wellbeing, I want to know what the research has to say. They seem to fall into two categories:

1. Focused-attention meditation. Here, the aim is to stay focused on something – like a mantra (a word or saying), the breath or an image.

2. Mindfulness meditation. Practitioners try to be aware of everything that they experience – including thoughts and physical sensations – without judgement.

I discover that Herbert Benson started his meditation research with, what at the time, back in the 1960s, was becoming an increasingly popular focused-attention form (outside conservative academic circles, at any rate): Transcendental Meditation. The Beatles embraced TM, many of their fans went crazy for it and India's Maharishi Mahesh Yogi (who named it, but based it on a traditional technique) became a megastar in his own right.

Risking ridicule from colleagues, even his entire career, Benson wired up a group of American TM practitioners to monitors, and found that using meditation alone they could lower their blood pressure – they could bring about physical changes that were 'relaxing'. This was a hugely influential finding. While the body and mind had long been separated in Western medicine, here was scientific proof that there was a fundamental interaction.

Since then, hundreds of scientific papers investigating the effects of TM on the mind and body have been published. A team at Stanford University, US, reviewed 146 studies and concluded that TM is twice as good at promoting relaxation and relieving anxiety as some other commonly used stress-busting techniques, including progressive muscle relaxation.

After dismissing hundreds of published research papers as being so poorly conducted as to be worthless, in 2012 another team decided that, based on findings from only the well-run studies, TM has 'medium to large' effects on 'emotionality', including anxiety.

So, yes, *promising*. And certainly worth considering.

I visit the website of the Maharishi Foundation USA, the group that teaches Transcendental Meditation in the US, and find a surprising (to me) number of celebrity endorsements. I thought everyone was all about mindfulness these days. But here are Ellen DeGeneres and Jerry Seinfeld talking about the difference it makes to them. Seinfeld is quoted as saying: 'I love energy. I love it. And I pursue it, and I want more of it. Physical and mental energy, to me, are the greatest riches of human life. And TM® is like a free account of an endless amount of it.'

Endless energy . . . I could do with that.

A little more searching reveals that it isn't only TV types who are into it. According to the *Guardian*, politician William Hague – perhaps the least likely TM aficionado – learned the technique in Sheffield as a sixteen-year-old and used to engage in bursts of TM to focus his mind.

TM, I go on to learn, is practised in twenty-minute sessions, twice a day.

Twenty minutes, twice a day . . . that doesn't sound too bad. At least, not in theory. And as far as I can tell, it involves nothing more than sitting down, breathing and focusing on a phrase. The effort sounds slight. The benefits seem large.

I decide to find out more about *exactly* what TM involves. The US site mentions regular introductory talks at various locations in New York. I'm heading there soon on a research trip, and one of those locations isn't far from where I'll be staying. So I sign up.

A couple of weeks later, at 1.30pm on a warm, damp Sunday, I arrive at a building on Madison Avenue in midtown Manhattan, right next door to the flagship Barneys department store.

I come out of the lift into a bright, anonymous, neutral-toned suite of offices. It's not what I expected. There are no garlanded posters of Maharishi Mahesh Yogi, no images of TM yogis with beatific expressions. The offices look the type you might rent by the hour.

One door stands open. A woman is hovering close by with clipboards. She smiles a welcome and hands me a board with a form. I take it with me into a small room, filled with rows of chairs. It's bland, too – apart from a framed photo of Maharishi Mahesh Yogi (I *am* in the right place!) and the mixed group of people who have gathered . . .

It *is* a Sunday, so there's plenty of sportswear around, but also a *lot* of hipster clothing. Most of the people here are young, in their twenties or thirties. Probably the oldest person in the room is at the front, bending over his laptop. In his early forties, I'd guess, but balding, he's very tall, thin and pale, his white wrists protruding from the cuffs of his formal shirt. While he finishes his preparations, I sit down next to a gum-chewing woman in neon Spandex, and check out my form.

It asks me to tick the most important reason for my decision to learn about TM. These are my options: to increase inner peace and/or calmness of mind; to reduce stress and/or anxiety; to improve brain functioning, mental clarity, creativity and/or intelligence; to develop higher consciousness, enlightenment and/or spiritual growth; to improve general health and wellbeing; to improve a specific health condition; other.

Higher consciousness seems a little ambitious for a Sunday afternoon, so I go for 'to reduce stress and/or anxiety'.

There are more questions to answer, but the tall, thin man is standing up. So I put my clipboard on my knee and pay attention.

He introduces himself as John Butler. Right away, he tells us, to my disappointment (and I get the sense this is shared) that we won't learn how to actually *do* TM in this session. That will come later. If we decide to proceed, we'll sign up for one-to-one sessions, be given our own personalised mantra and helped to 'transcend' in our very first meditation.

But all that costs money.

Today, in the free talk, we'll get to find out about what TM can do for us.

OK. I'm still interested.

TM is 'simple and effortless', Butler says. It's so easy, in fact, children can learn it. Even sceptics can learn it. 'They follow the instructions and they start transcending . . .'

Most people learn TM because they want to get rid of stress, he tells us, and adds: 'TM doesn't manage stress.'

I glance down at my form. *Ah* . . . But this is just a tease.

'TM doesn't manage stress. It gets rid of it. *Gone.*'

There's an appreciative murmur from the audience.

Butler tells us that the mind has layers. Consciousness is uppermost. But you can move down, through the layers, to a deep, still level. It's this deep, pure, concentrated level – this vast reservoir of energy, creativity and intelligence – that is accessed in TM, he says. 'TM causes us to, without any effort, experience thought in its most subtle states.'

I'm trying, at this point, to keep an open mind. Or at least, not to shut it down entirely. I'm a science journalist, so naturally I'm drawn to a more evidence-based approach to the mind – one that does not recognise a vast, untapped reservoir of intelligence, appealing as this might sound. But I can go with the idea of there being other types of awareness than conscious experience. Of course this is the case.

A bigger problem, for me, is what comes next: an attempt to place this 'reservoir' within physicists' understanding of matter. Butler talks earnestly about solid-state physics, neutrinos and leptons (all real), and claims that this deep level of consciousness sits at the base of the model of matter. He goes on to mix good data from journals with impeccable reputations with findings from publications with no reputation at all. At least, not for publishing good science.

The last section of his talk, clearly intended to be the clincher, clinches it for me. Only not in the way Butler intends.

He talks about an experiment, conducted in the summer of 1993, in Washington, D.C., in which a group of skilled TM practitioners, including Butler himself (he proudly shows us a photo) gathered with the aim of meditating together to reduce crime in the city.

The group used advanced techniques, he notes, not just regular TM, and, he tells us, to the critics' astonishment, the crime rate that summer dropped by eighteen per cent. (Actually, Butler says twenty-five per cent, but I later check the claimed figures, and it seems only fair to use the 'official' count.)

How did they do it? 'Imagine radio waves . . . it's a field . . . it spreads . . . My attention goes to another person and nourishes them. You can nourish a child, a cat, a houseplant . . . Regardless of whether or not we agree on the mechanisms, the results are there.'

Only they're not.

Whatever Butler claims, it's a matter of record that the crime rate did not drop that summer in Washington, D.C. In fact, I later discover, while the practitioners were engaged in their meditations, the weekly murder count rose. Further reading clarifies the situation (well, in a sense). There were, it turns out, eighteen per cent fewer homicides than the *organisers predicted* would have happened had the meditators not been there. This is their 'drop'.

Butler carries on talking, but – even before checking the data – I know I can't take TM seriously. I leave as soon as soon as he finishes, admittedly one of very few people in the room *not* to sign up for a one-on-one meeting.

As I dash into Barneys in search of some normality (after what I've just heard, the price of that handbag seems completely reasonable – I'll take two), I find myself thinking that it's all a bit of a shame.

Clearly, there *is* something to TM. It *does* seem to be a valid technique for calming the body and mind. In fact, it's the only meditation technique that the American Heart Association recommends that doctors consider for use in treating high blood pressure (though whether it's really superior to other types isn't clear, the AHA adds, as there's a lack of good research, and direct-comparison studies haven't been done).

Learning TM costs somewhere around US$1000 to US$1500, depending on where you live and if there are offers on. But at least there are decent studies to support at least some of the claimed benefits in terms of relieving stress and anxiety. It does work. Only not in the way Butler and the Maharishi Foundation USA say it does.

I guess I *could* just focus on the results, and still take up TM. To do it 'properly', I'd have to pay to get a personalised mantra. But I just can't credit that the particular word you use while meditating would make any real difference to the effects. So does TM differ fundamentally from other forms of mantra-based meditation? Could I get the benefits from something similar – but minus the crime-stopping claims? To answer that, I'll have to investigate how TM might actually work.

I'll look into that, but I also want to find out more about another form of meditation altogether: mindfulness.

When I later ask Herbert Benson about it, this is what he says: 'Different techniques go through different cycles of popularity. Right now, mindfulness is in many people's minds as the only way.'

'Mindfulness means paying attention in a particular way; on purpose, in the present moment and non-judgementally.'

So says Jon Kabat-Zinn, a modern pioneer of mindfulness in the West, and the man who stripped the spirituality from the technique. While mindfulness comes from Zen Buddhist thinking, Kabat-Zinn, an American who studied under Buddhist teachers and is now Professor Emeritus of Medicine at the University of Massachusetts Medical School, developed a secular eight-week course, originally with the aim of relieving stress in hospital patients.

Mindfulness Based Stress Reduction (MBSR), as he called it, is now taught to all kinds of people, including those who are physically healthy but dealing with everyday types of stress. If you see an advert for a mindfulness course near you, it'll probably be MBSR. At least, that's the course to look out for because there's evidence that it can work.

Here are a few findings from studies of people before and after learning mindfulness:

- Normal, healthy adults reported a drop in 'daily hassles' of nearly a quarter and a reduction in 'psychological distress' of close to a half. These improvements were still in place three months later.

- MBSR can alter patterns of brain activity in ways that should make you feel more positive, and find it easier to stay calm. Kabat-Zinn and his colleagues have found it leads to less right-side activation of the prefrontal cortex (associated with anxiety) and more left-sided activation (associated with wellbeing and calm).

- MBSR can leave a physical mark, expanding parts of the brain involved in regulating emotions and social thinking (according to research at Harvard).

Even people you might think of as being pretty impervious to stress seem to benefit. During the eight weeks before their deployment to Iraq, a group of US Marines who were trained in mindfulness meditation, and who practised it for thirty minutes each day, reported being better able to stay alert and in the moment (focused on what's happening *right now*) without becoming emotional.

Going back to my enquiries . . . I call the UK's best-known mindfulness researcher, Mark Williams, Professor of Clinical Psychology at the University of Oxford, and Director of the Oxford Mindfulness Centre. (Williams is also co-developer of an effective mindfulness-based approach to treating depression, and the co-author of *Mindfulness: A Practical Guide to Finding Peace in a Frantic World*, which describes techniques for addressing stress, anxiety, exhaustion and depression.)

I ask about any new research, and Williams tells me about a small-scale trial of a mindfulness course developed for schoolchildren. The hope was that it would enhance mental health and wellbeing, and the results, published in the *British Journal of Psychiatry*, were promising. Williams and his colleagues now want to run a much bigger trial. Their ultimate question is this: if – as his own work has found – mindfulness can work well to *treat* depression, what if it could *prevent* cases of full-blown depression or anxiety disorders? And, if so, when better to start than at a young age, in school?

My own son, Jakob, goes to a small, friendly school with a big emphasis on pastoral care. But I was talking to the Personal Health and Social Education teacher in the senior school recently, and she told me that a lot of the teenage girls there feel very anxious – about their bodies, about their friendships, about life, full stop. She's worried for them, and has been wondering whether courses of meditation might help. Some schools are also taking an interest in mindfulness because of research finding that, thanks to the emphasis on being in the moment, it can help to train focus on the task at hand – to strengthen the 'attentional muscle', as it's sometimes called.

What does Mark Williams think? Is mindfulness the answer, I ask. He pauses before replying:

'I – I think that probably the line should be not that mindfulness is better than anything else . . . I don't like the idea of coming along and elbowing everybody else out of the way and saying you're saved now you have mindfulness . . .

But mindfulness skills are attentional skills, and so they're foundational skills for learning everything. They can be used for enhancing even something like taking a penalty in football. The rugby player Johnny Wilkinson is a meditator. He uses meditation before he takes a kick.'

If mindfulness can help people cope better with stress, feel more positive and energised and help improve focus, this is something I *have* to try. But I'm still pretty hazy about exactly what it entails. It seems to involve meditations. But the emphasis on living 'in the moment' suggests it's something much bigger. A way of life.

I have a lot of questions. I buy Mark Williams's book, thinking I'll read it before going back to him with follow-up queries. But before I even open the book, I'm offered the chance to visit one of the schools involved in the recent mindfulness trial – a school that, I'm told, has embraced mindfulness so enthusiastically, classes are now on the curriculum, and Mindfulness Based Stress Reduction training is compulsory for new teachers.

This sounds like the perfect opportunity to learn about what mindfulness really means. And it explains why, one Tuesday morning, I find myself sitting in a classroom at Altrincham Grammar School for Girls (AGGS) with twenty-seven Year-8s, the Head of Religious Studies and the school's resident mindfulness lead, Rebecca Stokwisz, and a family-sized box of Maltesers.

AGGS is a grand turn-of-the-twentieth-century school – all polished parquet floors and long sash windows. It's state-funded, but selective, and it's in a wealthy area close to Manchester. The pupils are from relatively privileged back-grounds. They're expected to perform well, both academically and in terms of their behaviour.

Right now, the girls in this particular class (aged twelve to thirteen) are sitting in a circle, chattering to each other, their attention darting to and from that box of Maltesers.

Stokwisz, who is young and fashionably dressed, picks up the box, and hands out the chocolates. She asks the girls to hold their Malteser, raise it to eye level and *really* look at it: 'I want you to stay in your own bubble and not talk to the person next to you, but just hold it and notice any effect it's having on you,' she says.

There's a little sniggering. Stokwisz presses on. She asks the girls to bring the Malteser to their nose. The sniggering gets louder. '*Girls,*' she says firmly but pleasantly, 'stay in the bubble.'

At last, they're allowed to bring the chocolate to their lips, and then to take it onto their tongues. All this time, they're instructed to think about how this *feels*, and the effects it might be having on their bodies. Finally, they're allowed to eat the chocolate.

After the girls have discussed their reactions, Stokwisz begins a presentation on the whiteboard. The first slide is a quote from John Milton's *Paradise Lost*:

> The mind is its own place, and in itself, can make a
> Heav'n of Hell, a Hell of Heav'n.

Then, after a brief discussion of the power of mental activity to change the physical brain (the famously expanding memory regions of London black cab drivers are rolled out into service), Stokwisz asks the girls to point to the location of their mind. They point to their temples. She asks, 'Are our minds *really* located just in the brain?'

She asks the girls to sit 'well' – feet flat on the floor, hands in their laps. Then she gets them to extend their arms, palms facing each other, to close their eyes and to take their attention *into* their hands. 'Maybe you sense a tingling, or the blood flowing? Maybe you feel pins and needles? Maybe you don't feel anything, and that's OK.'

She asks the girls to take their attention across their fingers. Then she tells them to discuss what they noticed with their neighbour. A few talk about how their fingers moved. One girl says, 'I was thinking where I'll sit at lunch and I need to buy ingredients for brownies, and then I started thinking about homework and then I started getting stressed about exams.'

'What a lot you thought about in that short time,' Stokwisz says to her. 'With all that going on in our minds, no wonder we're so tired.'

She asks what effect exams are having on their bodies, and the girls scramble over each other to answer. One is so tired she can't sleep. Another starts thinking about all she has to remember, and then she gets a headache and worries the headache will stop her performing in the exam. One bites her nails. Another fidgets.

Stokwisz says, 'Mindfulness helps you to see the connection between your mind and your body. And it gives you tools to help.'

This was just a taster session. As I just witnessed, it combines the theory of mindfulness with training in how to 'do' it.

I sit down with Amanda Bailey, a former teacher at AGGS who is now Chief Executive Officer of the school's trust. It was she who was instrumental in getting the programme onto the curriculum at AGGS, as well as at other of the trust's schools.

Bailey tells me she grew up in a family of meditators. Her father practised TM. She tried it, but says she always felt she was doing it wrong. 'I think I had an expectation that I would be moving through different states of consciousness, and if that wasn't happening for me, I'd beat myself up. Even my meditation was something I needed to do better at. I went on a mindfulness course and I learned that you can't do it wrong. It was the first thing in my whole life that I *couldn't do wrong.*'

So what does it really *mean* to be mindful?

'Well, the more you practise it, the better you get. Though we're not trying to *get anywhere* with it, there *is* a discipline to it. We are trying to direct experience back into our body or our breathing. The mind wanders. That's what it does all day, every day. It's just that we're not aware of it most of the time. The more aware of the mind-wandering we can be, and the most practised we can be at bringing it back to the present within our body, or our breath, the less life will be on autopilot.'

Is it about making your thoughts more positive?

'It's not about changing thoughts from positive to negative. It's not positive psychology. It's about being aware of your experience as it unfolds, whether that be good, bad or indifferent.'

So if you notice your mind wandering off, you always try to bring it back to the present?

'We talk to the children about this. They might quite like to be lost in daydreaming. All I ever say to them is that daydreams can be wonderful things, and I'm not asking you to stop – and clearly even if I asked you to, your brain wouldn't. However, it's not always useful. If you find yourself daydreaming and you're meant to be doing your maths homework, it actually would be better if you got on with your maths homework.'

The main goal, it seems, is to be more focused on the present. As the Year-8s learned, mindfulness helps to put you back in touch with your sensory experience of the world. The promise of this, I understand, when I eventually read Mark Williams's book, is that it will help you to 'cultivate a direct, intuitive sense of what is going on in your inner and outer worlds, with profound effects on your ability to attend to people and the world in a new way, without taking anything for granted'.

And learning to see thoughts just as thoughts – just as your inner commentary, not as 'you' or 'reality' – helps you to free yourself from their grip. You don't need to believe you are weak or 'no good'. They're just negative thoughts. They're not reality.

The *meditations* seem designed to help you to develop mindful awareness, which Williams describes as the 'Being' rather than 'Doing' mode. When you're in this mode, you're able to sense more clearly 'the things that nourish you and those that deplete your inner resources', Williams promises. It's easy to become so focused on work and life goals that you neglect the activities that 'nourish your soul', he writes, leaving you feeling 'drained, listless and exhausted'.

Bailey says she meditates every day. So does Stokwisz. Ultimately, the idea is to sit in silence, observing thoughts as they arise and evaporate. But there are various types of guided mindfulness meditations for the non-Zen master to try (and plenty are available online, free to download). They focus on physical sensations – moving attention gradually around the body ('body scanning' – which the Year-8s practised with their outstretched arms) or keeping attention on the breath, for example.

Stokwisz tells me she spends forty-five minutes almost every day engaged in body scanning, gently returning to this focus whenever her mind wanders. (She tells me she also tries to walk to school 'mindfully' and to teach 'mindfully' – that is, she tries to pay close attention to what she's actually doing and experiencing in the moment.)

Forty-five minutes every day? That sounds a lot.

I ask her if she always enjoys it.

'I would say I enjoy it about eighty per cent of the time. But it doesn't really matter whether you enjoy it or not, because you're meant to go into it with no intention. Even if I think to myself, *I'm enjoying this*, that in itself is just a thought. Or if I'm thinking, *I'm not enjoying this*, then I think to myself: *I'm doing this for my wellbeing.*'

Hmm. Doesn't thinking *I'm enjoying this, but it's just a thought* take the joy out of life?

'No – the opposite. It makes it more precious. You appreciate that thought.'

And *not judging* negative thoughts really helps?

'If you pay attention to them, but don't judge them, over time they seem to happen less.'

Amanda Bailey had talked to me earlier about how the children are taught to see their thoughts as buses. If a negative thought comes along, you don't have to get on it. You can let it go past. You can't necessarily stop an unpleasant, negative thought from arising – but you *can* learn not to allow yourself to be drawn into a downward spiral of destructive thinking.

Learning to escape being sucked into negative thinking would clearly be a useful thing for many of us, I think. And it makes sense that learning to get better at reining in wandering thoughts and being in the present moment can help with focus (though mindfulness is certainly not the only meditative technique that trains attention).

But I'm keen to talk to as many people who practise mindfulness as I can, to find out more about how it helps them. So I'm grateful when other teachers at the school offer to discuss their experiences.

Ana Roslan, the assistant headteacher, who is Muslim, says that learning mindfulness has helped her to focus at work, and in prayer. 'Sometimes, when I'm praying, my mind does wander. I stop, breathe and carry on.' Since mindfulness originates in Buddhism, I ask if any of the concepts or techniques conflict with her religious beliefs. 'It helps with my faith, rather than conflicts,' she says.

Emily Bowyer, Head of Citizenship, is a committed Christian. 'I have a daily practice of prayer slash some kind of mindful exercise,' she tells me. 'So as I'm in prayer, I might do a body scan. Or I might have headphones on with a song and I'll sit and do the meditation with that.'

While she hadn't tried mindfulness before joining the school, Bowyer says meditation was something she was familiar with from her own faith. 'We have meditative prayer

– meditating on a Bible verse, meditating on a song. Personally, I think mindfulness sits quite well with that.'

I'd started out thinking mindfulness was 'just' a type of meditation. It's very clear to me now that it's a whole lot more than that.

You can 'do TM' for twenty minutes, twice a day. To 'do' mindfulness properly, everything has to change. At least, it would for me, because I'm not very mindful at all. The other morning, I walked into school with Jakob's PE bag on my arm, then walked it back to the car and took it home with me. I had to immediately drive back to drop it off. Today, I snatched up my keys from the table on the way out, got back and found they were James's keys for his work flat, not for our home. I had to call him to ask him to come back to let me in. Last week, I put petrol in my diesel car, and drove it for half a mile before the knocking engine made me realise what I'd done.

Not being mindful can be very expensive in terms of money, not to mention time, I've learned. And I don't think my ageing brain is entirely to blame. I'm distracted a *lot*. Learning to be more focused on what I'm actually doing would surely help me.

I can also appreciate that focusing on what you're doing might allow you to get greater pleasure from a walk or even work, or to make the most of a bedtime story with your child, or to really be there for a friend who's telling you about a problem. Mindfulness helps you feel 'really alive' is something I hear more than once.

And yet . . .

While I see advantages everywhere, I also see problems. At least, for me.

Children get a certain dispensation when it comes to daydreaming – it really is pretty normal when you're a kid – but adults are meant, I gather, to try stay in the present as much as possible. However, a lot of scientific research has found benefits to mind-wandering. Imagination, learning and creativity – they all improve with a healthy dose of mind-wandering. You'll hear that the opposite of being mindful is being mindless. I don't know . . . When I walk 'mindlessly' around the park, trailing after Lucas on his scooter, I'm paying not the least bit of attention to the sensations in my body or the flowers, or sometimes, honestly, to my son, but all kinds of really important stuff springs to mind. Changes I need to make to *this book*. A reply I've neglected to make to a friend's invitation to dinner. Genuinely important stuff.

We allow subconscious processes to take over in certain routine situations – while driving a familiar route, walking to work and sometimes, yes, even while we're with our kids – because they free up our minds to do other stuff, don't they? Like think.

While mindfulness accepts that thoughts can be valuable, there's a wariness of thinking that bothers me. Williams' book says: 'Thoughts can easily be shunted off in a toxic direction. It does not always happen – it's not inevitable – but it's an ever-present danger.'

Thinking poses an *ever-present danger*?

Perhaps you've heard this illustration of the joys of 'Being':

a herd of antelope charged by a hungry lion will scatter in every direction, their bodies and brains ringing with alarm. But as soon as the lion leaves, they settle down quickly and resume grazing, as though nothing ever happened.

Incapable of 'Doing', antelopes can only 'be'. Sheep too. And cows. Personally, I'd like to learn how to make my own Heav'n, not live so much in fear of slipping into Hell that I strive to spend as much time as possible in a state of awareness shared by a ruminant.

Still, I do like the concept of not boarding negative-thought buses. I resolve to practise this at night when they come looming. If ever there was a time you're most likely to see a string of these buses at once, isn't it at 3am? Though it's not just at night, of course. While I do sometimes think useful thoughts when in the park with Lucas, or getting the boys' dinner ready, or doing the shopping, I'm also guilty of wasting plenty of time in pointless thinking – in thoughts that make me sad and regretful, emotions that seem to slip so easily into frustration and irritability. So yes, I need to try to step back from the truly useless and destructive thoughts, and let them go.

I'm aware that a lot of people love mindfulness. Clearly, there are many who feel it has turned their lives around. I gave James a copy of Williams's mindfulness book, and he told me it really resonated with him. I'm just not sure I can accept the premises, even if I can appreciate some of the benefits. But maybe I'm being over-picky.

I came into mindfulness looking for a style of meditation. Could a twenty-minute body-scanning meditation on its own be useful? Or do you have to adopt the whole mindfulness package to enjoy the real benefits? Why not take what I want from mindfulness and leave the rest? And do the same with TM?

I think I need to take a step back.

My sister recently decided to start mindfulness meditations, so I ask her how it's working out. This is what she says:

'I've been using the Headspace app, which slowly lengthens the amount of time that you meditate. It starts off as ten ten-minute sessions, then ten fifteen-minute sessions and eventually twenty-minute sessions, etc. The biggest problem has been trying to find a time to do it. The recommendation is to do it first thing in the morning to feel the benefits all day long and get into the habit of doing it, but that's easier said than done when you get woken up by small children demanding breakfast, crying or generally requiring attention. So, I haven't managed to do it daily – but still have the intention of doing it daily, having started it a few months ago, which is more than I can say for most exercise or beneficial regimes I've tried!

In terms of how I've found it, so far, the sessions encourage you to be mindful – of how your body feels and your emotional mood, to focus on the breathing, to allow your mind to be free (to do whatever it wants to do, whether thinking or not).

I began the whole process by thinking I could quite easily relax and turn my mind off. However, from doing the first ten sessions, I've found a whole other level of mental calmness – a mental stillness where I'm not consciously trying to figure out how to solve some situation. While I haven't yet noticed that I'm calmer (I don't think I am yet) when faced with three people (two small, one large) at home all talking over each other and demanding attention, I have been able to draw on mindfulness to really enjoy more the time I am, for example, helping my daughter to learn to read or playing with my son. It's helped me learn to forget all the jobs that need doing, and which I'm lining up in order of priority in the mental background. I can see that I often spend too much time thinking about 'What next?' when I should simply be focusing and enjoying what I'm doing at that moment.

I've also found that it's helped me stop daydreaming so much! Focusing on effectively being present has stopped me going over past events – things done or said, whether positive or negative – or what may happen in the future. Of course you still have to plan for things, and do everything you can to ensure certain things happen, but there can be a lot of lost time in wondering about what or how events may turn out.'

So . . . my sister seems to like it. I decide I'll try mindfulness meditations, and just see how they feel. I'm all set to start that evening. But then I receive an email from an old school friend.

Jane had spent time in Mumbai, India, and I'd contacted her thinking she might know some regular meditators there who could give me different perspectives on their practice. She tells me: 'If you're looking at different approaches to meditation, you should talk to Adam's dad!' I email back, saying yes, I'd love to talk to her father-in-law, Mike, if he's willing.

Within the first few minutes of our conversation, Mike makes his position pretty clear:

'I had a misdiagnosis some years ago that I'd had a heart attack. I was fed dreadful chemicals, and I really wanted to get off them, so I decided that meditation was the way for me to do that. I've been medication-free for twenty years almost.'

Mike tells me that he and his partner recently returned to the UK after five years on the island of Lesvos, in Greece. 'We had five years of self-sufficient living. I wanted to prove to myself we could do it.' He'd been teaching t'ai chi for many years, and he continued this in Greece, with locals and expats. In fact, he still teaches – when he isn't doing interval training, or reading up on the effects of the mind on the body. 'I visit old people's homes and do some qigong and t'ai chi for the old folk,' he says, before adding: 'I'm seventy-five, myself.'

'So,' I say, 'I hear you've developed your own form of meditation?'

'Well, I refer to a book by a guy called Eric Harrison, and it's called *How Meditation Heals*. I used that as the basis. I think mostly when I started, the fight was to quieten the mind, which everybody has a problem with . . . Until I realised meditation had become a boxing ring, in which I was having this match between myself and this other self. So I went from that to just accepting what was going on.

'Eric Harrison points you towards picking a word or a

picture that's going to be your focus. So I paint the word "love" in my little TV screen above my forehead and put a frame around it. Then I just focus on it, and of course other things come into my mind, and when that happens, I think, where's the picture with the frame around it? Then I get my "love" back and focus on it again.'

Mike says he'll do this for about twenty minutes. He does it to relieve stress; and if he's in pain, he'll paint a picture of the aching joint in his frame.

'When we first moved to Greece, we were very busy setting up house and getting things built, and I found I wasn't doing any practice,' he says. 'That had to get reversed. I was very active physically, but there was something I missed about not meditating. It becomes a way of life, and a way of settling yourself and removing anxieties and tensions. If you're not doing it, you find yourself feeling tense, and getting short with people.'

*

After that conversation with Mike, who's borrowed and adapted until hitting upon a form of meditation that works for him, I find myself wondering if there's anything really special about the 'formal' types.

Could the mantra given to you in TM *really* make the meditation more potent? Does focusing on bodily sensations (as with mindfulness meditations) have significantly greater benefits than focusing on, for argument's sake, a vase on the mantelpiece?

Perhaps I should consider trying a focused-attention

technique three days a week, say, and mindfulness meditations on the other four? That way, would I be covering all the bases? Or just hedging my bets?

What I really need, I decide, is a fuller understanding of what the various types of meditation really 'do', in terms of interactions between the body and mind. Could a better understanding of this guide me to the purest, most psycho-active form?

And now we're almost ready to go back to Herbert Benson, the man I left hanging at the start of this chapter. But, I'm going to keep that conversation hanging just a *little* bit longer. Because first, there's this:

In research published in 2013, Benson and his team found that meditation doesn't just change brain activity, blood pressure and reports of how stressed people feel.

It changes the activity of certain genes.

And it does so within minutes.

This happens not just in experts, but in novices, who have never meditated before. (This reminds me of John Butler arguing that transcendence happens even for TM sceptics.) The effects are more pronounced in people who have been medi-tating for at least three or four years, but even first-timers show an *increase* in the activity of genes involved in the function of mitochondria (tiny components of a cell that produce energy) and the secretion of insulin (which regulates blood-glucose levels). There's also a drop in the activity of genes involved in triggering potentially damaging inflammation (which has been linked to depression) and stress-related pathways. And there's a boost to the activity of genes involved in the maintenance of telomeres.

The maintenance of telomeres . . .

Telomeres have been called the 'bomb fuses' of our cells. They're the caps of our chromosomes – the wiggly conglomerations of our DNA, found inside every cell of our bodies. As cells age, these telomeres get shorter. When they get too short, the cells can't divide any more and become inactive or die. So is this work suggesting that meditation could actually slow down the ageing process?

I call up Manoj Bhasin, who works on genomics at the Beth-Israel Deaconess Medical Center, and who was the lead researcher on this study. It's early days, he says. He and his team have yet to determine what real-world differences these changes in gene activity might make to people's health and to their lifespan. But in theory – *perhaps*.

I ask Bhasin if he meditates. He laughs. 'I'm the genomics guy. I usually work in cancer and neuro-regeneration. When I started this study, frankly speaking, I did not believe in it. But these genomic changes are very focused. I was surprised. Now my wife and I just sit down and try to relax – just take a break, to leave behind the day, for just ten to fifteen minutes each day. And I think I feel much calmer, much better.'

One important note: while the team did find that meditation creates these changes in gene activity in people who have never meditated before, long-term meditation (that's every day for six months or more) makes a lot of the changes *stable*.

The long-term meditators in the study had been using a variety of techniques including TM, mindfulness and yoga (which some people class as exercise, some as meditation, and many as both; for reasons I'll give later, I've chosen to look at yoga when I get to exercise in Chapter Two). But they *all* showed similar results.

Other research from Harvard has shown that *different* types of meditation can make the amygdala – the brain's 'alarm bell' – less reactive. The amygdala plays a crucial role in the 'fight-or-flight' response. It reacts to emotionally charged situations, especially negative ones. So it's the part of the brain that tells you to run away if your boss is stomping towards your desk – or to throw coffee in his face. A dampened response should mean more emotional stability (not to mention a greater chance of holding down a job).

I ask Benson about this. Yes, he tells me, the techniques that can create these improvements are different, but they have one thing in common. In fact, he says, in all his studies over the years, he has repeatedly found that what makes meditation 'work' to benefit the mind and the body is this: the letting go of everyday thoughts: 'It's about breaking the train of everyday thinking. That is fundamental,' he says. And he repeats, for emphasis: '*What you need is to break the train of everyday thinking.*'

Breaking the train of everyday thinking allows our bodies and minds to relax. Our heart rate slows, as does our breathing and our production of stress hormones. We enter a state that is the polar opposite of the fight-or-flight response to a threat. It's what Benson calls the Relaxation Response. And at least some of the physical and psychological benefits of regularly initiating this response seem to be enduring.

So am I right in concluding that *any technique* that breaks the train of everyday thinking will work, and work just as well?

Benson believes it will. In fact, he says, people have been using a variety of effective techniques for millennia. 'Meditation, repetitive prayer, yoga, t'ai chi . . . The basic techniques have always been there.'

So TM or mindfulness or yoga should be equally as effective, for precisely the same reason?

Yes, Benson says. 'Mindfulness is a wonderful technique for evoking the Relaxation Response. It's fashionable now, but thirty years ago it was TM. Before that, it was repetitive prayer. Some people have a terrible time sitting down quietly,' he adds. 'For them, yoga is a preferable technique. There isn't just "one" technique.'

I find this a hugely liberating conversation. What appeals most to me, in terms of a meditative technique, might not appeal most to you – but as long as your meditation is breaking the train of everyday thinking, it will help with the goal of feeling calmer and more in control of your emotions. *And* you don't have to accept an entire doctrine to get these benefits.

I wonder: what about watching a film or listening to music? If they break the train of everyday thinking, do they count? Manoj Bhasin gives me his thoughts on this: 'There are different ways to relax, but something like mindfulness or yoga is the concentrated form of that relaxation. We are saying: in that time, we aren't going to be doing *anything* but relaxing our body and our brain.'

So the next question is: how long do you need to spend in a meditative state?

I know Rebecca Stokwisz does forty-five minutes a day of mindful body scanning. TM organisations suggest twenty minutes twice a day. Could I find that kind of time? I suppose I might have to try.

But Benson and his team have investigated how long an individual meditation session should last to provide mental (and physical) benefits, and he says, 'Ten to twenty minutes a day. That's all.'

Ten to twenty minutes a day. I'm relieved. Of course, I am.

While mindfulness, TM and other types of meditation that break the train of everyday thinking should all evoke the Relaxation Response for the same reason, Benson has his favourite technique. He uses it every day, he says, and it's the technique he got the volunteers in the genomics study to adopt.

Some did it first thing in the morning, he tells me. 'They would get up, go to the bathroom, shower if that's their habit, and then sit and do this for ten or twenty minutes. The important thing is to make it daily.'

This is how to do it, exactly as Benson tells me:

First (and yes, I missed this from the introduction to this chapter, but only because I didn't want to flag it up at that point as a focused-attention form) he asks me to pick a word. He suggests 'peace', 'love' or 'calm', but it's up to me. 'Peace' sounds good, I tell him. He begins:

'So – close your eyes. Relax your muscles – your feet,
your calves, your thighs. Shrug your shoulders. Roll your
head and neck around. Sit at ease, without movement,
and breathe slowly . . .

Now each time your breath comes out, say silently
to yourself the word, "Peace". You are going to find all

sorts of other thoughts coming to mind. They're normal. They are natural. And they should be expected. When they occur, don't be upset, but simply say, "Oh, well", and return to "Peace".

Now I'm going to let you do this and I'll be quiet for one or two minutes, at the end of which time I'll ask you to keep your eyes closed, but to start thinking your regular thoughts. Now, on your out-breath . . . "Peace". Other thoughts come to mind, "Oh, well" . . .'

His voice fades to silence.

And I feel something unfamiliar: an energised kind of warmth that seems to spread from my chest and out through my body.

I've written countless articles for newspapers and magazines over the years. In the course of research, I've tried all kinds of things. I've even had my brain zapped by electricity. This is the first time I've ever felt anything this instantaneous and this *strong*.

Benson's warm, fragile voice rises up out of the phone again: 'Keep your eyes closed, and think your normal thoughts for a minute . . . Now open them. Did you feel anything different?'

'Yeah,' I tell him. 'I felt a *warmth*.'

'See how simple it is?' he asks, and his voice conveys real pleasure. That pleasure must come from what surely he sees as the giving of an invaluable gift. I sense that he knows how I feel because many other people, trying out this technique for the first time, must have felt it, and told him so.

'So that's it,' he tells me. 'So simple. And all it costs is ten minutes of your time.'

I can afford ten minutes. Surely everyone can, given what it buys?

Still, at this point I'm not claiming that Benson's technique is 'the answer'. I haven't even really tried body scanning yet, or mindful breathing, or Mike's method or anything else. And Benson himself has made it clear that various types of meditation will *all* work to relieve stress and anxiety and help with emotional control. Mindfulness, of course, is so much more than just meditation – and I think I'll come back to it when I look more closely at thought-based approaches to building a stronger mind (see Chapter Six).

But, for now, Benson's method *does* feel good. And this, I decide, will be the meditation technique for me.

The next question is: when to do it? If it's something that should be done every day, I'll need to find a regular time slot. First thing is no good, as my sister found, because 'first thing' is whenever one of the boys jumps on the bed, which can be any time between about 5.30 and 6.30am – and there's no way I'm setting an alarm for 5am to make sure I get my meditation in. But for anyone who *can* set aside ten minutes every morning, it's got to be better than scheduling meditation later on, when it might get disrupted by work, family or social demands.

I decide that on my three work days a week, I'll make sure I leave my desk fifteen minutes early, and do it right before I leave the house to collect the kids. On the other days? I guess it'll have to be right after the boys are in bed, or it'll never get done.

I note down my meditation plan. And I feel pretty good

– confident that it will help me. Step one of my plan for cultivating a calmer, stronger mind: *done.*

THE MEDITATION CHECKLIST

- Choose a technique that suits you. If you find it hard to clear your mind while sitting quietly, try something that involves movement, like yoga or t'ai chi.

- Do expect that it will take some time to get used to it. I haven't spoken to anyone who found it easy from the outset to stay focused on meditating for long.

- You don't *need* to meditate for longer than ten to twenty minutes a day (in one session) – but many people do report enjoying meditating for longer.

- You do need to aim to meditate every day.

CHAPTER TWO

EXERCISE YOUR MIND

It's a little before seven on a close, grey morning in New Haven, Connecticut, and I'm feeling stressed. Why? Because, of all things, I can't find the Yale Stress Center. I've got computer-calculated walking directions from my hotel. It should take six minutes. But it's been twelve already, and now I'm late.

I spot a car-park attendant down the street. I run over to him. (I'm already in my gym kit, which helps.) 'Do you know where the Yale Stress Center is?' I ask. He grins. Maybe this happens often. Just maybe he can't resist smiling at the obvious irony of clients turning up stressed-out. As he points in the direction of a nondescript, low-level block, with what surely anyone would describe as a *very* small sign out front, I hunt for a bin large enough to handle my oversized coffee and try to get my breathing under control. I'm about to go into a class on mindful yoga, and I suspect I'm not in the optimum starting state.

The yoga class is the just the first in a series of meetings and exercises organised by Dr Matt Stults-Kohlemainen, the Yale Stress Center's resident exercise specialist. If I want to learn how exercise helps with psychological strength, I can't help feeling this is the place to be. The centre is part of the school of medicine of the world-renowned Yale University. Its Director, Dr Rajita Sinha, is a professor of psychiatry at the university, and I've interviewed Matt before, so I know he's patient and helpful beyond the call of duty. Besides, his research and his clinical work are focused on how people can use exercise to help treat and prevent stress and anxiety, and so improve their psychological, not to mention physical, wellbeing. This is exactly the kind of stuff I want to learn more about.

After a few deep breaths, I take the lift to the second floor. It's early, and the place seems deserted. I pass door after door, all closed. At last, I find one standing open. A friendly-looking woman with a grey bob and flawless skin appears in the corridor. This must be Anne Dutton, who'll be taking the class. I introduce myself, and apologise for being late. She smiles, 'Don't worry, it's that kind of day.'

The small, bland office space has undergone a mini-makeover. Shimmering voile has been draped over the regulation plastic blinds. On the walls there are Japanese pictures, and plaques that read 'Love is the beauty of the soul' and 'Life is all about making memories'. The lights are switched off. It's gloomy – or peaceful, depending on your perspective.

Two women, waiting on their mats, smile a welcome. There's Jenya, a slim woman with a dark ponytail, and Cindy, her bobbed hair pushed back by a band. I guess they must be roughly the same age as me. I confess to them that I've never done yoga before. 'Then this is the best class to start with,' Jenya promises.

In a quiet, gently musical voice, Anne asks us to sit comfortably 'and in a position that is alert, and to turn your attention to how you are feeling at this moment – what sensations you're aware of in your body – and to the emotional tone of the moment.' This must be the mindfulness aspect. 'Consider any thoughts that are on your mind, that are preoccupying you . . . So turning towards that moment and the information it has for you, think about what would be supportive and helpful for you right now. Anything you noticed about yourself? Any messages about what your body needs and your heart needs?'

My own heart is still pounding from all the caffeine and the lingering stress of being late. I wait for Cindy or Jenya to reply. Jenya says she's noticed how full her mind is of 'what I think Iris Murdoch called the debris of the day before'. (This is the Yale campus.)

Anne nods in understanding. She guides us into the 'hero's pose'. We sit on a block, shins reaching back. Then she demonstrates how to arrange our fingers on our faces, so we can easily block off one nostril, and breathe through the other, then switch. It feels a little uncomfortable. Jenya sniffs. 'Shall I get you a tissue?' Anne asks.

After the breathing exercise, we do a series of stretches. While not painful, they're not exactly easy. 'Feel the energy shooting out of your hands,' Anne urges gently. 'Feel the effects on your body.'

We move into balancing exercises, doing squats, engaging our cores. Then we're into full sun salutations – supposedly smooth movements up and down, arms spread. It feels good to stretch the whole body. And it feels good to listen to Anne's constant calm guidance and encouragement. Whenever her benignly mesmeric voice stops, my mind wanders to the construction noises outside.

More stretches. Anne helps me to tip my pelvis into position. 'I'm not sure my body bends that way,' I tell her. She says, 'It's OK – it's that internal feeling of energetics that's therapeutic. That feeling of extending energy. It's normal to feel "my body can't do that" in yoga.'

Over the next hour, I feel this quite a bit. Then it's time to lie flat on our backs, in what I learn is called 'corpse pose', and to be aware of our breathing. Anne says, 'Take a moment to extend gratitude to yourself and to the others who have supported you with their own efforts . . . Namaste.' And it ends.

Ninety minutes have passed in what feels more like twenty.

I can't remember the last time I engaged in ninety minutes of what could reasonably be called exercise. In fact, this is probably the first time. Like many people, I see five free minutes in a day as a valuable time slot (an opportunity to put in a load of washing and dash off an email), and it feels insanely luxurious to have spent an hour and a half stretching, and relaxing, and breathing.

Before my visit, Anne had warned me that I wouldn't be able to talk at length to her clients immediately after the class, as they had places to get to. So I'd emailed a few, to ask them what they feel they get out of the classes.

Cindy's been attending Anne's classes for about two years. She wrote:

> 'Afterwards, my body moves much more easily and
> gracefully . . . It improves my posture. It makes me feel
> prettier. I am standing taller and straighter and feel
> more in charge of my day. That strength in and of itself
> is a stress-reducer because I feel better equipped to cope
> with issues. The few minutes of rest and meditation at
> the end are a little luxury. I like how Anne refers to it
> as a mini-vacation for your mind. We are treating
> ourselves to a bit of time away from everyday life.'

One of the problems with scientifically evaluating the impact of yoga on wellbeing is that there are just so many forms. Anne describes what I just experienced as 'a blend of form and vinyasa, with an emphasis on alignment, action and attitude'.

In the West, I'm told the form of yoga most commonly offered is hatha. There are many forms of hatha – ananda, anusara, ashtanga, bikram, iyengar, to name a few – but they all emphasise physical posture, breathing techniques and relaxation or meditation.

A team including psychiatrists at the universities of Harvard and Boston reported that a twelve-week course of hatha-type yoga, involving one session three times a week, significantly boosts levels of a neurotransmitter (brain signaling chemical) known as GABA (gamma aminobutyric acid). Low levels of

GABA are associated with anxiety, so there's reason to think that raising them could be beneficial. The healthy volunteers in the study – people who had no psychiatric or medical disorders – reported feeling 'better', with significant improvements in their mood. According to the US National Center for Complementary and Alternative Medicine, part of the National Institutes of Health, there are 'studies to suggest' that yoga can reduce stress, and help relieve anxiety, depression and insomnia.

I ask Anne about the intentions of the class I just attended. 'My personal intention has not much to do with stress,' she confesses. 'It's to bring people into intimate and clear connection with all levels of their being.' To bring mind and body closer together. 'A blend of alertness and ease are the two pillars.'

I did enjoy Anne's class. But the problem I already have with it is this: it takes quite a long time. Anne believes you need to practise yoga for a minimum of one hour and fifteen minutes for the body to really respond. When she works with private clients, she'll often do two-hour blocks.

My friend Jane has a colleague, Sara, a biostatistician, who works for the same pharmaceutical company as her, near Boston, US, and who does yoga every day. Sara says she got into it by accident. 'One day I came to the gym at 6am to realise the aerobic class was cancelled. The only class I could join at the time was a yoga class. I didn't want to start my day with a disappointment that I'd got out of bed early for nothing, so I joined it. And I got hooked. I'm a full-time working mom, but I've always managed to have an exercise routine. When I started practising yoga, though, it improved my way of handling stress.' I ask her how long she spends on yoga each day. She says: one to two hours. *How does she fit it in?* 'I always exercise first thing – 6 am – when everybody else at home is still sleeping. When the kids were very young, I used to do it using videos in the living room. It takes a lot of discipline, but once you and your body get used to it, it becomes part of your everyday life and you feel weird on days you don't.'

After Jenya and Cindy head off to work, Anne and I sit down to talk a little more about her work at the Yale Stress Center. As well as her own style of yoga, she teaches mindfulness to clients. I ask her about her background. It turns out she grew up in Japan, so was aware from a young age of Zen, 'which isn't really any different from mindfulness', she says.

While at college in the US, she had a bad car accident. 'I was in a wheelchair for six months. That was difficult. I realised I needed some powerful tools to help me. At first, I went around churches – I was brought up a Christian – and monasteries, but I couldn't find anybody who really knew what I was saying. The churches told me to pray to God, but that would still be "me" praying to God, and I had lost my sense of me as an intact "I". So I went to Japan . . . I was looking for a tool that would dig down deeper below the level of cognition, because my thoughts weren't helping me. I went on a pilgrimage of eighty-eight temples in Shikoku, in a remote rural area. I encountered a monk. I was reading a book and he walked up. We didn't speak, but there was something about his face . . .'

To cut what I find a completely fascinating story slightly

short, Anne ended up finding a lay Zen teacher and also attended Komazawa University, a Zen Buddhist university in Tokyo. She spent eight years in Japan, studying meditation. From Japan, she came to New Haven to study for a Masters in Buddhist Studies at Yale. Then she became a freelance academic, and taught meditation. 'I was very involved in retreats. I did eighty of them or so, but my legs still hurt. I wondered why, and I thought – oh, yoga! It was invented to prepare the body for meditation. At first, I hated it! It was so uncomfortable. So then I did about eight teacher trainings, until I finally understood it.'

After seven years as a yoga teacher, Anne heard about the Mindfulness Based Stress Reduction course at the University of Massachusetts. She says it took her about six years to complete all the levels. Afterwards, she taught yoga and MBSR in the community and then, in 2012, the Stress Center opened, and she joined. While Anne talks, I'm mentally totting up all these years of study and practice. It comes to . . . well, quite a few. But I see virtually no lines on her face. She looks unbelievably young for her age.

Anne reaches up to a shelf behind me and takes down a book. Some time around the year 400, a man called Patanjali compiled the Yoga Sutras, 196 Indian sutras – sayings – that form the foundational text of ashtanga yoga. 'Patanjali talks about spokes,' Anne says – as in the spokes of a wheel. 'Working with the breath is one spoke. Meditation is another. There are all these pieces for living a well-balanced life. I'm a proponent of that. Physical postures are very helpful because we are bodied. But if we just go to a workout class, we won't get some of the same benefits as something more comprehensive.'

Yama
Social Restraints

Niyamas
Moral Observances

Samadhi
Spirituality

Asana
Postures

Dhyana
Meditation

Pranayama
Mindful Breathing

Dharana
Concentration

Pratyahara
Turning Inward

I could talk to Anne all day. I'm bursting with questions about what life at a Buddhist university is like, and what she learned in Japan. But right now, I'm trying to focus on exercise. And while I find myself agreeing that a well-balanced life surely relies on more than one 'spoke' (after all, that's what this book is all about), I know from brief journalistic forays into the field of exercise and neuroscience that more vigorous activities than yoga also have their own benefits for the mind. And now it's nearly nine o'clock, and time for my first meeting with Matt Stults-Kohlemainen, to find out more about what these are.

Matt grins a welcome. With his big blue eyes and rich brown hair, he wouldn't look out of place in a boy band. When I discover he's actually thirty-five, I'm surprised. What with him and Anne, I can't help thinking there must be a youth-enhancing bonus to being an expert in stress. A little later that morning, we get to this. But right now, I've got a gadget to strap on.

Matt hands me a couple of sticky circular electrode pads connected with a wire. I go into a small room across the hall and, following his instructions, apply one electrode to the dip at the front of my right shoulder, and the other on my lower, left side, above the waistband of my leggings. If I'm going to learn about how physical activity works for the mind, I'm going to have to get a little sweaty, he's warned.

This electrode kit, manufactured in Finland and known as Firstbeat Bodyguard, is a mini-electrocardiogram. At the time of writing, the Yale Stress Center is trialling it on staff, with a view to using it with patients. Throughout the day, it'll record the electrical activity of my heart. At the end, Matt promises, he'll be able to tell me when I was physiologically stressed – engaged in the fight-or-flight response – and when I was in recovery, enjoying what Herbert Benson terms the Relaxation Response (see Chapter One). He'll then be able to compare the data to my schedule, to see what I find stressful, and the impact, if any, of various types of exercise and relaxation practice on my body. While this particular gadget won't tell me much about the ongoing benefits of exercise for the mind, it should help to show the immediate, acute impacts of exercise on stress.

As Matt explains what he has planned, I feel intrigued, but also a little apprehensive. Well, mostly I am apprehensive about one part: the exercise test.

Exercise and I parted company when I turned fifteen – the minute I was no longer required to endure sports at school.

At university, the only exercise I got was walking to lecture halls or the pub and back to college (and that was only because I couldn't afford a car). Aged twenty-eight, a friend and I went to a drop-in gym in London, out of some sense that it might be a 'good thing'. After seven minutes slow jogging on the treadmill, I was uncomfortable, out of breath and bored. So I gave up. I remember thinking, who would willingly put themselves through this? Depending on how you look at it, I was lucky in one respect (or unlucky, given the impact it had on my will to exercise): I was naturally fairly slim. The only reason for exercising, I felt, was to look good, and for me, I decided, as I skipped off to the local bar to join my colleagues in yet another liquid dinner, it just was not worth the time or the pain.

Four years later, there was a hiccup in my anti-exercise agenda. I got together with James. We'd been friends at university, despite the fact he was passionate about sport, and had seemed always to be in cricket whites or rugby gear, while I was busy dyeing my hair and writing bad plays. At thirty-three, he still loved all sports, and he was running regularly. He suggested we go for a run together.

It was, as you'd expect, a disaster. My legs seized up, my lungs contracted to nothing. It was pain, pure pain.

But you can't live with a man who's mad about sport and not be forced at least to think about it. At that time, we were living in Sydney, home of the beautiful body, and I was getting older. I felt more impetus to go to the gym (occasionally). But then, after having two children in fairly rapid succession, I got straight back out of the habit. Aged thirty-eight, when Jakob was two and Lucas five months, we moved from Sydney to Sheffield. It was freezing – it *is* freezing. And since no one ever sees me out in shorts, never mind a bikini, why exercise? There isn't the time. And though I know that theoretically it's good for my body, I find myself thinking about doing exercise in the same way as contributing to a pension fund: I *know* it's important, but right now, you know what, I just can't do it.

So there I am, in Matt Stults-Kohlemainen's office, all wired up to the mini-ECG, and worrying about the exercise test. But as he prepares to explain to me how exercise has a transformative effect on the mind as much as the body, I also find myself thinking: *OK, let's have it. I'm forty years old, and this could be my big chance to be properly convinced.* I've never cared that much about physical achievements. In that, Matt and I are very different. He's a former collegiate track and cross-country runner, and he was a United States Marine from 1999 to 2008. But, he tells me, he uses exercise to improve his mental state – to help him in his academic career, his relationships and in his life in general. And to me, that sounds like something really worth listening to.

Go to the doctor complaining about depression or anxiety and stress, and the odds are you'll be offered pills, Matt says. But, he argues, if you could package up all the benefits of exercise in a pill, it would be prescribed to treat these problems by every physician in the country: 'Exercise has as strong an effect as most medications, and has way fewer side effects.'

He points to the exercise bike in the corner of his office. 'There's data that says the chances of dying on a bike like this, even in a high-intensity work-out, are less than getting struck by lightning in a two-storey building. The lightning would have to strike through two storeys to get to you!' (Though of course, it's important to exercise 'responsibly' – that is, within your limits, increasing your exercise level only gradually, and under professional guidance, if you think you need it; and to stop if you feel pain or experience any symptoms that might suggest a heart attack.)

The most common risks from exercising 'too much' are tendonitis (inflamed tendons) and other musculo-skeletal injuries, Matt tells me. (I feel reasonably confident that I will never be exposed to these particular risks.) The side effects of Selective Serotonin Re-uptake Inhibitors (SSRIs), such as Prozac – drugs that are commonly used to treat depression and chronic anxiety – include confusion, hallucinations, vomiting blood . . . and anxiety (and note, this is among the 'common' side effects). *Anxiety*? Hold on—

Yeah, Matt says, the role of serotonin in depression, stress and anxiety is complex. Serotonin, a neurotransmitter – a chemical messenger between nerve cells – is often described as the brain's 'happy chemical'. But more serotonin is not necessarily a good thing. In the short term, more of it is associated with more anxiety. Being told to stand up and give a talk in public triggers the release of serotonin. So does exercise.

Exercise *is* in itself a stressor, Matt says. But short bursts of stress are no bad thing. 'We can thrive on the experience of stress,' he says. 'Without stress, we become bored.' What scientists now think matters most for long-term psychological (as well as physical) health is what happens afterwards: after a stressful event, does your body recover quickly or slowly? Research shows that 'quickly' is what's desirable – and one fundamental psychological benefit of exercise is that it helps this to happen.

To really understand the beneficial effects of exercise, it's useful to know a little about what happens in the brain and body during a stressful event.

My own biggest sources of stress (as well as joy, yes, of course) are my kids. Every single school morning, no matter what I do to try to prevent it, we seem to run late. I wake up thinking, *This morning will be different.* But Jakob's developed an invisible ulcer on his tongue and won't eat his breakfast, Lucas drops soggy Weetabix on his only clean pre-school top, I can't find Jakob's reading book because it's at the bottom of the pile of bedding they've dragged from all our rooms for a 'duvet show', I can't locate the one particular car from Lucas's immense collection that he insists he has to take out with him, and now his face is crumpling, the tears are coming . . . For you, maybe it's something different: an irascible or incompetent colleague you can't avoid; a long commute, and frequent traffic jams. We all experience these kinds of regular, insidious stressors – profound threats to our equanimity and our psychological wellbeing.

So, as the 'threat' – the source of stress – presents itself, your sympathetic nervous system ramps up, priming you for fight or flight. This is what happens inside your body:

There's a burst of activity in the amygdala – the part of the brain that detects a 'threat'.

The amygdala instantly sends a distress signal to the hypo-thalamus (a tiny control centre in the brain), which activates the sympathetic nervous system via signals to the adrenal glands.

The adrenal glands pump out the hormone adrenaline.

Adrenaline raises your heart rate, blood pressure and breathing rate. It also triggers the release of sugar and fat from temporary storage sites, to provide your muscles with fuel, so you can run away or tackle those wild beasts – fight or flight. (And I'm honestly speaking here with reference to the evolutionary origins of this response, rather than my kids.)

After this surge of adrenaline, if the stressful event continues to bother you, the hypothalamus sends signals to the pituitary gland, which tells the adrenal glands to release cortisol – the second major stress hormone.

By now, the hippocampus (a separate brain region) is laying down memories – a threat being something you'll probably want to remember, simply from a survival perspective. And the amygdala has sent signals to the prefrontal cortex (PFC) – the seat of rational thought – giving you a chance to come up with a sensible plan to tackle the threat.

While the threat exists, this route between the hypothalamus, the pituitary and adrenal gland (known as the HPA axis), keeps cortisol churning out. When the prefrontal cortex decides the threat has passed (say, that presentation actually went all right), the hippocampus can put the brakes on cortisol production. Relief! The parasympathetic nervous system engages, putting you into recovery mode.

In people who are chronically stressed (and while I don't feel we need to see a doctor about it, I'd probably classify both James and myself in this group), physiological reactions to stress change. To use the terminology of scientists who work in the field, they become 'dysregulated'. They don't rise and fall as normal. When it comes to cortisol, for example, instead of a surge, and then a sharp drop once the source of stress has passed, cortisol levels rise a bit and don't drop back properly. In fact, those levels stay slightly elevated all the time, even at night. 'It's a blunted response,' Matt says. And it's not good for you.

For a long time, scientists have known that chronically high levels of cortisol interfere with learning and memory, harm the immune system, and damage health. In 2013, two papers published in the influential journal *Science* identified high cortisol as a possible trigger for mental illness.

People who don't recover well after a stressful experience are said to have a poor 'parasympathetic response' – because it's the job of the parasympathetic nervous system to calm you down. If you can boost that system, you can, in theory, help people cope well with stress. And regular exercise, it turns out, is an excellent way of doing this.

Matt and his colleagues have taken groups of regular exercisers and non-exercisers into the lab, and asked them to give a speech in public, or count backwards out loud – anything to get them stressed. 'What we see with cortisol is that the exercisers react more strongly, so they have a higher spike,' he says. 'But then when the stress ends, they recover much faster.'

Boosting recovery from stress is far from the only benefit of exercise. Work over recent years has shown that there are many ways it can help you deal better with stress and anxiety, and improve psychological health in the long term.

First, the 'hard' science (but if acronyms make your eyes glaze over in the way the sports pages of the Sunday papers do mine, feel free to skip this bit; I will come back to a few of these factors in other chapters in any case):

One crucial benefit is that exercise dampens down activity

in that HPA axis. A Princeton University team has found that regular physical exercise tweaks the response of the hypothalamus to stress, triggering the firing of 'calming' neurons, so warding off anxiety.

As you no doubt already know, exercise also stimulates the production of endorphins, which, as well as being painkillers, also have a mood-boosting effect. In the immediate short term, exercise also boosts alertness. If your brain's slowing down, a few star jumps by your desk could be a healthier option than a bar of chocolate. (Perhaps I should confess that I first learned this one from the TV series *Elementary*, but real-world exercise/brain specialists confirm it.)

Then there's something called Brain-Derived Neurotrophic Factor (BDNF). This chemical, which has been dubbed 'Miracle-Gro for your brain' triggers the growth of *new* brain cells, and protects brain cells in regions involved in mood from the damaging effects of cortisol. (Some anti-depressants, including Prozac, also raise BDNF levels.)

Exercise also boosts the number of mitochondria – energy-producing powerhouses – in brain cells, theoretically helping to delay mental fatigue. It reduces tension in your muscles, helping, in turn, to reduce feelings of anxiety. It can rein in the production of serotonin in parts of the brain where you don't want too much of it – like the amygdala. And, if all this isn't enough, it helps with levels of inflammation.

People who exercise regularly have a sharp 'inflammatory response' – there's a surge in markers of inflammation in the body, but then a dive (according to new work by Matt and his colleagues). Non-exercisers have a blunted response – so their baseline levels are higher. Chronically raised levels of various markers of inflammation are associated not only with some physical diseases, like cancer, but also depression. (There's one really interesting study finding that a rise in markers of inflammation associated with work stress can be completely counteracted by exercise.)

If your eyes are beginning to glaze, I'm nearly done. But I can't ignore the 'softer' benefits, because they matter too:

Exercise is a distraction. If you're fussing and fuming, you're paying attention to the stressor (whether that's a work project you're struggling to finish or the prospect of a weekend trip to relatives you're not that fond of). 'Exercise helps you to take your mind off problems – it helps you to recalibrate your attention,' says Matt. 'If you're attending to negative cues – if every little thing is setting you off – that's not productive. Say you then go and do a yoga movement, you're focusing on your breath, your posture, your alignment. These are positive things to think about.' (More mindful things, I guess.)

There's also the 'mastery hypothesis' to explain the benefits of exercise. The idea here is that exercise is a challenge and if you meet that challenge, there's a boost to your self-esteem and confidence. 'So when you're confronted with stressors, you may shrug them off a little bit more,' Matt says.

Finally, there's another, physical boost to your capacity to deal with stress. A bout of exercise improves your blood pressure for two to three hours afterwards, helping to blunt your reaction to any stressful events in that time. If you exercise regularly, this effect may even stretch to four to five hours. So if you know you have a stressful meeting, an exam or even a date lined up, you could aim to schedule a bout of exercise a couple of hours beforehand to help you cope. 'I've certainly done that,' Matt says.

I ask Matt to tell me more about how he 'uses' exercise in his life. He laughs. When he gets stressed, he becomes a total exercise junkie, he says. He remembers one particularly stressful period in his life: 'I'd wake up at 5.30am and work out every morning, then I'd come home and run, then I'd go to the gym. I was working out for many hours a day.'

I know people who are a bit like this all the time. I'm sure many of us do. My friend Sunny is married to a man with an exercise compulsion:

'Aaah, the exercise thing . . . yes, it is in fact a 'thing' in our relationship. My husband, Ryan, is one of those people who needs to exercise every day. Every. Day. Without fail. He can't go a day without it. He would either swim, run or cycle virtually every day. And if he doesn't, he becomes a vile beast – irritable, grumpy, moody, angry and surly. He's like a junkie who needs to get his fix! Many a time on the weekend we've been having lovely quiet family time at home (me with a cup of tea in hand reading a magazine, kids playing Lego or colouring in and him supposedly reading the newspaper) and he starts to get all jittery and irritable until I scream, "Oh for goodness sake, just go for a run!" He's out that door quicker than a cheetah. I do feel that his exercise impinges on our family time or my 'alone' time. With three small children, we often seem to tag team in order to do the things we want to do solo on the weekend (him exercise, me sleep . . .).

Sometimes it feels like a competition. He'll say something like, "Man, I really need to do some exercise," which effectively means me getting left with our three small children for a few hours . . . which I resent. However, if he doesn't get his exercise fix, he's unbearable. So it's a Catch-22.'

An 'addiction' to exercise can be a real problem, Matt says. If being forced to skip exercise for a day makes you stressed, that's not necessarily a good place to be. Now, he says, he's much less of a junkie. He takes breaks from his desk job to take two half-mile walks every day, one in the morning, one in the afternoon. One day a week, he works out at home with rubber bands and light dumbbells, as well as doing exercises that involve what he calls 'functional movements' ('Think starting a lawnmower, without the lawnmower . . .'). Then, 'One day a week, I do housework.' *Housework*? (This is a former US Marine, remember.) He smiles. 'Very hard. I make it exercise. I scrub the floors; I do squats with my laundry basket.' Four days a week, he goes to the gym and does forty-five minutes of resistance training. On only one day a week does he engage in what he calls 'a hard cardiovascular workout'. 'That's forty-five minutes, about thirty of which are hovering around eighty-five per cent of my maximum heart rate.' And there I was thinking that jogging after Lucas on his scooter counts as tough . . .

Still, Matt does emphasise that if he's feeling 'overly fatigued', he'll take a day off – which typically means he'll exercise six days a week, rather than seven.

With patients at the Stress Center, Matt encourages variety when it comes to exercise. He digs out a sheet of paper for me showing an 'exercise pyramid', developed by a team at the University of Missouri, for adults aged eighteen to sixty-four. It's a bit like a food pyramid, only in place of carbs at the bottom there's 'Lifestyle' – biking, yard work, household chores and walking; in the middle there's 'Aerobic Activity' – walking, jogging, swimming or a sport like basketball; further up, as the pyramid narrows, there's 'Strength and Flexibility' – yoga, stretching, strength training; and at the very top is 'Inactivity' – sitting, the exercise equivalent of gorging on sugar.

If my goal is maximum mental strength and wellbeing, I ask how long I should be spending on all these different activities? This is what Matt says:

- Lifestyle-type exercise should take place every single day, though not necessarily in huge doses. Research shows that just a fifteen- to twenty-minute walk has a massive impact on how stressed or anxious you feel (the same impact as a session of t'ai chi), but should be done regularly for maximum long-term impact.

- Strength and flexibility training – which includes yoga or lifting weights – should ideally be done at least twice a week.

But what I'm most worried about is the final section – 'Aerobic activity'. It's only the second step up on the pyramid, so I'm expecting Matt to say 'a lot' and 'very often'. Realistically, I'm not at all confident I'd be able to work out for forty-five minutes every day, as he does:

- Aerobic activity – Matt says: 'The guidance for physical health is 150 minutes of moderate intensity aerobic exercise a week. And for psychological health? It turns out that it's the same.'

Carol Ewing Garber at Columbia University has led the work on this. She's looked at total durations of physical activity (not just 'exercise' because walking up the stairs or gardening count – so long as they make you breathe harder and get your heart rate up) and depression and found that little bits of moderate-level activity go a long way to preventing depression, but that there is *no additional effect* beyond a total of about three hours a week.

There are no official exercise guidelines for psychological health, but based on the research, Matt recommends five thirty-minute sessions per week. While there is some evidence that really vigorous exercise – *if* you're fit enough to cope with it – may be most effective at boosting levels of BDNF (that 'Miracle-Gro for the brain'), the sessions don't *have* to be hard, Matt says, and they don't have to be at the gym. Brisk walking is OK, if that's a physical challenge for you. *Any* kind of walking is OK, if it's a challenge – so, if it gets your breathing and heart rate up, and maybe leaves you with a little sweat on the forehead. But these sessions do need to be regular: while you may feel pretty good after one bout of exercise at a level that's enough to challenge you, to get the long-term mental benefits, of course, you need to do it again, and again – and again.

And if you can do it outdoors, so much the better. For an illustration of how even gentle exercise in the tranquillity of nature can change your outlook, I don't think you can do better than this, drawn from a piece I read in the *New Yorker*:

Ittetsu Nemoto is a Buddhist priest who conducts death workshops for the suicidal at his temple in Seki, a small town in remote, rural Japan. He tells the people who attend his workshop to imagine they have cancer, and have three months left to live. He asks them to write down what they would do in this time. Then they're told to imagine they have one month left, then one week, and finally ten minutes. Most people start crying. Some realise they have spent so long thinking about wanting to die, they'd forgotten even to think about how to live.

The author of the article describes the different ways in which Nemoto tries to lead desperate people away from death and towards life. She reports the story of a man who'd been living as a hikikomori – one of as many as a million young people in Japan who stay holed up in their homes, too afraid to leave. Nemoto has a rule that anyone who wants his help must come to him; this man eventually mustered the courage to make the journey. The temple is a long walk from the nearest train station. By the time he'd completed that walk, the unfamiliar sunshine and exercise had improved his state of mind so much, he turned around and went home, 'cured', at least for the moment.

Scientists, too, have accumulated evidence that exercising outdoors (and just *being* outdoors in natural environments) can improve mental health. A team led by researchers at the European Centre for the Environment and Human Health analysed data from studies that had investigated the benefits of indoor versus outdoor exercise on psychological (as well as physical) wellbeing. They found that exercising in nature was associated with bigger improvements in energy and 'positive engagement', as well as 'revitalisation' and bigger reductions in tension, confusion, anger and depression.

There are groups that promote this. The Conservation Volunteers, an organisation formed to look after green places, suggest you join one of their Green Gyms: 'Want to improve your health and wellbeing but not too keen on running machines or lycra? Then why not take a look at our award-winning alternative . . .' suggests the jauntily written website of the UK branch. 'You could be helping the environment as well as yourself!'

Scientists speculate about why exercising outdoors may be better than indoors. One argument is that as we evolved to exist in natural settings, our brains find it easier to process country scenes, compared with urban environments, and there is some preliminary brain-scanning evidence that supports this. But also, if you're outside on a sunny day, sunlight can lower blood pressure, and so, in theory, improve your ability to cope with stress.

As well as his daily walks, Matt does his weekly 'hard cardiovascular workout' in a natural environment: Sleeping Giant State Park in Hamden, Connecticut. And he goes alone. There's some evidence that if you exercise on your own, rather than with other people, you get a bigger boost to your psychological wellbeing afterwards, he tells me. 'I always go on my own to a state park,' Matt says. 'I just can't do it at a gym, because I know I'm not going to get the same response.'

Why should exercising alone be better for your mental state? No one knows for sure. It could simply be that you're more distracted if you're in a gym – there are TVs everywhere and maybe friends or acquaintances to chat to – and these diversions make the exercise seem less unpleasant, so there's less of an upswing in mood when you stop. Still, some people find it very hard to exercise without multi-tasking, Matt says, 'and if this is the case, I would encourage them to do whatever it takes to exercise, because the physical health benefits alone are so great'. While it's best to run outside on your own, clearly it's better to jog on a treadmill next to a friend than do nothing.

Speaking for myself, I know that when I did go to a gym, I used every technique I could think of to separate my mind from my body, to distract myself, so that as far as was possible, I wasn't really doing the exercise, my body was. My legs might have been moving, but I was just listening to some of my favourite songs.

Many of us use music when we exercise. Research confirms it can help us to pump our limbs faster and harder, without extra discomfort. The theory is that a fast beat revs up our bodies, preparing us for exertion. And there is some work confirming my own perception – that music can make workouts *more* enjoyable, at least for certain people.

Still, Matt, as well as others at the Stress Center, are keen on what they term 'mindful exercise', which turns out to be the diametric opposite of what I've always done. They argue that for maximum psychological benefit it's better to 'approach' – that is, really be aware of and consciously experience – all the sensations in your body, whether negative or positive.

James DiLoreto, who sees clients at the centre while he is finishing his post-grad training to become a certified psychologist, says, 'Even if you're feeling discomfort on the bike, if you come into your body and allow yourself to experience it, you'll notice these feelings are temporary. They have an up and a down. And by viewing them not as good or bad, your approach to them can change.'

So maybe if you're mentally strong, like Matt or James DiLoreto, and can embrace the fatigue and the pain, there are benefits to exercising without music. I'm not sure I'm there *just* yet. And as I think this, I glance warily at the bike to which James has just referred. I know it's almost time for my exercise test. But first, Karyn Gunnet-Shoval is going to help me to understand 'mindful exercise'. She works as a clinician at the centre, and she's going to take me on a therapeutic intervention she uses with clients: a mindful walk.

In contrast to Anne, who radiates calm, Karyn is petite, intense and highly animated. Anne's smiles are slow. Karyn's are lightning strikes. While she talks (which she does quickly), she leans forwards, physically projecting herself into my briefing.

'There are two different intentions with walking,' she says. 'The first is for exercise.' This exercise component will, she explains, be quite fast. The second, is mindful walking. She goes on:

> 'Both are extremely important. With walking, we
> might be thinking about all the things we need to get
> done or that are stressing us out. In mindful walking,
> we're really focused on the here and now. We want to
> be in the body, in the moment. I want you to think:

How am I breathing? Am I feeling any pain in my leg or my foot? Often anxieties and stressors are going to come up and people push them away. Say to yourself, I'm going to be in the moment. Be aware of your thoughts, and then come back to the moment. You might even feel bored. Notice that thought and let it pass by. Think: *If I'm stressed, is my heart rate going up? How can I slow my pace so that my heart rate is not all over the place?'*

Karyn explains that she'll take me on the walk in the way she takes her clients: she'll lead, I'll walk behind. We won't talk. I'll follow her quickly to nearby Amistad Park, and then mindfully around it.

Before we leave the centre, she asks me to close my eyes. Then she guides me through a five-minute mindful breathing exercise. I breathe normally, but focus on the sensation of the breath wherever I feel it most – in my nostrils, in my chest . . . Then we're off.

It's a short walk to the park, but she *does* walk fast. I feel slightly self-conscious, trailing behind her, as she strides ahead, but no one passing by seems to notice. Or maybe they're just used to it. I try not to think about this. I try to feel my feet on the path, and the breeze, which after the sultry start to the day, has turned cool, and is fresh on my skin.

When we get to the park, Karyn's pace slows dramatically. I try to focus on the weight of my body, and I feel a twinge in my hip. I notice the trees, remember I'm not really meant to be looking at my surroundings, and try to bring my thoughts back to my internal state. I notice a couple of women on a bench, and I can't help wondering what they're so intently talking about. Again, I bring myself back. It's not a battle, exactly. But it is constant.

After two slow laps, Karyn leaves the park, and ups her pace. We walk fast to a nearby cafe and sit down. About thirty minutes have passed since we left the Stress Center. Again, she takes me on a body-scanning, breathing-awareness exercise. I try to ignore the couple at the table next to us, and listen to her voice as she guides me. I feel the air in my nostrils . . . And we're done.

After buying a banana (I'm hungry after all this), we walk fast back to the centre. 'Our bodies are set up to deal with stress before anything else,' Karyn tells me, as we head for the lifts, 'including illness. That's why stress is so bad when you're ill. And physically our posture is important. If we act in a tense way, shoulders up, body tight, the same stress response will be there, leading to chronic stress. We need to learn to relax our minds as well as our bodies.'

I know what I said in the last chapter about seeing the benefits in 'mindless' rather than 'mindful' walking. But after the walk, I do feel relaxed – and I can't help wondering if that will be reflected in the data being collected by the Bodyguard electrodes. That sense of relaxation is short-lived, however. Karyn escorts me back to Matt's office. And there's no escaping it now. It's finally time for the aerobic exercise test.

James DiLoreto is here and is going to take notes. Matt gives me a heart-rate monitor, and I nip across the hall to strap it to my chest. Back in the office, he gives me the wristband that will display my heart rate. Before I even get up from my chair to walk to the bike, that rate starts to rise. It's unnerving to see my body responding to something my mind is doing its best to pretend isn't about to happen. But just the anticipation of exercise, and the anxiety I'm feeling, is enough to send my heart into overdrive. It was at 80 bpm; now it's 99. As I get onto the bike it's 105, and I haven't even started to put pressure on a pedal.

'Push and pull, Emma. *Push and pull!*'

I'm pedalling hard, and Matt's clapping quickly, urging me on. 'You can do it!'

Before I started the test, Matt asked me to rate my level of wellbeing on a scale from -5 to +5 (where 0 is feeling neutral). Then came a three-minute warm-up, my heart rate monitored as I kept the revolutions per minute to 50.

After completing the scale again, plus another ranking of perceived effort, I'm now on the first of four sprint-tests. Matt's added a little resistance, and I have to pedal as hard as I can for twenty seconds. I lean forwards, gripping the handlebars, determined not to be the weakest subject he's ever had. I get up to a speed of 133 RPM – and then it's time to rest. I indicate my scores on both the scales (up on effort, one down on wellbeing), and we go again.

This time, I get to 141 RPM. I've beaten my previous score. I feel good! I score up for both effort and wellbeing. The third time, I get to 142 RPM – better again. And I still feel better than average! The fourth test is really hard. I'm pretty much at maximum effort. I only get to 141 RPM. But that's not much below 142 and I'm kind of enjoying the challenge. I give myself +3 for wellbeing.

Matt asks me to cycle slowly, while I recover a little. Once my heart rate's dropped back from a high of 170 to 130, I'm allowed off the bike. Hot, with burning thighs, I stumble back to my chair. Matt then takes me through a guided mindful body-scanning and breathing exercise. This isn't meant to be a relaxation exercise of itself, he tells me. Now the exercise 'stress' has ceased, my body will have shifted into the recovery 'relaxation' state, so this exercise is designed to help you pay attention to those changes – to be mindful of them. Afterwards, he asks me to rate my wellbeing. I'm still feeling +3.

'That's interesting,' he says. Most people, it turns out, feel steadily worse and worse as the test progresses. But afterwards, they get a sharp rebound – reporting a much higher wellbeing score than before they started. 'There's something magical about the recovery,' he says. Well, usually.

But I knew why I felt better after the second test: I'd beaten my first score. I don't think of myself as being particularly competitive. At least, not unhealthily competitive, *especially* not when it comes to any kind of physical effort. But I guess my ratings say otherwise. When I competed against myself and won, it felt good.

Still, Matt's observation that most people feel steadily worse as the exercise test progresses is important. Exercise at a level that's challenging probably won't feel good while you're doing it. If you're on the treadmill, and you're feeling worse than you did before you came to the damned gym, and wondering *why* did you decide to put yourself through this? – that's normal and it doesn't mean the wellbeing-promoting effects of exercise aren't working for you. Because it's only afterwards you're going to feel better. And many people, as Matt has seen, do feel much, *much* better than they did before.

Before I leave the Stress Center, it's time for me to find out my results.

First, from the exercise test, I know I'm not fit. But although I sit while I'm working, there's no time for sitting in the mornings, or after picking up the kids. At weekends, we're often at the park. Every night, I carry at least one of the boys up the stairs to bed. I'm always picking up toys and vacuuming and hauling washing from the machine. Maybe, I can't help hoping, all that might help . . .

Matt takes into account my age, my heart-rate scores, my RPMs while I was cycling and what I've told him about my usual exercise patterns. He works out that I'm 'moderately fit'. Not great. But actually not awful.

Now it's time to download the data from the Bodyguard sensors. The technology is proprietary, but one of the key measures is heart-rate variability – the relative change in heart rate over time. More variability is good. It reflects a better-functioning parasympathetic nervous system (the branch that calms you down). Less is bad.

Matt sends all my data off to a server in Finland and, a

short while later, a graph appears on his monitor. The jagged lines are colour-coded. They don't look that great. There's an awful lot of red – which I don't need Matt to tell me probably means 'stressed'. There's very little green – 'recovery'. In fact, during the past five and a half hours, I've been pretty much consistently 'stressed'. Yes, I'm in an unfamiliar environment and I've been interviewing and even exercising, but I haven't *felt* stressed. Are my results normal?

There is a difference between threatening stress and challenging stress, Matt underscores – a concept I've already come across: work, for example, may be a challenge, if you enjoy it; it may be a threat, if you don't. And there is a difference as far as the body is concerned – threatening stress narrows the arteries and veins carrying blood around your body. Challenging stress doesn't have this effect. So challenging stress may not be as physically damaging – and certainly it's nowhere near as psychologically injurious.

One of the problems with the Firstbeat sensors, and similar technologies, is that they can't yet tell the difference between a welcome challenge, or even excitement, and a genuine threat. On one of Matt's own recent graphs (there's an awful lot of green – but then he's extremely fit, and more mindful and so on), there's a red spike in the evening that has him perplexed for a minute. 'Oh – I was reading *Game of Thrones*! I think of that as exciting, not stressful.'

Going back to my own graph, while it is almost all red, my results do show something positive. My single, sky-scraping spike into utterly relaxed green came at the point when Karyn took me through the meditation after the mindful walk. Yes, I'd felt relaxed. But to see my heart's activity in total agreement was fascinating.

As I say goodbye to Matt, wishing him luck with all his 'challenges', my brain brimming with everything I've found out, I decide that before I design my own routine, I'll talk to some friends to find out more about how other people incorporate exercise into their daily lives.

My friends span the extremes, from those who do absolutely no exercise, bar walking to and from their cars, to one who runs sixteen miles to and from work every day and competes in *twenty-four-hour* running races over the peaks of the Lake District. There seems no point (for me) in talking to the exercise-obsessed, but I need people with knowledge and experience. So I go to a couple who run triathlons, and exercise pretty much daily – my school friend Jane, who we met in Chapter One and her husband, Adam. They live in the beautiful, historic town of Lexington, Massachusetts, not far from Boston. The summers are lovely, but the winters are severe. I whinge about the climate in Yorkshire – I couldn't even *think* about going out for a run in November. But they seem to manage. Jane says:

> 'I enjoy exercise, rather than see it as a chore, espe-
> cially if it's outdoors. I look forward to the sense of
> freedom that running and cycling bring about – but I
> hate thrashing up and down an indoor pool. From a
> physical perspective, exercise helps me feel strong,

toned and capable. Psychologically, I get a positive outlook about my self-image and wellbeing, and it gives me a focus in my life. Exercise, of all types, definitely helps reduce stress for me, especially after a difficult day at work. I like variety, or I get bored. I do strength training once a week, run once a week, cycle to work once or twice a week, cycle at the weekend, walk four miles to town and back, sometimes do yoga, sometimes swim. I actually can't imagine my life without exercise.'

Adam says:

'Exercise hurts. Sometimes a lot. But it's incredible! I'm a "Type-A", high-energy person, so for me exercise is all about getting fitter, faster, better, healthier. Different types of exercise have a different effect both before and afterwards. I really have to want to go swimming to get started. But the after-swim feeling is lovely – totally relaxed, chilled, without a care in the world. Running is different – more of an intense fatigue. Not a relaxed tiredness. I feel more alert and active afterwards. With biking, it's an all-over body fatigue, but with what feels like energy left. I don't think I could live without exercise. I love the outdoor aspects and the freedom it brings.'

I think about all this. Yes, I live in the northern UK, which gets cold and wet. Very wet. But Sheffield, as British cities go, is extremely pro-sport. It's home to Jessica Ennis, the face of the British Olympic team at the 2012 summer games. Sebastian Coe, head of the committee that won those games for London, started running seriously while at school here in Sheffield. If Yorkshire had been a country in those 2012 Olympics, it would have ranked twelfth on the medals table.

Climbers also love the countryside around Sheffield. I can't tell you exactly why; my mind tends to wander when they talk about it. But there's no denying it: less than half an hour's drive from my house is everything from climbing to mountain-biking, canoeing, to horse-riding. And as in any city, of course, there are gyms. Although even Sheffield's gyms are over-achieving – I decide to visit the one nearest my house, to check out their rates, and I discover banners and posters announcing that this. The Hallamshire Tennis Club – and gym – is home to Jonny Marray, who in 2012 became the first British player to win a Wimbledon doubles final since 1936. And if that wasn't enough, Nick Matthew, three times world squash champion, also trains here. I mention this to my mother-in-law, who regularly plays tennis at the club. 'Oh yes,' she says. 'Nick Matthews's dad used to train Victoria!' That's Vicky, James's sister, who used to play squash for England . . .)

Still, I remind myself, that for maximum psychological benefit, I just need to find a way to manage 150 minutes of 'moderate to vigorous' exercise per week, which should include a couple of sessions of resistance-training or stretching. (Though something I feel I should stress here is that being inactive when you're not actually exercising is still not great. There's a lot of evidence that sitting is bad for your physical health. If I could afford one, I'd think seriously about buying a treadmill desk, so I could walk slowly while working.)

After some consideration, I decide not to take up an outdoor exercise 'activity'. I know what Matt said about exercising outdoors, and I remember what he and Jane both said about variety, but I also know that if exercise is going to happen for me, it's going to have to be grounded in a simple routine. And, as with meditation, the more basic and manageable the routine, I decide, the better.

So, I go for this:

I join the local gym. I decide I'll go once on Tuesdays, and once at the weekend. I'll jog or run on the treadmill for twenty minutes and then lift weights for twenty minutes.

And I join an adult fitness class. Every Friday morning, I take Lucas to SportStars – an excellent class for young kids, involving running, kicking, throwing, jumping and a lot of giggling. And every week, I spend the full forty-five minutes of his class eating an almond croissant and switching between watching him having fun and reading my copy of the *New Yorker*. But the people who organise SportStars run adult fitness sessions at the same time, on the playing field outside. I've seen the gym-togged mums drop off their kids for their class, and done my best to pretend they don't exist . . . Reluctantly, I sign up.

So far, that's three sessions of forty or so minutes, including two with some weights. I'm almost there.

Now, what else?

In Sydney, I lived close to the city centre, and I walked everywhere. Here, I pretty much always use the car. I recently came across a study finding that people who switch from driving to work to cycling, walking or even taking a bus, develop a higher level of wellbeing (rated in terms of impact on feelings of worthlessness, unhappiness, sleepless nights and being unable to face problems). In theory, we could walk to school but, as I said, we're always running late, and who wants to drag complaining young children up a long hill. In the drizzle. Or the snow.

Still, I decide that we'll walk to school twice a week, so long as it isn't snowing, pouring with rain or threatening to pour with rain. (No point setting myself goals I'll never achieve.)

That's five thirty-minute sessions.

Then, carried along on the wave of all this planned achievement, James and I make another decision. It's something we've been thinking about for a while, since we left our beloved poodle-cross dog with close friends in Sydney. We decide to get another.

I very rarely take breaks while I work. But with a dog, there'll be no excuses for not walking every day. It'll be a whining, licking incentive to get up from my desk, go out to the Botanical Gardens, which are conveniently close to my house, and walk fast *outdoors*. On the two days I have Lucas at home with me, we'll take the dog to the park with us, and I'll commit to *walking fast*. So if it is snowing, or pouring with rain, I'll still be getting in my minutes – and many of them will be outdoors.

And I think I have it. A workable exercise plan.

Still, making a plan is one thing. Sticking to it is quite another. I'm going to look more closely at ways to help me actually achieve my goals a little later, when I get to mental toughness (see Chapter Six). For now, though, Matt and James have a couple of suggestions:

James advises to really focus on how you feel now – and how you can hope to feel if you follow your plan (he uses this approach with clients). Bear in mind that there's a wealth of hard scientific evidence to show that exercise *does* make people feel better in all sorts of ways. If you feel lethargic, if you find it hard to get going, if you feel stressed or anxious or you're plagued by low moods, there is plenty of work to show that (unless the cause of all this is an underlying medical problem that needs treatment) exercise really could help to turn this around.

And if you're unsure about how easy you'll find it to stick to your exercise plan, Matt advises to make it as detailed as possible, and to really visualise the process: create a timetable, so you know exactly what time you have to leave the house or get to bed, to have enough sleep to enable you to get up half an hour earlier to exercise before work, if that's your intention. Exercising is hard, he accepts. The more you can make it an automatic part of your week, the easier it'll be to stick to a plan.

THE EXERCISE CHECKLIST

- 'Lifestyle'-type exercise (gardening, housework, a stroll to the shops) should take place every day.

- Strength and flexibility training – which includes yoga or lifting weights – should ideally be done at least twice a week.

- One hundred and fifty minutes per week of 'moderate- to vigorous-intensity' exercise will provide you with the maximum psychological benefits. It might help to break this down into five thirty-minute blocks. But if you do very little or no exercise right now, you'll need to build slowly up to this level.

- If you can exercise outdoors, there seem to be added psychological benefits.

- If you can engage in mindful exercise, there may also be benefits – but if music helps you, use it.

PS Remember how I was struck by the youthful appearance of Matt and Anne? Anne I suppose I'm not too staggered about. She's spent years of her life studying meditation and yoga, and I'd put the odds of her smoking, eating junk food and partying all hours at essentially zero. But Matt was in the US Marines – hardly a relaxing experience – and he's done a lot of sport. Shouldn't that take a toll? Maybe, but there's evidence that people who exercise regularly have younger-looking skin, he says. One theory to explain why goes back to the work on the genomic effects of meditation by Herbert Benson and his colleagues at Harvard. The Relaxation Response may slow the ageing of cells. You can trigger it with meditation. And you can help it to happen with regular exercise.

CHAPTER THREE

URISH YOUR MIND

Robert Burton was a seventeenth-century Oxford don with a fascination for cartography, navigation, mathematics, chemistry, pharmacology and medicine. Oh, and he wrote plays. Today, he's best known as the author of *The Anatomy of Melancholy*, first published in 1621. His life's work, it was an encyclopaedia on the affliction: 'What it is, with all the kinds, causes, symptomes, prognosticks & severall cures of it.'

On a recent trip to London, I visited the Wellcome Library, home of a first edition, and spent a fascinated few hours leafing through the volumes. Burton certainly had some clear ideas about the causes of melancholy – or depression, as we'd call it now. 'Be not solitary, be not idle,' is one you'd hear today. And he was convinced that particular foods act as threats or bolsters to psychological wellbeing. Some of these you also hear today:

86

Bread that is made of baser graine, as Pease, Beans, Oates, Rye, or over hard baked, crustie and blacke, is often spoke against. [Bread is bad – yes, you definitely hear that.]

Milke and all that comes of milke, as Butter and Cheese, Curds &c increase melancholy (Whey only excepted). [Dairy is bad – yes, you hear that too.]

Burton also cautions against the consumption of most meats. Hare, in particular, is singled out. It is 'hard of digestion, breeds incubus . . . and causeth fearful dreams'.

Fish too are bad news, however. To engage in 'solitary living and fish eating' is effectively to write yourself off.

The idea that what we eat and drink affects our mood and psychological health dates back well before Burton's time, of course, and still holds today. And all that conflicting health advice I mentioned in the Introduction so often concern what we consume, with any given food going, it seems, from hero to zero and back within a week or less. On the same day I happened to see a story stating that there are no benefits for the brain from taking omega-3 fatty-acid supplements, my mother-in-law dropped by the house and demanded to check the fish fingers in our freezer. It was *imperative*, she told me, that they were fortified with omega-3s – she'd read a piece by an expert on it in her paper that morning.

Given the abundance of claims and counter-claims, this part of my plan – to find out how my diet might affect my mind – is probably the one about which I feel most apprehensive. And to make things more difficult, the number of claims is massively outnumbered by the tally of academic papers on the subject.

Take just one nutrient, resveretrol, which is found in the skins of grapes and is present in red wine (a nutrient that's inspired an entire *diet*, for heaven's sake). There are more than 20,000 journal papers on the impacts of resveratrol on health, so how am I meant to make sense of all the results? And yet, if I'm going to go beyond the contradictory headlines, and really get to the bottom of what the science actually tells us, somehow I'll have to.

First, though, I want to work out which foods and ingredients are most often claimed as either beneficial or bad in terms of psychological wellbeing.

Barring stuff I just *like* (a list topped by dark chocolate, any kind of cake and Yorkshire puddings), and things I consume *because* of their mind-altering properties (alcohol and caffeine), I'm not sure that any particular food makes me feel happy, or depressed or anxious.

But I do sometimes experience 'brain fog', that blurry, awful feeling of trying to force thoughts to the surface. And there are times I feel so overwhelmed with fatigue, even the pavement looks an appealing spot for a nap. Yes, I have young kids. I'm woken in the night at least a couple of times a week. They never get up after 6.30am, so if I go out in an evening, I know I'm going to be sleep-deprived the next day, and that sleep debt will probably carry over for another day or two. But I wonder if there's more to my brain fogs than physical tiredness. Certainly, I have friends and family members who are convinced that what they eat and drink affects how they feel. And if there *are* common dietary triggers of sluggishness or low mood or anxiety, or feeling *great,* maybe I just haven't made the connection in myself — and it's time I did.

*

The kitchen smells of spicy carrot and chocolate. There's a printout of a 'mood-boosting' menu on the countertop, and I'm working my way through it:

Carrot soup and pine nuts and walnuts

Escabeche of mackerel

Lamb with kale, cauliflower and garlic

Beetroot and chocolate cake with blackberries and crème fraîche

'Working my way through it' on a Thursday night means: bought carrot soup, smoked salmon from the freezer, garlic-smeared lamb chops with supermarket-prepped kale and cauliflower and bought beetroot and chocolate cake, a punnet of blackberries and crème fraîche hurriedly emptied into the only clean and vaguely appropriately sized non-Tupperware dishes I can find.

I hear a key in the front door. James walks into the kitchen. The bought soup might as well be rotten fish guts for the glance it gets. When we have guests, he almost always does all the cooking, and he's very good at it. But it's a *Thursday* night, and there's only half an hour before our friends are due. I've invited Kate Douglas – an editor on *New Scientist* magazine, and an open- yet tough-minded judge of health claims – and her husband Ed, an accomplished climber and mountaineering journalist and writer, who believes that what he eats and drinks affects how he feels.

This particular menu is the creation of two David Kennedys. One is a professional chef in Newcastle. The other is Director of the Brain, Performance and Nutrition Research Centre at the University of Northumbria. I found the menu on the Internet. (More on the rationale for the ingredients a little later.) For now, buying their time with dinner (even this hasty attempt at it), I want to ask Ed more about his own experiences with food – and talk through with them some of the issues surrounding food and mood.

I pass round the carrot soup (which James has poured into espresso cups and garnished with herbs from the garden – really, who'd know it was Tesco's?). Ed says:

'I can't drink coffee after noon, or I can't sleep at night. Dark chocolate – I can't eat that in the evening, or it'll keep me awake. Otherwise, it's *very good*. Cake is also good. I don't feel good after red meat. Alcohol we try to avoid three days a week. Alcohol makes me wake up at 3am, and I really don't like that because then I start having an existential crisis . . . Omega-3 supplements I take every day. They're a mood leveller, I've read.'

Ed tells us he's taken omega-3 supplements for years. They make him feel psychologically better, he says. 'But that might just be because it's part of my routine. I think I probably *associate* taking them with feeling better.'

Kate says she thinks the only major dietary influence on

her mood is whether or not she's hungry. 'If I don't eat, I get ratty.'

Ed raises an eyebrow. '"Ratty" doesn't really do it justice.'

She laughs. 'No . . . I get irritable, bad-tempered and snappy.'

Kate, too, has tried taking omega-3s. 'I started taking them at the same time as Ed, but I gave up. I didn't notice an effect on me.' In fact, she says she's tried all sorts of dietary modifications to see what might happen. 'I've even tried drinking my own urine. I'm that interested in self-experimentation. But I just haven't found anything that's really had an effect on me.'

So what does this mean? Is Ed imagining some of the impacts? Or do foods and nutrients affect different people in different ways? Kate certainly believes it's the latter: 'People's reactions to food and drink and stress and all the rest are all so individual.'

The soup cups cleared, we move on to the salmon, and Ed talks about how he craves different foods at altitude. Sardines at sea level? Awful. But shift him hundreds of metres up a mountain, and they taste delicious. He just can't get enough of them. They make him feel great. And the same goes for really salty and fatty foods. At altitude, where there's less oxygen, whether his mind's feeling in control or not, his *body* is stressed. So clearly, there's a link between the state of his body, the food he desires, and how those foods make him feel. While few of us are as likely as Ed to find ourselves at the top of the Matterhorn one week and halfway up Everest the next, other experiences – like exercise and fasting, not to mention feeling anxious – do put our bodies into states of stress, at least in the short term.

So, it isn't just differences between people to bear in mind, then, when it comes to the impacts of food on how we feel, but differences *within ourselves*, depending on what state we're in, physically and psychologically: have we been exercising or fasting, are we 'feeling fat' today and so on.

James, Ed and Kate all use exercise to 'allow' them to eat fatty, sugary foods. Kate and James are most extreme. 'I feel bad about eating too many sweet things, unless I've *deserved* them,' Kate says. So a carb-laden cake in the morning could make her feel bad – guilty and low – but after spending lunchtime at the climbing wall, the effect is the opposite. Ed says he'll eat bits of sweet things all day without feeling bad about it.

One of the problems with looking to science for links between food and mood and emotional wellbeing is that it has real difficulty identifying idiosyncratic impacts. Big studies generally seek across-the-board results – a similar change in at least most of the people involved. This approach can separate genuine treatments from quackery. But the greater the scope for individual differences in reactions (and when it comes to diet, that scope seems to be huge), the harder it becomes for studies to find useful connections.

So if something makes you feel good, should you just go with it? Like Ed with his omega-3 pills? My problem here is that while many dietary changes (cutting out coffee, say, eating more curry, or even drinking your own urine) are cheap, or even free, many are not.

The supplement industry is a multi-billion-dollar business. If omega-3s, say, only work because you *believe* they do, that's something, clearly – but it's an expensive something. Some of the foods that I know have been claimed to be mood-enhancers, like blueberries and oily fish, are also expensive. And changing your diet might incur other costs. Switching to gluten-free foods for a 'clearer mind', say, as a few of my own friends have done, can mean eating products that are higher in sugar and fat.

So, while bearing the problems in mind, before I start shelling out hard-earned money in pursuit of the ultimate diet for the mind, I want to find out all I can about whatever the science *can* tell me.

The Food and Mood Project, an organisation in the UK that received funding from the mental-health charity Mind, put out a questionnaire asking about the effects of diet on mental- and emotional-health problems, like mood swings, anxiety, feelings of depression, difficulty with concentration, and irri-table/aggressive feelings.

For various reasons, the 200 people who completed the questionnaire weren't exactly representative of all of us (not least because they reported actually having mental-health problems). This was also a small group. And it was just a survey. But I'm still interested to see what they had to say.

Eighty-eight per cent said that changing their diet 'improved their mental health significantly'. One-fifth said that by changing their diet, they had seen large improvements in mood swings. About a quarter reported improvements in panic attacks, with about the same figure for anxiety and also for depression. '[I am] totally sure it was dietary related – nothing else externally changed that much day to day – but I notice how I feel when I lapse with wheat, sugar, dairy. Awful,' reported one participant.

The people questioned were asked to identify dietary 'stressors' – things that they felt made their moods worse – and 'supporters' – foods that helped:

DIETARY 'STRESSORS'

- Sugar

- Caffeine

- Alcohol

- Chocolate

- Wheat-containing foodstuffs

- Additives

- Dairy

- Saturated fats

Cutting down on sugar and on caffeine were the two strategies that came out top as being 'helpful' or 'very helpful' for emotional or mental health.

DIETARY 'SUPPORTERS'

- Water

- Vegetables

- Fruit

- Oil-rich fish

- Nuts and seeds

- Wholegrain foods

- Fibre

- Protein

- Organic foods

(Omega-3s were listed most frequently among supplements that 'definitely helped' emotional or mental health'.)

This seems a pretty reasonable starting line-up for me to check out. To it, I add other foods and nutrients that commonly crop up in reports relating to psychological wellbeing. These include: certain vegetables and fruits (like blueberries); certain vitamins; gluten in particular; and carbs in general. Oh, and resveratrol.

If the papers on resveratrol alone could fill my house, floor to ceiling, the research on all those other food types could probably stretch to the moon and back (I think I exaggerate only slightly). So I decide to focus on research that looks at the impact of food on the *brain* – and then, by extension, the mind. Which doesn't exactly slash my workload.

Then I remember that the effects of nutrients on the brain is precisely the field of the *Professor* David Kennedy who co-created my 'mind-altering' meal. It's time, I decide, to ask for help.

It's graduation day at the University of Northumbria. The city-centre campus courtyard is packed with students in mortarboards and gowns, clutching rolled degree certificates in one hand and plastic glasses of beer in the other.

I weave my way between them to the Faculty of Health and Life Sciences. Kennedy's office is on the fourth floor. Bearing in mind my new resolution to exercise more, I take the stairs. As I climb up them, doing my best to control my breathing, I pass a series of posters requesting volunteers for various studies, including 'NON-REGULAR EXERCISERS NEEDED FOR MEMORY RESEARCH!' (ah, how unfortunate that I no longer belong to that group!), and I eventually get to the Brain Performance and Nutrition Research Centre.

I know from the centre's website that it does two things. Firstly, it carries out 'contract research' – it's paid by the manufacturers of nutritional supplements to conduct research on the impacts of various nutrients on the brain. (The companies hope, of course, that the research will produce results that they can use to make scientific claims in support of their products.) Secondly, it uses money left over from this corporately funded research to explore the questions about diet and brain function that really intrigue the team.

If, at this point, you're thinking, *Hold on, so this is a guy whose research relies on money from companies who hope he'll find that their supplements work. So doesn't he have a conflict of interest?* I'll note now that what Kennedy had to say was not along the lines of, 'Hey, what journalists really don't convey is just how amazingly useful supplements are for your psychological wellbeing'.

So, I get to the office, and a man in his forties, with black-rimmed glasses and a slightly rumpled shirt hurries along the corridor towards me. Kennedy is on a departmental away-day, and he's nipping out over his lunch break to talk. We go to a meeting room and sit down.

Kennedy turns out to be welcoming and friendly – until he gets on to the topic of journalists.

I raise the issue of the multitude of daily claims about diet and the brain in the newspapers. 'It's usually rubbish,' he says flatly.

Perhaps I should feel defensive about this attack on my profession, but I'm glad. I want some straight talking to help clear through all the confusion.

'What I tend to find with journalists is, it doesn't matter what you say to them, they'll print what they want to say anyway,' he goes on.

But academics don't escape his ire, either. He talks about a piece in a British broadsheet paper. A scientist who Kennedy knows extrapolated from a test-tube study to make a claim for the impacts of one particular nutrient on the human brain. 'It was basically rubbish,' Kennedy says.

What about nutritionists? I ask him. There's no shortage of articles and books by nutritionists on the impact of diet on our mood and brain health. 'They come out with all kinds of claims as well!'

We've got off to a good start, I think. No-nonsense is what I want.

I ask him why so much 'rubbish' is reported in the media (journalistic incompetence and over-hyped claims from some academics, press officers and nutritionists aside). Why don't media stories convey what's actually been scientifically substantiated about diet and the brain?

'To be honest, there is very little that is substantiated,' he says. 'But the thing that's really annoying is you get fads for things. You'll get a single piece of research, or a couple of papers, that rewrite the book. Like with caffeine. And dairy. You get a complete swinging seesaw, which is pretty much always not based on the evidence.'

What he means is the balance of good evidence – which might give rise to a 'substantiated' claim.

So while the results of one new paper in a decent journal might seem to many journalists worth heralding as a 'breakthrough', good scientists are far more cautious. And the bolder the claim, the more they want to see other studies getting the same results, before they'll begin to consider it as genuine. Plus, if most of the decent research tends to support one argument, a single paper arguing the opposite does not, for a scientist, 'rewrite the book'.

So little of the nutritional research that's talked and written about is decent work done on actual people, Kennedy complains. 'You have a tip of the iceberg – that's the research on people.' The rest, he says, is stuff on cells in test tubes, or on animals, which may well end up going nowhere when it gets to the human stage. Yet the results are reported as being applicable to us.

OK – so bearing *all* that in mind, I'm ready to ask him if we can run through my list of foods and nutrients.

Note: David Kennedy is an 'expert' in this field. But there are, of course, other 'experts'. And because the evidence is so often inconsistent, and so little has actually been done on people, there's disagreement. Kennedy's is not necessarily the last word on this matter. But it's one I feel confident taking as a reputable starting point. To his comments, I'll also add a few of my own, in square brackets, and underneath.

CAFFEINE

The claims:

• It improves mental focus.

• It makes you anxious.

Kennedy's take

One of the things that consistently has the best beneficial effect on brain function is caffeine. Caffeine is structurally very similar to adenosine [a neurotransmitter – a chemical that transmits signals between nerve cells]. It does promote arousal, and can provide a boost to brain function (including focus and concentration), though whether or not you need to be a little withdrawn to get clear benefits is unresolved. [The morning after a night without coffee can be enough to make many of us 'a little withdrawn'.]

The negatives have been overblown [depending on the dose – yes, if you drink six double espressos, you may expect to feel jittery]. It doesn't make most people anxious. There is evidence that a subset of people have a specific genetic predisposition to being made anxious by coffee.

My notes

Of course, caffeine *can* interfere with sleep, though clearly, not everyone is affected as badly as Ed. Or perhaps some are, but they're in denial. James can drink a double espresso after dinner and still sleep well, but I think he's chronically sleep-deprived, and would probably sleep even if his blood were replaced with Red Bull. My mother drinks tea all day and frequently wakes at 2am. She'll make herself another cup and swears it helps her get back to sleep. I've tried to suggest that all that tea could be the reason she's waking at 2am. She won't buy it.

Recently, I was talking on the phone to an acquaintance, Mark – a banker with Macquarie Group, at their London base. He happened to mention all the cans of caffeinated beverages stacked on the traders' desks. 'You'll see guys here with like eight cans of Diet Coke piled up on their desk, and it's gone by the end of the day. This is a high-pressure environment.

People are self-medicating. I did give it up for a while, and started drinking decaf. Caffeine affects my concentration span definitely, so when I'm having full-on days, I need to drink it to try to be as productive as I need to be. But it's a trade-off. When I gave it up, after two or three days, I started sleeping eight hours at night, instead of waking at five every morning.'

I've given up coffee twice in my life, both times when I was pregnant. As soon as I felt able to, I went right back to it. I know it improves my focus and concentration span. If I don't drink more than a couple of cups in total, and none after lunch, I'm fine. I think if you're one of the subset of people who get so jittery it's unbearable, you'll already know about it. But for me, in moderation, given what the science says, I can't see a problem with it.

DAIRY

The claims:

- Dairy products, like milk and cheese, can make you depressed.

- Dairy can help prevent mood swings, and relieve depression.

Kennedy's take

Dairy's good for you, for a number of different reasons. The whey proteins are good [as Robert Burton identified, back in 1621!]. They are broken down into bioactive peptides – proteins that affect body functioning – and have a variety of beneficial effects, but the principal one is that they protect against insulin resistance. What you don't want when you eat something is a really sharp increase in blood-glucose levels and then a plummet [which happens in people with insulin resistance]. Dairy levels that off a bit.

My notes

Some people are, of course, intolerant to lactose, a sugar found mainly in milk and dairy products. According to the NHS, only one in fifty people of northern European descent have some kind of lactose intolerance, though most people of Chinese descent have the problem. I avoid ice cream, because it gives me stomach ache, but that doesn't mean I'm lactose-intolerant. My diet is generally pretty low in fat, so when I suddenly dump a load of it into my stomach, it's not surprising (I've been reliably informed) that my body struggles to digest it.

CHOCOLATE

The claims:

- It's a psychological 'stressor'.

- It makes you feel good.

Kennedy's take

If you eat milk chocolate, the negatives of all the fat and calories in it will outweigh the benefits – or certainly balance them. The darker it gets, the more beneficial it becomes. The reason chocolate is good for you is that it contains flavonols. We've found improved cerebral blood flow [more blood flow to the brain – which, in theory, should help brain function] from about 500mg of cocoa flavonols. You'd have to eat pretty much a whole 100g bar of really dark chocolate to get that, though.

My notes

Not long ago, I interviewed Richard Hammersley, Professor of Health Psychology at the University of Hull, about chocolate, among other things. He said he was cautious about the idea that the chemicals in chocolate could have any meaningful impact on our brains at the level we consume it in a normal diet. But he said: 'Chocolate is very special, in terms of its sensory properties – its taste, mouthfeel, texture and so on. It melts at body temperature, which is quite unusual for foods. So it provides a sensory experience that many people find extremely pleasant – which is likely to affect your mood.'

Well, I'd agree – I find it pleasant. But about half the people in that Food and Mood Project survey (see p. 93) reported that cutting out chocolate made them feel better. Chocolate does contain some caffeine, so perhaps people who are sensitive to caffeine do feel less anxious when they avoid chocolate. But Hammersley has another explanation, and it refers back to what Kate, Ed and James all told me:

Let's suppose that you are trying to avoid chocolate because you know it's fattening. And you're restraining your diet because you're a bit concerned about your weight. So, mid-afternoon, you have some chocolate – not an unusual scenario. The chocolate improves your mood because it tastes nice, alleviates the hunger you were feeling because you haven't eaten enough other stuff, and because you associate it with treating yourself. Where do we go from there? It depends on how you feel about eating the chocolate. A common pattern would be that once you've eaten it, you start to feel guilty about going off your diet, and you really shouldn't have eaten it, so the beneficial effects on mood might vanish within a few minutes . . .

When it comes to chocolate, my own preference is for dark, rather than milk. It's still not exactly low in calories, but even if I'm not going to eat enough for it to actually do much for my brain, it does make me feel good. Maybe only temporarily, but I'll take anything I can get. Based on what I've learned, I'm not going to stop eating it.

OILY FISH

The claims:

• Omega-3 fatty acids, which are found in relatively high levels in oily fish, like salmon and sardines, can combat depression and boost memory.

Kennedy's take

There's some epidemiological evidence [garnered by studying disease patterns in different populations] in support of the idea. But when you look at the intervention studies, there actually isn't much good evidence. This all started with a couple of very small studies in children, which said that omega-3s improved cognitive [mental] function. This was built up by the press into: all children should have fish oil. The government even proposed giving every child in the country fish-oil supplements – right up until the point where they did a review that showed them it actually had no noticeable effect on cognitive function.

My notes

As Kennedy says, there's some interesting suggestive evidence. There's work finding that people with depression have lower levels of omega-3 fatty acids in their blood, for example. But there's also plenty of other work finding no such link. Two big reviews of all decent research into whether fish-oil pills support a healthy brain or treat depression have concluded that they do neither. *But* . . .

There's controversy over what the dosage should be. The fish oil used in research is usually a mix of two fats: docosahexaenoic acid (DHA) and eicosapentaenoic acid (EPA). Some researchers say there's evidence that a supplement containing at least sixty per cent EPA alleviates depression, whereas 50/50 mixtures may not. It may also be the case that if you already eat fish (or other foods containing essential fatty acids, like walnuts) that supplements won't provide any noticeable added benefit, which could muddy the results.

So where does this leave me? Studies investigating how much fish people eat, rather than whether or not they take supplements, seem to produce the most positive results. And researchers tend to agree that eating oily fish is a better way to get these fatty acids than out of a bottle. There are added benefits to choosing salmon for dinner, of course. One, you're not eating something *un*healthy, like a big greasy burger. Two, oily fish contain another nutrient that's being linked more and more to psychological wellbeing: vitamin D.

VITAMIN D

The claims:

- Too little vitamin D hikes the likelihood you'll develop depression.

- Vitamin D supplements can help not only with depression but managing stress.

Kennedy's take

The evidence that vitamin D is related to brain function is reasonably good. But the evidence in regard to *giving* vitamin D to people isn't that good. There's no stand-out research.

My notes

Vitamin D is well-known as being crucial for bone health. But over the past decade, there's also been an explosion in research linking low vitamin-D levels to a higher risk of everything from multiple sclerosis to breast cancer to contracting a winter cold. It's become clear that all kinds of cells have receptors for vitamin D – including immune cells, and cells in your brain. The adrenal glands *use* vitamin D in regulating the production of the stress hormones adrenaline and noradrenaline, in theory providing a link between levels of the vitamin and your susceptibility to feeling stressed.

Most of the work on people is only suggestive, though. There's research finding that people with low vitamin D levels do worse on tests of brain functioning, or are more likely to be depressed. Critics point out that depressed people spend more time indoors, and we get most of our vitamin D not from food, but by exposing our skin to sunlight. The results of studies involving actually giving vitamin D supplements to people to see what happens just aren't consistent: some show improvements; others don't.

Personally, having researched and written a detailed feature on all this, I feel pretty convinced by the work on the impact of vitamin D on the immune system that getting enough vitamin D is important for physical health. The jury seems to be out on impact on mental health. But since vitamin D is present in things like sardines, mackerel, salmon and eggs – healthy foods, in many ways – I can't see a downside to eating more of them.

B VITAMINS

The claims:

- Vitamins B6, B9 (folate) and B12 are needed to clear something called homocysteine from the system. Homocysteine, which is produced naturally in our bodies, is toxic to brain cells.

- Low levels of B vitamins are associated with depression (and also dementia).

- Giving people B vitamins improves the health of their brains.

Kennedy's take

There is a huge literature looking at the effects of B vitamins on brain function. And there is no evidence that giving those three vitamins either solely or together has any impact. Every review – including Cochrane reviews [highly regarded reviews of the available evidence] – has shown no evidence of *any* efficacy whatsoever.

My notes

Kennedy is pretty definitive about this. In fact, he's clearly very irritated that researchers are still spending public money on B-vitamin studies, given the repeated failure to find a convincing link between supplements and better brain function. I can't find any solid arguments against his viewpoint.

MULTIVITAMINS

The claims:

• Each of us is probably lacking in something, so a multivitamin should address slight deficiencies.

Kennedy's take

The only vitamin research that really shows any brain benefits has involved multivitamins. The benefits are subtle. [By which he means 'small'.]

The reason we seem to find these effects with the multi-vitamin is, I assume, because if you look at the British national nutrition surveys, what you find is that small but significant parts of the population are deficient in each of the vitamins. So if you paper over only the gaps in two or three vitamins, you're still left with the rest.

But, if you can give normal members of the public a

multivitamin and improve their brain function at all, that means there's something wrong with their nutritional status to start with. With regard to vitamins, *we should be able to get what we need from our diet.*

My notes

We *should* be able to get what we need for our brains from our diet, with perhaps the exception of vitamin D. But even people who think they eat 'well' don't necessarily always cover all the vitamin and mineral bases all the time.

Like a lot of people, I'm sure, I think I eat a reasonably healthy diet (too many biscuits aside). I mean, I know what I'm *meant* to eat. But *do I* eat at least five servings of fruit and vegetables every day? No. In all honesty, not even close. And how often do I eat oily fish? Maybe once a fortnight.

I don't really want to take a supplement. I don't like the idea of being on any kind of regular 'medication', no matter how innocuous. I decide that I should improve my diet – but if I find that in practice I don't, I'll think about taking a multi-vitamin (while bearing in mind warnings to take care not to consume more than the recommended daily amount of vitamins and minerals, because there's work showing that high doses of some – such as vitamins A and E – can cause harm).

Now I want to talk to Kennedy about another food – or rather a group of foods – that were reported in the Food and Mood Project survey as being good for mental and emotional health, and which I know I'm meant to eat for *physical* health: fruits and vegetables.

I mention this, and Kennedy's eyes light up. This turns out to be his passion. In fact, he tells me, he's recently written a book all about why and how plants can have such an influence on our brains and minds, their vitamin content aside. As he talks, all the irritation with journalists who get things wrong and scientists who persist in pursuing what he sees as long-dead ends falls away – and a topic I've never really considered that closely before comes vividly to life.

Plants, I learn, contain three main groups of chemicals that mess with our brains.

You don't *need* to know what they're called. But if I list them, it'll make it easier to explain why blueberries have a fundamentally different impact to a sprig of rosemary, for example. So, they are:

• alkaloids

• phenolics

• turpenes

ALKALOIDS

'The alkaloids provide us with pretty much all of our social drugs – morphine, cocaine, ephedrine, caffeine, nicotine,' says Kennedy, with animated enthusiasm. 'They're all alkaloids, and they're all produced by plants as defence mechanisms against being eaten. Alkaloids are toxic to insects, and the reason they have an effect on humans is that we have essentially the same brain as an insect, just more complicated. We have many of the same neurochemicals, and the same receptors.'

Caffeine, he's already told me, mimics the structure of a neurochemical called adenosine, which is used to pass signals between nerve cells. Adenosine slows us down. When we drink coffee, caffeine rushes into the brain and latches on to receptors on cells that normally receive adenosine. Adenosine can't then bind to these receptors, because the caffeine is already there, so it can't slow us down. Messages between nerve cells speed up, and – thinking we're in the middle of some kind of emergency – the body then produces the 'fight-or-flight' hormone adrenaline, ramping us up even more.

'Insects have *exactly* the same receptor,' says Kennedy. 'If you give an insect caffeine, it speeds up. Morphine will reduce pain in insects, cocaine will make them overactive, nicotine will improve their memory.'

OK – so plant alkaloids may be things we consume, but (caffeine aside) generally not as part of a day-to-day diet. But what about the phenolics?

PHENOLICS

This group includes polyphenols, which are naturally and widely present in plants, and which many of us consume every day.

Tomatoes, berries, citrus fruits, bran, maize, onions, coffee, kale, broccoli, leeks, red wine, turmeric (often used in curries) and tea – these, and more, all contain polyphenols in varying levels, depending on the type.

While some research has focused on certain types of food (and the specific polyphenols they contain), championing turmeric, say, or blueberries – Kennedy strongly suspects that *all* polyphenols do pretty much the same things to us.

'I'm becoming sceptical about singling out single ones as being special,' he says. The reason you hear about some more than others, he thinks, is down to this: seeing interesting results from a study by scientists on turmeric, say, other scientists then decide to look at it – and the number of academic papers and media headlines on this one ingredient snowballs. But all the attention doesn't mean the polyphenols in turmeric have any special super-powers.

Flavonoids belong to the polyphenol group. They're in the skins of many berries, as well as coffee and tea (and chocolate). While they're frequently touted as being 'health-boosting antioxidants', this isn't correct, Kennedy says.

'The antioxidant hypothesis is still the one that predominates in supermarkets and newspapers,' he says. 'We're told we should eat lots of antioxidants because they will mop up all the free radicals in our bodies. But actually that isn't the case.' (And Kennedy is far from the only academic to hold this opinion. Search 'Antioxidant myth' online and you'll find *plenty* on it.)

The fact is, we simply cannot eat or drink enough polyphenolic antioxidants to have any significant impact on levels of free radicals inside us. And while polyphenols do seem to stimulate the body's *own* antioxidant mechanisms, 'the evidence that that's where the benefits come from is very, very thin these days,' Kennedy adds.

The current leading theory, he goes on to say, is that poly-phenols interfere with a process in cells that leads to inflam-mation – and chronic inflammation is damaging to the brain and the body.

There is another area of research when it comes to poly-phenols, though: work suggesting they can boost levels of BDNF – the 'Miracle-Gro for the brain'.

Kennedy is interested in all this, but doesn't do this type of research himself. However, this is exactly what Sandrine Thuret and her team engage in at the Nutrition, Neurogenesis and Mental Health Laboratory at King's College London. This group believes 'there is tremendous potential for diet to boost brain power and improve mental health' by stimulating the growth of new brain cells – and she's interested in flavo-noids, like those in blueberries, cranberries and dark chocolate (as well as omega-3 fatty acids).

But at the moment, no one's in a position to say anything very specific, or very useful. Yes, there's reason to think poly-phenols are good for us. But, 'Eat blueberries for breakfast to ward off depression'? No one can say that with evidence-based authority.

So, that's alkaloids, and phenolics. Which leaves us with turpenes.

TURPENES

'If you smell a flower, you're pretty much smelling turpenes,' Kennedy explains.

Our herbs – sage, mint, basil, rosemary, oregano – all

smell good, thanks to their turpenes. Turpenes curb the activity of an enzyme that breaks down a neurochemical called acetylcholine. The main drugs used to treat dementia do exactly the same thing. Not only that, but a lot of turpenes have an effect on receptors for GABA, producing a calming effect. 'Valerian, renowned historically as a calming agent, has its effect via GABA receptors,' Kennedy says.

Kennedy's own work has produced some promising results for extracts of sage on attention and mood in actual people. But it's at an early stage. He certainly isn't advising that we go chucking sage all over our pork chops in the belief it'll brighten up our mood.

Before moving on from fruit and veg, there's one last nutrient I feel compelled to ask Kennedy about: resveratrol. 'Red wine can boost your brain power!' is a line I've seen more times than I care to remember. So – can it?

Kennedy, it turns out, is well aware of all the research on resveratrol. His team has done some of it (including work that led to the 'Red-wine-can-boost-your-brain-power!-type headlines in the national press, feeding his caution when it comes to journalists). Resveratrol is a polyphenol. As he's already mentioned, he doesn't think any polyphenol is particularly special.

But what his team *has* found in one study is that resveratrol itself (i.e. *not* red wine, which includes a lot of other ingredients) increased blood flow to the brain, which, might – feasibly – boost brain function. *But* the volunteers in these studies didn't actually show any improvements on brain-function tests. (Kennedy has also found that other polyphenols – including flavonols from cocoa – can also boost brain blood flow.)

So, I say, polyphenols can boost blood flow – which may, *in theory*, have some benefits, perhaps supporting long-term psychological health, as well as thinking abilities. But wouldn't taking a brisk walk do the same?

Kennedy nods. 'Yeah. The best intervention is probably exercise. Above everything. Forget the diet. Just exercise.'

This from the man obsessed with the impact of plants on the brain. The man paid by companies to conduct research into the potential effectiveness of supplements on brain functioning.

Forget the diet. Just exercise.

I ask if he takes any supplements for his brain.

'No. My kids get vitamin supplements. I'm like everybody else – I think I have a reasonable diet. I'd never remember to take them anyway. And they're expensive.'

OK . . . when you're thinking what to cook for dinner, do you bear all the research in mind?

'No,' he says. (That said, he does advocate, as you might expect, a broad and varied diet, with fruits and vegetables playing a prominent role.)

But speaking of what you might make for dinner, what happens to polyphenols when you cook fruit and veg?

It's complicated, he says. Heat seems to wipe out some, and boost levels of others. He's reviewing all the work on this at the moment. At this stage, he can't offer any clear guidelines.

Then something else diet-related occurs to me. My friend Kate talked about how if she's hungry, she gets 'ratty'. I do, too. And 'eating regular meals' was high on the list of strategies that support mental and emotional health reported in that Food and Mood Project survey. I ask Kennedy if he's done any work on the effects of the timing or frequency of meals on the brain and mind.

He says he has, but his research has produced conflicting results. 'Personally, I'm not a believer in the idea that breakfast is the most important meal of the day,' he adds. 'I'm not hungry when I get up in the morning and I don't want breakfast. I don't think it would benefit me to eat it.'

This talk of timing prompts me to glance at my watch. I realise it's time for Kennedy to get back to his away-day. We've talked all through the lunch break. And my stomach is rumbling. My brain's starting to slow. I need something to eat . . .

As I take the lift back down (I know, but honestly I'm feeling a little weak), I think: *I'm with Kate*. I need to eat regularly or my mood dips. I get irritable. I lose focus. But there are people who go even further in the opposite direction than Kennedy, of course. They don't just skip breakfast. They fast.

Not long ago, I looked into fasting for a feature for *New Scientist*.

There seems to be good evidence that *either*:

a) slashing your normal daily intake of calories, *or*

b) going without food completely for a day or two a week

can stimulate your brain to make new cells, which should have mental and psychological benefits.

I spoke at the time to Mark Mattson, an expert on all this at the US National Institute on Aging in Bethesda, Maryland. He told me: 'If you look at an animal that has gone without food for a day, it becomes more active. Fasting is a mild stressor that motivates the animal to increase activity in the brain.'

Mattson's own animal work has shown that alternate-day fasting, with a single meal of about 600 calories on the 'fast' day, can boost the production of BDNF (yes, that 'Miracle-Gro'), which supports the health of brain cells and encourage new ones to grow – by 50 to 400 per cent, depending on the brain region.

Mattson guesstimates that twenty to thirty minutes of vigorous exercise a day could produce a similar boost to BDNF as a day of fasting.

Is fasting *plus* exercise twice as good as only one or the other? I asked him.

It's not clear, he said. But work by one of his students on mice suggested it might be.

Mattson believes that advice to start a day with a good breakfast is flawed. Studies suggesting breakfast is important were conducted on schoolchildren who usually ate it, but were asked to skip it, meaning their poor performance could be due simply to the crummy effects of skipping a meal (it can take six weeks to get used to this kind of change, he says). Mattson himself misses breakfast and lunch five days a week, then has dinner and normal weekend meals with his family. He says he feels *more* alert than he used to, not less.

For that feature, I did try going without breakfast. It wasn't good. I knew Mattson had told me it would take six weeks or so to get used to such a big shift, but I felt *awful* – and I had work to do, and kids to look after. I just couldn't contemplate feeling that way for six weeks. Fasting, I decided, was something that'd have to sit alongside reading all seven volumes of Proust's *Remembrance of Things Past* – something I'd really *like* to do, but at some blissful imagined point in a future when there are no urgent demands on my time.

I come back to that Food and Mood Project's finding that eating regular meals helped a lot of people. I think regular meals are important for my sanity, though they won't be for everyone's.

I decide to be more careful about eating, and to have even more regular prophylactic snacks. I guess these should be something healthier than biscuits . . . If I eat something *before* I start to lose focus, maybe it'll be easier to avoid the draw of the cookie cupboard. In fact, perhaps I should avoid the draw of the cookie cupboard altogether. Because while this isn't a topic Kennedy has investigated – and so wasn't one he was keen to discuss – if I'm looking into foods and psychological wellbeing, I cannot avoid some key constituents of biscuits.

There's the sugar, of course. But depending on who you listen to, *wheat* is either the latest dietary scapegoat – or pure poison. And, along with sugar, it falls squarely into a class of foods touted with equal verve as mood-boosters or mood-destroyers: carbs.

Back when my days were entirely my own – i.e. pre-kids, and when I was freelance – I used to know instinctively when it was about four in the afternoon. My faltering attention and growing weariness would take me downstairs for a couple of biscuits, preferably slathered in chocolate. (Post-kids, I still eat biscuits. Just more of them. And any time is fine.)

When we're feeling peckish, many of us go for a carb-based snack. It makes sense.

Sucrose – table sugar – is separated in the body into glucose, and also fructose. A cookie contains sucrose and maybe added fructose, plus flour, from wheat, which contains its own carbs, which are broken down to release glucose.

Glucose is our body's preferred fuel. But we can use fructose, too. So it's no wonder we especially like the taste of sweet things.

As Richard Hammersley says, 'Animals and people are pretty much born liking a sweet taste. So therefore it's feasible that things that taste sweet might improve your mood.'

So – a biscuit provides a jolt of glucose fuel and tastes nice. How else might it help my mood?

One claim is that carbs help speed tryptophan into our brains. Tryptophan is an amino acid – a building block of protein. It's converted in our brains into something called 5-HTP, which can then be converted into serotonin. Some anti-depressants, including Prozac, are thought to work because they raise levels of serotonin in parts of the brain. So, theoretically, more tryptophan in the brain could mean more serotonin, which might put us in a brighter mood.

Since tryptophan is a protein building block, you can get

it from protein-containing foods. But just eating a chunk of chicken or an egg isn't going to bathe your brain in serotonin. That's because tryptophan released from something you've eaten has to compete with other amino acids to get across the blood-brain barrier, into the brain. A surge of insulin can divert competitors out of the blood, into muscle, giving tryptophan an easy passage into your brain. And what can trigger a surge in insulin? Eating carbs.

Richard and Judith Wurtman at MIT, US have found that a 'typical American' breakfast containing 69.9 g of carbs plus 5.2g of protein (waffles, maple syrup, orange juice, coffee with a little sugar) resulted in a blood amino-acid balance that should, in theory, mean a lot more tryptophan gets into the brain than a breakfast containing 15.4g of carbs and 46.8g of protein – turkey ham, Egg Beaters (a mostly egg-white egg substitute that comes in a carton), grapefruit, American processed cheese and butter.

It's probably worth pointing out here that while some people take tryptophan supplements in the hope they'll help with depression, many researchers, including David Kennedy, believe this to be pointless. 'Normal foods will give you all the tryptophan you need,' he maintains.

While one big analysis of the available data did find that tryptophan or 5-HTP supplements can alleviate the symptoms of depression, there can be serious side effects, the authors noted, including dizziness, nausea and diarrhoea, and taking tryptophan has also been associated with the development of a fatal condition. Regular anti-depressants are preferable, the study concluded.

But back to the Wurtman 'pro-tryptophan' breakfast. That's a high-carb, low-protein meal. Waffles. Maple syrup. Orange juice. All the stuff we're told not to consume. This kind of diet may possibly raise tryptophan levels, though this is debated (what isn't in this field?), but if eaten on a regular basis, it's not going to do your ability to regulate your blood-sugar levels any good. And problems with blood-sugar control are bad for your brain, and your psychological wellbeing.

But Richard Hammersley does agree about the desirability of a protein/carb balance in breakfast – partly because of the impact on mental alertness. 'You want to have a reasonable-sized breakfast that has some protein in it,' he says. With his cereal or toast, he has an egg or a bit of cheese. 'The reason I do that is that with minimal protein I find I get hungry again about two hours later, and I find that affects my alertness.'

OK. So those are the general *positives* claimed for carbs. What Kennedy *would* say about the class of foods as a whole is this: 'There's nothing wrong with carbs per se. They're good sources of energy. Our problem is that we eat way too many of them.'

However . . .

. . . there are scientists who believe that sugars are particularly toxic to our brains. There's at least one high-profile neurologist who says we should be eating no more carbs daily than those contained in a single piece of fruit. Carb critics maintain that we didn't evolve to eat a lot of the stuff, and we don't need to (we can get energy from fats, they say) and that even mildly raised blood-sugar levels damage the brain.

Grains, such as wheat, are often singled out as particularly heinous sources of carbs. Wheat, barley and rye contain the protein gluten. The theory that gluten is a vastly under-appreciated cause of anxiety, depression and lethargy, not to mention gut problems, headaches and dementia, has been widely reported. Perhaps you've heard the argument that while full-blown, gut-wrenching coeliac disease afflicts around one in a hundred people, gluten sensitivity is more common than doctors generally believe – that perhaps as many as forty per cent of us can't process gluten properly, leading to damaging inflammation in the body and the brain (and the rest of us are in harm's way).

But although this argument might have been widely reported, it is very controversial.

There has been a small study finding that people with irritable bowel syndrome who were unknowingly given gluten then recorded higher scores on a questionnaire measuring depression. But there's also work suggesting that people who react to wheat-based products aren't responding to the gluten, but to a set of sugars, called FODMAPs, which are found not only in wheat but in many fruits, vegetables and dairy products – including onions. Focus on gluten, then, and you might be ignoring the real culprit.

And what about the idea that all carbs are bad?

If you did restrict your carb intake to a piece of fruit a day, there might be some of the same benefits that come from fasting. But some fasting researchers are convinced that it's extended periods without protein – *not carbs* – that underpin the health benefits. And a low-carb diet has also been associated with feeling grumpy. And a lot of specialists out there are very sceptical of the idea that the level of carbs in a 'reasonable, balanced' diet – that is, a healthy one as recommended by the NHS, for example (see http://www.nhs.uk/Livewell/

Goodfood/Pages/eatwell-plate.aspx), advocating *'plenty* of potatoes, bread, rice, pasta and other starchy foods' (my italics) – would do us any harm. And there's some indication that the Mediterranean diet (high in vegetables, poultry and fish, but still containing plenty of carbs, like pasta and whole grains) is even better.

A LOW-CARB CAUTION

There's plenty of evidence that you shouldn't follow low-carb or low-calorie diets if you're trying to become pregnant. The idea that a pregnant woman's lifestyle and experiences can affect the gene settings of her unborn child, with lifelong implications for the child's health, has gained a lot of support. Children born to women who didn't get enough to eat (which would be your body's interpretation of a very low-carb diet, and some fasting regimens) are at higher risk of developing obesity, as well as a range of other health problems. There isn't room here to go into the reasons for this, but if you're interested in finding out more, I've included a few references at the end of the book – see p. 337.

This is clearly a really complicated field.

When it comes to carbs as a class, I can't help noting that the history of drastic dietary recommendations isn't exactly untarnished. 'Eat no eggs – the cholesterol's a killer!' turned out to be bad advice. 'Cut out all fat!' led to a steep rise in our consumption of sugar. 'Ignore fads!' – even those propagated by 'experts' – would seem a sounder mantra.

But that doesn't mean there's nothing to some of these claims, of course.

You may be one of those people who reacts to the sugars in wheat, some fruits and vegetables with brain fog and bloating. (My sister avoids apples, pears, onion and garlic for precisely these reasons.) Maybe your diet is far too high in simple sugars and other 'high-GI' carbs, and you're prediabetic, or even diabetic, without knowing it – so you're routinely at risk of getting irritable when your blood-sugar levels drop below normal levels, or losing mental energy when they get too high. Perhaps you are genetically highly sensitive to caffeine, but hadn't realised it, and even a small cup a day, which for other people would pose no problems, *is* exacerbating your anxiety.

The people who took part in the Food and Mood Project survey were asked what they'd say to people contemplating dietary changes. These are a few of their comments:

- 'Try it! It's such a simple and harmless way to explore and it beats taking drugs as a first choice from the doctor.'

- 'Try something for just one week – e.g. no sugar/no caffeine. It's such an eye opener.'

- 'Go slowly, change one thing at a time and monitor the effects. Tell yourself, 'If this does work, I'll know quickly – if it doesn't, I'll try something else.'

- And this: 'Be honest with yourself – I always believed I was a healthy eater, but the reality was different. My reality now matches and I follow it. The result is a new me.'

I think I'm like that last respondent: not honest with myself about my diet. If I try changing it to make it fit with what health organisations recommend as a balanced diet, surely I should feel more alert, and suffer less with lapses of concentration and dipping mood? *But* when we do make changes to our diet, any effects may be down to more than the chemicals in the food making it into our bodies.

In fact, there's an exploding field of research focused on the idea that our diets could affect our physical and psychological wellbeing profoundly, but indirectly.

One particular evening in London prompts me to find out more.

It's eight o'clock, the sky's still blue, flags are fluttering along The Mall, all the way down to Buckingham Palace and the Royal Society's summer soirée is in full swing.

I'm surrounded by the greats of the British science world, dressed impeccably in black tie, and by science journalists, noticeable for being dressed somewhat less impeccably and for being distinctly more brazen in their search for waiters bearing bottles of champagne.

The party is to celebrate the launch of the Royal Society Summer Science Exhibition, designed to showcase the most exciting cutting-edge science and technology research. I grab a glass of champagne and wander around the stalls. After getting my 3D photo taken at one (weird, but brilliant), I pause at another, which bears a poster announcing: 'You're never alone . . . Immune-bacterial interactions in the gut.'

The young team at the stall is from the University of Oxford. I tell them I read somewhere that ninety per cent of the cells inside each adult are bacterial, not human, and is that actually right? One of the researchers points to a simple graphic on the next poster. It's of an old-fashioned balancing scale. The text reads:

DID YOU KNOW???
You are made up of approximately:
10 trillion human cells
100 trillion bacterial cells

Underneath is written:

PRObiotics are microbes that are ingested to improve
gut health
PREbiotics are foods that can change the bacterial
composition of the gut

This is something I haven't really considered so far in my exploration of the impact of diet on the mind. But I need to.

The Oxford group turns out to be mostly interested in the potential role of gut bacteria in inflammatory bowel disease – a group of diseases that includes Crohn's disease and ulcerative colitis. But there's a comment relating to the bacteria inside us that's been niggling at the back of my mind. It's something that Thomas Insel, Director of the US National Institute of Mental Health, mentioned in an email to me, after I'd contacted him to ask for comment on a story. The story was about schizophrenia and viruses. It had nothing to do with diet. But Insel wrote:

> You may want to broaden your scope to look at the microbiome and mental illness. No one is writing about this, but it is clearly going to be one of the next frontiers for neurodevelopmental disorders, based on recent animal research. It is too early to settle on a specific infectious agent. Microbiomics give us a chance to look broadly at prenatal and postnatal exposures. One catch is that we will need to wait twenty years to know if the offspring develop schizophrenia. But this seems more in line with the state of the field.

The microbiome is the complement of microbes that live inside us, mostly in our gut. As Insel says, some researchers are looking at whether particular gut bacteria could influence the development of schizophrenia. But there's a lot of other work being done on gut bacteria and psychological health, particularly anxiety and depression.

I look into it.

And I come to this conclusion: a lot of it *is* at a pretty

early stage. Suggestive, rather than conclusive. There are plenty of animal studies. For example, 'anxious' mice become more relaxed when they're given transplants of gut bacteria from 'calm' mice. The reverse also holds: transplants of gut bacteria from anxious mice make calm mice more stressed.

There's also a mouse-research finding that consuming various strains of lactobacillus (a 'beneficial' bacterium) boosts brain receptors for GABA (some anti-anxiety drugs, including Valium, also work on GABA). Bifidobacteria (a group of bacteria that normally live in the intestines) also seem to be capable of reducing anxiety.

But what about humans?

A lot less has been done in people. A team at the University of California, Los Angeles divided a number of women into three groups. One was given a yoghurt containing a mix of several probiotics twice a day for four weeks; another got the yoghurt, minus probiotics; the third got nothing. Brain scans before and afterwards showed changes in regions associated with emotion in the women who ate the probiotics. In theory, these changes might help the women deal better with stressful events. But it's early days.

The Oxford team told me that in their work, they're leaning towards looking at prebiotics, rather than probiotics, the idea being that it's a more effective way of beneficially altering the types of bacteria that live in the gut. (Prebiotics are types of fibre that we can't digest, but which nourish 'good bacteria'.)

So what should we eat, if we want our good bacteria to flourish? I do some research. Acacia gum (gum arabic) and raw chicory root would, it seems, be excellent choices, if they were palatable . . . And among foods you or I might actually eat, raw garlic and wholewheat flour, bananas and leeks score relatively highly. All come, of course, from plants.

I go back to Kennedy on this.

Yes, he says – 'the phenolics manage pathogenic and symbiotic microbes, particularly bacteria'.

The phenolics – that huge class of compounds found in many of the plants that we eat (see p. 112). One of the jobs of phenolics, it seems, is to protect the plant from being infected by microbes. So, if we eat them, and they end up in our gut, they could influence *our* gut bacteria?

'Yes. And this is where the complication comes. We didn't take any account of gut bacteria until the last decade or so. Polyphenols are snipped up [cut into chunks] by gut bacteria. But polyphenols also change the gut bacteria.'

It may even turn out that all the focus on what polyphenols are *converted to*, or what *they do*, in the body isn't the main reason they're good for us, he says. Kennedy is open to the idea that their main benefits may be down to their influence on gut bacteria – and so what the gut bacteria actually produce, in terms of anti-inflammatories, or other chemicals.

But eating more polyphenols – more fruit and veg – should modify our gut bacteria in a healthy way?

'I wouldn't say that,' Kennedy says. 'It's so unknown at the moment. We don't understand it yet.'

Still, I can't help thinking that surely this is another reason to consider how much of my diet is sugar and fat, and how much is fruit and veg. And it makes me think of what I give to Jakob and Lucas.

When my boys were babies, I made all their meals. I puréed steamed multi-hued vegetables and organic farmers'-market fruits with the best of them. Then, at about two, they each entered the 'fussy phase'. And were very happy to stay there.

I have a photo from our summer holiday in Spain last year, with my sister and her husband and their two kids, who are about the same age as mine. We're at a restaurant. There's Jakob, turning his nose up at a plain pasta sauce with 'black rocks' in it (a tiny, practically invisible, smattering of pepper). Then there's my nephew, Idris, aged three, with squid tentacles poking out of his mouth. I really don't know what went wrong.

Persuasian, blackmail and threats have resulted in a situation that I think is acceptable, if not desirable: they will both eat carrots, Jakob will eat mashed potato and broccoli and Lucas will eat peas. They'll both eat a tomato pasta sauce (with absolutely no pepper). Other than that, they turn their noses up at veg – unless it's cooked beyond recognition or chips. When it comes to fruit, Jakob will eat strawberries and Lucas will eat blueberries. Both are OK with bananas. That's it. Jakob won't even eat raisins. When they want a snack, they get chocolate biscuits at worst and Cheerios at best.

Kids need energy. While I'm not a neurologist, I'm convinced they need carbs. But surely I can do better than Cheerios and biscuits? At the very least, I could enforce a banana-then-biscuit rule. Couldn't I?

I decide I'll just do it. And after dinner, they'll have to eat fruit before they get anything else, even yoghurt. And I'll try to do the same.

But I'm not quite ready to draw a line under diet just

yet. I know this is taking a while, and you might be thinking 'too much information', but I'm determined to find out all I can about diet and the mind, so I really know where I am with it, and can move on. And there's one final topic that I need to deal with before I can do that. It's something I consume pretty much daily. As Richard Hammersley says, 'Let's not forget that alcohol is a big part of the British diet'.

*

This was Robert Burton's take on the impacts of wine on melancholy: wine, he said, is 'a great cause, especially, if it be immoderately used . . . Yet notwithstanding all this, to such as are cold, or sluggish melancholy, a cuppe of Wine is good Physicke.'

I guess I must suffer from 'cold, or sluggish melancholy' because for me, a cup of wine is definitely good Physicke.

Over to Richard Hammersley for the modern perspective: 'A common problem is that people who have had a – quote – 'stressful' day have a few drinks at night. And they wouldn't think they were alcoholics and they probably don't feel particularly intoxicated – and this would be completely without comment in most middle-class circles. So they have half a bottle or even a whole bottle of wine in the evening. But we know alcohol has knock-on effects to the next day. Alcohol affects sleep quality, which affects mood.'

You take those first few sips of wine, and the alcohol affects the GABA system, making you feel calmer, and more relaxed. But it also wreaks havoc with your heart-rate variability – that indicator of bodily stress. Back at Yale, Matt Stults-Kohlemainen showed me a Firstbeat readout from a colleague who'd worn her sensor at work and then at a wine-tasting afterwards. When she started drinking, her physiological stress levels soared.

There is some evidence that a low dose of alcohol (in one particular study I came across, this meant one 360ml beer) can *increase* total sleep time, and reduce night-time waking. But, while the effects will, of course, vary from person to person – and certainly depend on how much alcohol you're used to drinking – more than this may well interfere with sleep, as my friend Ed noted when he and Kate were over for dinner.

The worst effects happen, I gather, when the alcohol has largely been metabolised. So if you don't generally drink much, then you have two large glasses of wine in the evening (which, as Hammersley points out, could actually contain as many as three or more units), if the alcohol is cleared four to five hours later, *that's* when you're more likely to wake up. As Ed said, who wants to risk waking at 3am and having an existential crisis?

So if I'm going to cut back on alcohol, is there something else I should drink instead? Like water?

The number-one 'dietary supporter' identified in the Food and Mood Project survey was water. I do a little research, expecting to find all sorts of data showing that I drink far too little of it. What I actually find surprises me.

New Scientist (which I generally trust, because I know how it operates) evaluated the evidence, with input from academic experts. Let me pass on some of the highlights:

- The idea that we need to drink eight glasses a day, totalling about two litres, is based on no scientific data. No one even knows where the myth comes from. If you're not sweating a lot, you'll probably need to drink about 1.2 litres a day.

- This 1.2 litres doesn't have to be in the form of pure water. Contrary to popular belief, tea and coffee and even mildly alcoholic drinks (like a wine spritzer with a lot of soda) will hydrate you. (In support of this claim, there's research finding no difference in hydration levels between adults who got their water from caffeinated rather than uncaffeinated drinks.)

- The idea that by the time you feel thirsty you're already dehydrated is a myth.

The conclusion of this feature? Relax and trust your body . . . drink the drink of your choice whenever you're thirsty.

And now, *at last,* I think I'm ready to go back through everything I've learned, draw some conclusions and make some decisions.

Part of me feels disappointed that there isn't a big transformative change to be made – that eating twenty walnuts, perhaps, or three eggs a day could halve my stress levels or super-charge my mood. It's a small part, however. Mostly, I'm relieved by what I've found out. I wouldn't want to be a slave to a special 'mind diet', and for most of us, I can't see that there's any need to be.

So, I am going to eat more oily fish. And I am going to plan to cut back on bread, cut out sugary snacks and eat nuts when I'm peckish instead. I'm going to keep to my regular high-carb breakfast of porridge and fruit, but add some protein – maybe a bit of smoked salmon. And I'm going to increase the family's fruit and veg intake. I'm going to make sure that I – and James and the kids – do get the recommended minimum of five portions per day (a portion being 80g).

What about supplements? I already give the kids multivitamins. Children's needs are different to adults', and the UK Department of Health does recommend a vitamin A, C and D supplement between the ages of six months and five years. And for James and me? Buying more salmon and fresh vegetables may cost even more than multivitamin pills, but I'm more comfortable with this approach.

I know a lot of people do fast in one form or another, and enjoy it – and there's good evidence for the benefits. But I'm not going to do it. As I said, there's just no way I can go through six weeks of feeling rubbish right now.

And ultimately, after all the to-ing and fro-ing, trying to make my way through the mire of diet/mind claims and counter-claims, ultimately I think the only clear guidelines are pretty straightforward ones.

I'm conscious that the list of recommendations below is not particularly exciting. It's not obviously appealing (unlike 'Red wine can boost your brain power!') and it's not as catchy as 'Cut out all carbs!' But, as far as I can tell, it has other virtues: it's based on the balance of good evidence, and contains no out-on-a-limb kind of claims – which, in the field of diet, the brain and psychological wellbeing, is as close as I believe it's possible to get to 'fact'.

THE DIET CHECKLIST

- Ignore faddy diets. Aim to eat a 'healthy, balanced' diet – perhaps a Mediterranean diet, or at least the kinds of meals that would fit with the NHS's 'Eat well plate' (http://www.nhs.uk/Livewell/Goodfood/Pages/ eatwell-plate.aspx).

- Do try to eat a broad range of vegetables and fruit. There's probably nothing particularly special about some of the 'brain-boosting' fruits and veg you often see mentioned in the media – like turmeric or blueberries. Variety is best.

- Sugar, caffeine, alcohol, chocolate and wheat are the foods most often identified as being potential mood-wreckers. If you're keen to modify your diet to see if it makes you feel more emotionally balanced, you should probably start with these.

- If you can't honestly say that your diet is 'healthy and balanced' you *may* want to consider taking a multivitamin.

- Be very cautious about taking other nutritional supplements. Some may be dangerous. Others may do nothing but deplete your bank balance. (For a very readable report on this from the NHS, see http://www. nhs.uk/news/2011/05May/Documents/BtH_supplements. pdf. Michael Lean, Professor of Human Nutrition at the University of Glasgow, says in the report: 'I deal with many patients who are led by clever marketing or packaging to spend huge amounts of money on so-called "health" supplements and products for which there is no evidence, and which do nothing at all.')

PS The justification for the 'mood-boosting' menu on p.89? Kennedy looked a little awkward when I asked him about it. It was put together for a dinner, just to get people thinking about the possible impact of diet on the brain, he stressed, rather than as a way to boost your mood right there and then. But here's the rationale: carrots contain vitamin A, required for healthy brain function; walnuts are full of polyphenols and also alphalinoleic acid, which is readily turned into omega-3 fatty acids in the body; mackerel contains omega-3s; kale, cauliflower and beetroot contain dietary nitrate, which is turned into a molecule that can increase blood flow; chocolate and blackberries both contain polyphenols.

CHAPTER FOUR

REST YOUR MIND

My degree was in psychology, so when I worked as a daily news reporter on the website of *New Scientist* magazine, it wasn't surprising that I'd be the one chosen to cover the annual conference of the British Psychological Society (BPS). My editor liked psychology stories because the public likes psychology stories. Who isn't interested in the positives (willpower and creativity, happiness and resilience) and the negatives (psychopathy and narcissism, post-traumatic stress disorder and depression)?

Who isn't? Well, psychology is often regarded as pretty soft as science goes, and I had 'hard-science' colleagues (people into things like theoretical physics and cosmology) who felt that it often produces findings we essentially already know. They'd take the piss. 'You're going to the BPS? What are the top stories? Unemployed people are more likely to be depressed! Obese people tend to have a poor body image! Lack of sleep makes you grumpy!'

And yes – it will come as a revelation to no one that a lack of sleep is bad for your emotional health. We all know that a disturbed night leaves us brain-fogged, irritable and struggling to concentrate. But I want to go far beyond what's self-evident when it comes to sleep – to find out how to modify my sleep patterns to maximise my chances of having a clear, calm, but alert mind; and to learn how to work with my body's natural 'circadian rhythms', or to change them, if necessary.

For me personally, I expect the presence of young, sleep-shy kids in my house will mean some of this won't be a lot of use right now. Interesting theory, rather than lessons I can put straight into practice. But when it comes to sleep, I know I need all the help I can get. And if you don't have young kids (or they sleep well), hopefully you'll be in a position to make the most of what the science has to say.

So what *does* it have to say?

First, a fundamental question: how much sleep do we really need?

I want a professional opinion. So I contact a retired US Army colonel called Stacey Young-McCaughan. Now a professor at the University of Texas, she's written about the role of sleep in the health and psychological resilience of military personnel, a group that I imagine will have been thoroughly studied.

I've never spoken to a colonel before, and going by – well, going by my extensive knowledge of . . . TV dramas, I expect her to be brusque, with a deep emotional wound and a penchant for solitary fishing and cutting one-liners. When I get her on the phone, though, Young-McCaughan sounds delightful. The kind of woman you might eat a cupcake with. Anyway, back to the research:

You often read that adults need seven to eight hours sleep a night, I say. I guess that's right?

'What's your shoe size?' she asks me. 'Take a roomful of people and go round them, asking them what their shoe size is, and you'll be able to arrive at an average number. But there'll be a range, and it's similar for sleep. We don't have good ways of telling how much sleep individuals need. It's kind of trial and error. How much can you live on, and your family doesn't want to kill you because you're so irritable and crabby?'

I think about my own family. Before she had kids, and something – maybe just sheer necessity – made her feel able to cope well on less, my sister used to need nine hours a night. My sister-in-law, Vicky, has told me she feels fine on six, but is worried she isn't getting 'enough', because she's heard that we need seven or eight. (I'll have to let her know Young-McCaughan's view on all this as soon as I get the chance.)

But first, another question: what about those people who say they can function well on even less sleep – on four or five hours a night?

'I think there definitely are people who can get by on five hours of sleep,' Young-McCaughan says. 'And people who say they can do that definitely act normal. Hey, but you're a mom of young children. How's your sleep these days?'

Ha! Yeah, I tell her, unfortunately for me I'm *not* someone who can get by on five hours a night. At least, not regularly. And not today. Lucas woke at 1.30am, for no obvious reason.

I took him back to bed, and he quickly settled down. Then Jakob got up at 3am, not distressed exactly, but wide awake. (Me, concerned about whether perhaps he's worrying about something at school: 'Are you thinking about something?' Jakob: 'Umm . . . I think I'd like to go to the circus?') *I* spent the next hour thinking about *precisely* the kind of problems you can solve at 3.30am, like, how the hell are we going to pay off the credit card, then at 5.05 am, Lucas clambered on top of me, cooing, 'I love you, Mummy', and I didn't have the energy or the will to fend off the cuddles and send him back to his room. 'I know you're awake now, but I'm not,' I mumbled. 'You have to lie still.' I might as well tell the Earth not to turn.

With my brain on go-slow, I'm finding it difficult to organise my thoughts here. You know as well as I do what it feels like. But this is what the sleep laboratory studies have to say:

Sleep 'deprivation' – which can mean anything from being awake all night to getting 'too few' hours, in relation to your individual needs – causes:

- drowsiness

- irritability

- an impaired ability to concentrate

- schizophrenia-type symptoms

Drowsiness – well, of course.

As for irritability, brain-scanning research at the University of California, Berkeley, shows that a lack of sleep cuts down on the conversation between two regions that really need to talk: the amygdala and the prefrontal cortex. The amygdala – your brain's 'alarm bell' – is the bit that fires in response to something emotionally charged, like a hostile boss striding towards your desk. The prefrontal cortex – the thinking part – can overrule the amygdala's urge to chuck your cup of coffee at him and ditch your job.

Without clear input from the prefrontal cortex, you're far more likely to overreact, whether at work, with your partner or with the kids. So this finding strikes me as really important. I already know that exercise and meditation can help support the ability of the prefrontal cortex to prevent an overreaction. And here's the evidence that sleep is vital for this.

What about the next point: problems with concentration?

I do some reading and find too little sleep makes it harder for the brain to filter out what's important from what isn't. In the words of Ulrich Ettinger, a professor at the University of Bonn, Germany, 'the unselected flood of information leads to chaos in the brain'.

It was Ettinger's group that also noticed symptoms usually associated with schizophrenia in sleep-deprived people. After being kept up all night, the volunteers reported alterations in their sense of time and smell, and even odd mental leaps – such as believing they could read thoughts. 'We did not suspect that the symptoms could be so pronounced after one night spent awake,' Ettinger said. (In fact, the overlap with the symptoms of schizophrenia was so great that the team thinks sleep deprivation should be used as a model for studies of new drugs to treat psychoses.)

So, that's what too little sleep can do in the short term. But what about the long term? Because for many of us with sleep problems, whether they have a clear, immediate cause (like young kids) or not, this is an ongoing issue.

Surveys regularly report that about a third of adults in the UK and US suffer from ongoing insomnia, defined as trouble getting to sleep, waking up in the night or waking up too early (or all three). Medical organisations are generally more conservative, putting the figure at ten–fifteen per cent. Still, that's at least one in every eight to ten people who can't get the sleep they want and need.

One of the reasons I wanted to talk to Colonel (Retired) Young-McCaughan is that soldiers on deployment routinely get very little sleep. Do they provide any useful hints for the rest of us? What happens in the long term? And do we *really* need what we feel we need – or could we manage our hours down? Could reduced sleep possibly be like fasting? You feel rubbish to start with, but give yourself long enough – perhaps as a regimen, rather than the fractured madness of early parenthood – and you can adapt? My extant knowledge of how soldiers sleep suggests perhaps you can.

I first heard about Gary a few years ago. New to Sheffield, I met another mother, Dawn, at a playgroup. Her baby was the same age as Lucas. She invited me to join her weekly mothers' group meetings. I leaped at the chance. In the course of general chats with these women, I asked about their partners – who they were, what they did. Back came the usual kinds of answers: IT, teaching, graphic design. And then there was Niki. Her fiancé fought pirates in the Gulf of Aden.

Niki told me that before going into private security, Gary had been a corporal in the British Army, and had served in Iraq. When I later met him, I felt the same way as I had with Anne Dutton, the yoga and mindfulness expert at the Yale Stress Center; I was so fascinated by his life and his experiences, I could have talked to him all day. Among other things, I asked him how much sleep he'd got during combat, and how that had affected him.

'During the Iraq war, I had literally three or four hours' sleep in any twenty-four-hour period,' he told me. 'I got used to it.' After how long? 'A few weeks. Not even that. I was there for about five months. I was hammering myself with lack of sleep, and it didn't bother me.'

So when you got back home, did you stick to three or four hours a sleep a night?

He smiled. 'No. No – I don't have to!'

Engaged in door-to-door hunts for wanted men believed to be in Basra (a group that at the time included Osama bin Laden), Gary had had no choice but to cope on a bare minimum of sleep. Seven hours a night simply wasn't an option. He says he adapted, and mentally and emotionally, he was fine.

I find this intriguing. But he's just one man.

A search of the scientific research reveals these insights:

- People who report chronic insomnia are more likely to develop depression.

- Short-term problems with regulating emotions become ongoing.

- People with chronic insomnia find it harder to 'turn on' brain regions relating to the task in hand, and turn off 'mind-wandering' brain regions, so it's harder for them to focus day-to-day.

- Sleep-deprived people have higher levels of a hormone called ghrelin, which stimulates you to eat, and lower levels of leptin, which tells you you're full. (This doesn't directly affect mood. Unless, like millions of people in the UK, you're on a semi-permanent weight-loss diet, of course – in which case, slipping from that diet is highly likely to make you feel low.)

But that research was all on civilians. I ask Young-McCaughan what the military science says. How does reduced sleep affect the emotional and mental functioning of US soldiers?

To my surprise, it's not clear. In fact, she says there are still big gaps in understanding what sleep disturbances, including reduced total sleep, either during combat or recovery back in the garrison, actually mean for the soldiers' psychological resilience – and this type of research is badly needed. Perhaps some of us are like Gary, and we can adapt to cope well with little sleep in the short term. I can't help suspecting most of us are not. So why am I even mentioning Young-McCaughan again?

Because military research *has* revealed some fascinating differences between people in *how* we sleep, she tells me.

These findings come from research carried out behind the closed doors of one of the US military's most notorious training grounds.

Camp Mackall, North Carolina is home to the US Army's survival school. Here, soldiers take part in a training programme known for its near-torturous brutality. This is Survival, Evasion, Resistance and Escape training – SERE.

SERE is designed to prepare soldiers for some of the most difficult challenges they may ever face, so naturally it's tough. For several days, they have to live in the wild with only a knife and a canteen for carrying water, while being hunted by the enemy. Then comes the Resistance component. At a mock prisoner of war camp, complete with concrete cells, razor wire and fake graves, 'prisoners' are put through interrogations so realistic they experience 'intense and uncontrollable stress', in the words of one journal paper.

For the scientists who worked on that paper, which include Dennis Charney, now Dean of the Icahn School of Medicine at Mt Sinai, New York City, SERE was a perfect laboratory for studying the real-world effects of severe stress on people. Charney and his team got permission to give various tests to regular and Special Forces soldiers before and after the full SERE training programme, and before and immediately after mock interrogations.

This first finding isn't directly to do with sleep. But it is to do with managing stress, and I find it really interesting. I can't skip it.

They found that blood levels of a brain chemical called neuropeptide Y (NPY) were strongly linked with the soldiers' ability to cope. Those with *more* NPY performed *better*. Also, the Special Forces soldiers, known for being especially cool under stress, had significantly higher levels of NPY, compared with regular troops, before and after the training. Twenty-four hours after the programme had finished, NPY levels in the Special Forces soldiers were back to their baseline, while those in regular soldiers were still way below.

The Special Forces soldiers, with more NPY, simply coped better with stress, and recovered faster. Charney and his team are now working on a nasal NPY spray as a treatment for stress disorders. Might such a spray one day help the rest of us cope better with day-to-day stresses? We'll have to wait and see.

But now I'll get back to the findings on sleep. And to research into the differences between regular people and Special Forces soldiers.

For many people struggling with insomnia, the 'debris of the day' is a big problem. Who hasn't struggled to fall asleep, or back to sleep after waking in the middle of the night, due to worrying over an ongoing problem, or perhaps a row? Special Forces soldiers, probably. As Young-McCaughan explains the sleep results of this study: 'These people were out on these really intense missions. But the ones who did the best, they'd be out, fully functioning, they'd come back – and they could immediately turn off and go to sleep.'

There could be a few reasons for this. Maybe they've learned psychological strategies for letting go of worries, like stepping outside of your thoughts. Or maybe they just *don't* worry.

I think Gary falls into this category. I once asked him if he'd killed people while on active duty. He replied that he had. I asked how that had affected him. He said it didn't. Not really. His view was that he was doing a job. In a situation of 'him or me' or 'him or my fellow soldier', he'd made the choice instantly, and felt no compunction about it. He had no trouble sleeping. (Gary, incidentally, is no psychopath. He's a loving dad, seems a decent man, and is a respected leader of others. He has, I guess, the perfect mental build for a soldier.)

So, of course there are differences in psychological outlook between people, which can affect how well we sleep, and I want to come back to this. But Young-McCaughan reads something interesting into the ability of the Special Forces soldiers to crash when given the chance: 'They had really strong circadian patterns of hormones, and sleep ability.'

Circadian patterns . . . I remember learning at the Yale Stress Center that the biggest surge of the stress hormone cortisol comes first thing in the morning, to help us get going. It doesn't take much digging for me to find that there are daily patterns to levels of various other hormones too, including some relating to our alertness and our desire to sleep – and that disruptions to these patterns can wreak all kinds of havoc with our sleep, psychological functioning and mood.

So it's circadian rhythms that I want to explore next.

Our lives are shaped by the spaces we live in and move through – the rooms and the streets, the hills and valleys, the cities and deserts. They are shaped just as powerfully by our engagement with time. Yesterdays and tomorrows may seem to stretch in an unending line, but within each day is a cycle that is echoed by the ebb and flow of our inner life – our attention, alertness, energy and mood. This internal rhythm is produced and regulated by a neurological mechanism called the circadian clock, and we are all born with it. The crucial ways it affects our adjustment to internal and external reality is the focus of the new scientific field called chronobiology.

As introductions go, this strikes me as a nice, neat, poetic one. Michael Terman, Director of the Center for Light Treatment and Biological Rhythms at Columbia University Medical Center, US and Ian McMahan at the City University of New York, who wrote the book from which it's taken (*Chronotherapy: Resetting your inner clock to boost mood, alertness and quality sleep*), go on to talk about the origins of research into the circadian clock, and how it keeps time. From hills and valleys, cities and deserts, the reader is taken down into a cold, damp, pitch-black cave.

Summer, 1962. Two hundred and fifty feet below the French-Italian Alpine border, a twenty-three-year-old spelunker called Michael Siffre set out a tent, a sleeping bag, a few books, a torch and a field telephone in what would be his home for the next two months. He had no watch or clock. His intention was to live 'beyond time'.

Siffre kept records of what he did in this beyond-time. 'Time passed without my being aware of it in the darkness and silence . . . I felt I was on another planet.' Every time he woke, ate or prepared to sleep, he sent a message to his friends up above. When he finally surfaced, his sleep and waking patterns were analysed.

What emerged were patterns that occurred in a cycle that lasted twenty-four hours and thirty minutes. Something inside Siffre was keeping time – even if that time didn't exactly match the solar day. Similar results have since come from people housed in laboratories designed to exclude all clues to time. The research shows that, on average, our natural sleep/wake cycle is twenty-four hours and thirty minutes long, though it can vary between people from 23.9 to as much as twenty-six hours.

Clearly, even the *average* among us have half an hour extra on the calendar day. So if we stuck strictly to a cycle governed by our inner clock, we'd gradually shift from doing what we do in the day today to doing it in the night, and then back into the day. But we don't. So what resets our clock, to keep us in synch with Earth's spin? The answer, Terman says, is the daily cycle of changing light.

When we don't allow light to regulate our cycles properly, he argues, the result can be mood disorders and depression. In fact, body-clock mechanisms are involved in all the biological processes that have been proposed as underpinning depression, he writes. 'When the sleep pattern gets out of sync with the circadian cycle,' he warns, 'there can be precipitous drops in mood.'

I find that a researcher at the University of Pittsburgh, US reviewed the available research on how circadian rhythms may control mood. There's a lot of work out there finding that serotonin, dopamine and noradrenaline (brain chemicals that are targeted by anti-depressant and mood-stabilising drugs) have a circadian rhythm to their levels. And it seems that melatonin (the somewhat sinisterly named 'hormone of darkness' and a crucial player in driving the sleep/wake cycle) at least helps to regulate those levels. This supports the idea, then, that a healthy mind requires a well-functioning circadian system.

But managing that system effectively involves more than being sure to expose ourselves to some light. And while we all have roughly twenty-four-hour cycles, of course we aren't all biologically driven to be asleep and awake at the same times.

This is from my sister-in-law, Vicky:

'I'm terrible at getting to bed, and love my alone moment after hubby and kids are in bed, all fed and watered, and I get some me time. I know watching TV is the worst thing to do, but I do like watching catch-up stuff with a cuppa in the peace and quiet. I then start doing stuff – washing, making lunches for work. It's like a second wind, and I feel so energetic and awake. I get to bed late, usually between 12 and 12.30am. I get up at 6.30am most school days and find it's not a big problem and I don't feel less energetic. As long as I get six hours' sleep, I'm good to go.'

Most of us are familiar with the concept of larks and owls. Larks like to go to bed early and wake early. Owls stay up late, and sleep late – or would like to. Vicky is unusual in that she seems to be both, staying up till after midnight and getting up at 6.30, ready to hit the day head on. (She also cannot lie still on a sun lounger for more than two minutes. I've seen her. She literally starts jiggling. Oh, to have her energy.)

Before my kids interfered with my natural sleep cycle, I'd go to bed at about eleven and get up about seven. That makes me, in the bird-centric terminology of circadian scientists, a hummingbird. I'm not really sure why a hummingbird, rather than anything else. But you're probably one too. Terman estimates that around seventy per cent of us are.

The virtues of being a lark have long been celebrated. 'Early to bed and early to rise, makes a man healthy, wealthy and wise,' wrote Benjamin Franklin in the eighteenth century. The world isn't really designed around larks, however, but around the majority. Most pubs shut at eleven. Most working days begin at nine. What more could a hummingbird want? In theory, people like me should fit in fine (from a circadian perspective).

But what if you're an owl, and you go to bed late, when you feel tired, but then you're obliged to get up earlier than you'd like? If you have to be torn from sleep by an alarm clock every morning, you're in trouble, says Terman. Because that cortisol surge that helps to get you going in the morning doesn't happen when you physically wake up. It happens when the body clock thinks it's wake-up time. So if that's an hour or two later than the scream of the alarm, you'll be getting up groggy, and staying that way for a while.

One of the myriad problems of being a teenager is that, as the hormones of puberty hit, they go from being lark-ish kids to being owls. And yet, except in a minority of chronobiologically aware institutions, the school start time does not alter. This may change, however . . . In October, 2014, GCSE students from 106 schools in England were invited to begin their day at 10am, as part of an Oxford University study. This followed a pilot study at Monkseaton High School in North Tyneside in 2009, which found that delaying the school start time by an hour produced a nineteen per cent improvement in grades in core subjects. Still, there would be practical challenges to shifting the national school start time, of course – it would be very difficult for many parents to manage, unless the working day started later, too.

Some owls are able to tailor their lives to their sleep patterns, of course. But what if you can't? Or you're a lark who feels exhausted and low by mid-afternoon, yet you've another three hours left at work? Many people naturally become extreme larks as they get older, and this too can be distressing. Genes and hormones direct your sleep/wake preferences. But you *can* tweak them, Terman argues, using light.

When light enters the eye, signals don't go only to the brain's visual system. They go also to a small bundle of cells called the suprachiasmatic nucleus. This is the body's 'master clock'. There are biological clocks in various other parts of the body, but this master clock keeps them in synch.

Roughly speaking, if you need, or want, to adjust your master clock so you wake up spontaneously earlier than you do right now, a period of bright light, or a dawn simulator, in the morning could help, Terman says. If you want to stay awake later, and be more alert in the afternoons, a bright light pulse or a natural dusk simulation in the late evening might work. (For more on Terman's advice on regimens and dawn/dusk simulators, visit his website – see p. 339 for details.)

Of course, not all of us need to switch bird species. Many of us are hummingbirds, and yet still, we suffer from insomnia and daytime sleepiness and low mood. While stressing that insomnia has many culprits, it's worth considering mismanagement of your master clock, Terman argues. If your cycle isn't precisely twenty-four hours, you'll need daily light input to adjust it. Yet many of us, even in sunny places, don't get that. We put sunglasses on before leaving the house. We squint. We spend a lot of our time indoors, exposed to light that's a small fraction of the strength of the sun.

If you live somewhere sunny, at least you have the option of starting your day with natural light. When I worked at home in Sydney, and before I had a dog, or children, there wasn't necessarily any *need* for me to go outdoors for perhaps a couple of days at a time. But when I did start the day with a swim at a nearby outdoor pool, I felt great. I put it down to the exercise and the heart-catching beauty of Bondi Beach, virtually deserted at that hour, stretching out before me. But perhaps I was also helping to align my body clock with the day.

If you live somewhere less blessed with sunshine than Sydney, you run a greater risk of your body clock slipping out of synch – and also of developing depression. This happened, at least to a certain extent, to my friend, Michelle. A few years ago now, she moved with her husband and baby daughter from Philadelphia in the US (harsh winters, pretty good summers) to Sweden. Northern Sweden in winter, she says, is gloomy almost beyond imagining. She lives in the south, which does at least get a few hours of light in the middle of the day in winter. But still, she finds it hard.

'Where we lived in the US, winters were actually colder than here in southern Sweden, and we are familiar with the darkness of winters of England, but the utter bleakness of Swedish winters is unremitting. Perhaps if one has always lived in this environment, then it is normal, but we find it a shock to the system physically, mentally and emotionally. All functions seem to slow down. We virtually hibernate in winter. Our activity levels drops and low moods hit hard. The saving grace is when it snows heavily and the white of the snow lightens up the dark world. On snowy days, we also get to see the blue skies, which are few and far between. But should there be a wintry day with blue sky and some sunlight, you are sure to find Swedes sitting outside, wrapped up warmly but holding their faces to the sun as if trying to absorb as much light as possible until the next time.

To bring some of the blue sky into our life, we started using a blue-light device during our second winter. We noticed an immediate improvement in our mood and in our ability to get up in the mornings and switch on. We tend to use it first thing in the morning while waiting for the kettle to boil or while eating breakfast. Twenty minutes is usually enough.'

Did Michelle suffer in winter from full-blown SAD – Seasonal Affective Disorder, a type of depression? I don't know. But she certainly suffered. And she did find that light therapy helped. In fact, there is research evidence that light therapy at any time of day can relieve depression, and not just depression associated with living in near-darkness.

Now back to the majority: all those people who don't live in Sweden or Sydney. Or who do, but don't necessarily use light to their advantage? I ask Terman what common body-clock mistakes people make?

He says:

'They keep their bedrooms so dark that there is no dawn or sunrise penetration. On the one hand, this successfully eliminates night-time light pollution, which disrupts sleep directly, and also destabilises the circadian clock. On the other hand, a dark bedroom at wake-up time – with reliance on an alarm clock – encourages the inner clock to slip later, delaying the onset of morning alertness. Obviously, the use of window shades (even blackout shades) has benefits and costs, and their use will vary seasonally and with latitude of residence, considering the wide variations in sunrise time.'

Blackout blinds, then, aren't all good or all bad. If you're being woken at 4am by sunlight streaming through your window, and you don't need to get up till 7am, they may be more beneficial than harmful.

What else do people commonly do wrong?

'They skip breakfast and start eating voraciously at midday. This forces desynchronisation of a secondary clock system located in liver tissue, which times daily digestive function. When the liver clock and the hypothalamic clock [the master clock] get out of sync, it's a formula for malaise and sleep disorders. It's therapeutic even to have a small protein-based breakfast after waking up, even if you're not at all hungry. This will start shifting the two timing systems into accord.

They leave evening room light too bright. This includes bright illumination from computer displays and TV screens. This excess of photic stimulation encourages the circadian clock to drift later, out of sync with the desired/required workday sleep schedule. And that's a formula for triggering or exacerbating depression.'

Terman's comments on breakfast put in mind of Richard Hammersley's comment in the previous chapter that he finds it best to eat a little protein with his breakfast – and his own observations, and those from the Food and Mood Project survey, that eating regularly can help with emotional regulation.

I then ask, apart from using light, rather than abusing it, is there anything else you can do?

There are sleep-promoting supplements out there, he tells me. Melatonin is a popular one. Our bodies naturally produce it in the evening, and as levels rise, we get sleepier and sleepier . . . Melatonin can also reset the inner clock. But Terman is cautious. The supplements available at the moment are too strong to achieve the ideal circadian effect, he says.

Anything else? I ask him.

Once you've got your sleep/wake pattern and circadian clock nicely synched, don't mess it up with occasional late nights, he advises. So-called 'social jetlag' spells bad news for mood. (I can only report the advice . . .)

And when your sleep/wake cycle and your master clock *are* synched, so you're doing what you can in this respect for your psychological health, does any circadian rhythm of mood emerge? Anything that it might be useful to be aware of?

In fact, there is a pattern, Terman says: unless otherwise interfered with, mood (and alertness) tends to follow the rhythm of core body temperature, with a low point towards the end of the night, and a gradual rise to a peak in the evening.

Most of us also have a natural dip in body temperature and alertness levels in the afternoon, between about 2pm and 4pm. (You'll often hear that this is caused by a big lunch, but the circadian influence is far more potent, I gather.) Larks have a longer and bigger dip than owls – and alcohol will make everyone's dip worse. But there may be a way to avoid the dip. There's research showing that if you do some exercise or have a hot shower when your body temperature's starting its afternoon descent, you can keep your attention levels high.

After all this reading, and my conversation with Terman, I feel I understand now how important it is to try to keep my inner clock in time with the day. And I start to think about what changes I should be making to try to achieve this. But let me note first that Terman is convinced of the benefits of 'fresh air' for a good night's sleep, in addition to a well-managed circadian clock. 'One answer to the predicaments of modern urban life would be to move to a sunny tropical clime, preferably next to a beach or a waterfall', he writes in his book. So that's the *medical advice*?

My sleep resolution is, therefore: to go and live in a sunny tropical clime, by the beach.

And until that time:

Not to fall asleep on the sofa in the evening. To try to go to bed at the same time every night. Unless I'm going out. (I'm not going to stop going out – it's rare enough as it is.) Even if we don't always walk to school, I'll try to make sure we get *some* time outside in the morning. And walking the dog every lunchtime – part of my new exercise programme – will conveniently also help to channel some extra light in the direction of my master clock.

In the evening, I don't look at the computer anyway. I'm too tired. I do dim the lights, and put on a lamp. Lucas sleeps with his main light on, but I don't know if I can do anything about that. If I turn it off and switch on his night light when I go to bed, he comes through at two or three in the morning and demands to have the big light back on. For now, it'll have to stay on. But I'm aware that it's not ideal. I'll try to come up with strategies to get him out of it.

I also decide that when I am tired after a poor night's sleep, I should try going with it, instead of fighting it. I don't think I get depressed when I'm sleep-deprived, so much as ratty. So if I've had an awful night, I resolve not to try to make the kids eat beef stew, wholegrain rice and three veg for their dinner. I'll give them what they love – canned pasta in the shape of

TV characters and grated cheese – because whatever the anti-inflammatory, brain-boosting benefits of broccoli, surely they're bound to be counteracted by the pro-inflammatory effects of a foul-tempered mum crying, 'Why can't you just eat it? It's healthy!'

OK. I have a plan.

But in my questioning of Michael Terman, I realise I've missed something . . .

Terman made it clear that a 'good night's sleep' begins when the so-called sleep pressure that builds during waking hours reaches a high point in the mid- to late evening, just as the circadian timer sends a signal to trigger the release of melatonin, the 'hormone of darkness'.

Before this confluence of events, it's very tricky to fall asleep, as anyone's who's tried to get an unusually early night before an early flight knows well. Unless you're already sleep-deprived, of course, in which case the sheer overwhelming force of sleep pressure may be such that you're able to fall asleep before than your normal bedtime. (I can. And frequently do.) Dropping off on the sofa at 8pm is bad news, of course – unless your working day starts at dawn. But what about *earlier* in the day?

While being awake all day and asleep only at night is the norm in the UK for adults and older kids, in many parts of the world it isn't. And in writing about sleep before, I've come across work suggesting psychological benefits stemming from something young children everywhere and some adults in Spain do every day: taking a nap.

The Intercontinental Hotel, Park Lane, London. I'm wearing a white dressing gown and slippers. A therapist called Pearl leads me from the darkly soothing spa reception area, along a corridor dotted with red uplights, to a small room containing a large bed. The bed's covered with towels.

'You'll lie down here,' she tells me. 'It'll feel hard, but then I'll start it up, and it'll fill with water. The water's heated to thirty-five degrees celsius. It'll feel like you're weightless.'

I lie down, my head on a pillow, and Pearl drapes towels, then a heavy cover on top of me. 'I'll be back in twenty minutes,' she promises.

I hear her press a button and, accompanied by oddly bark-like noises from the pumping mechanism, the mattress rises beneath me. After a few minutes, I find myself lying, cocooned, on the softest, warmest bed I've ever experienced. Piped music is playing. Gentle piano. Some birdsong. A couple of crickets join in. I close my eyes, and feel myself relax . . .

The past three nights in a row, my sleep has been disturbed by sick children. So perhaps it's no surprise that, though it's 2.30 in the afternoon, I'm finding myself easily drifting towards sleep. I don't completely drop off. But I get to that early, jerky stage, just as consciousness gives way.

Then the door opens, and another therapist smiles and asks me how I feel.

'Wonderful. Relaxed,' I tell her, surprised that twenty minutes have passed already.

Later, when I'm dressed, and back in the reception area, I talk to Radhika Khandke, the spa's manager, about the 'nap experience'.

'It's really popular with people who are jet-lagged – people who are travelling and need a quick pick-me-up,' she says. 'They may come off a flight and want to relax before going to do some shopping, to get into the time zone.'

Do most of them report actually falling properly asleep?

'Some do,' she says. 'Some say, "I thought I'd fall asleep, but I stayed awake" – but they felt like they were in a really deep state of relaxation.'

Twenty minutes isn't long, of course. Clients who do actually fall asleep during one of the sessions get no more than a 'power nap'. But the benefits, as you will see, may be profound.

✳

About eight years ago now, I signed a contract to write five science-based thrillers for kids. The series was called *STORM*, published in the UK with E. L. Young as the author. (*I know* – but if I can't promote myself in my own book, where can I?) I had to write 80,000 words in six months, every six months, for two and a half years. Since my advance wasn't astronomical, to make ends meet, I also had to keep up with some journalism.

I worked out that for the first draft of each book, I had to write ten pages a day, three days a week. Ten pages might not sound like a lot. And they were thrillers for kids. I'm not claiming to be Hilary Mantel, or anything. Still, I did find it mentally draining. But I quickly noticed a pattern to just how full or empty my mental reserves seemed to be.

Between about 9am and midday, the words flowed OK. Between midday and three, it was pointless trying to write anything, even with the help of multiple Tim-Tams (an Australian biscuit that's a bit like a Penguin, but nicer). And 4pm to 7pm were my golden hours. The brain-clamp was released and the paragraphs poured out.

Clearly, I realise *now*, my circadian rhythm in body temperature and alertness underpinned all this. I didn't know then that taking a hot shower or doing some exercise might at least have helped with the slump. But it bothered me that I wasn't doing much between twelve and three. Even if I did some journalism, or necessary chores, they felt like wasted hours.

Then, one lunchtime, with five pages down and five more looming ahead of me, I lay down beside my laptop. (I feel I write fiction best in bed, with the curtains closed and only a lamp on. No doubt, Michael Terman would disapprove, but there we go). I fell not-quite asleep, but was on the verge of it. It was a slow-motion bungee jump into unconsciousness. I dipped into it. I experienced perhaps five minutes of hallucinations and jerky sensations. Then I returned to normal consciousness. And I felt refreshed.

Instead of messing about for a few hours, doing chores or research for features, I went back to my laptop. While the words didn't flow like they did from four till seven, they came, which was something. I immediately made this a habit. Five pages. A dip to the edge of sleep. Back to work. I was more productive this way. I got more done in a day, and my first drafts were finished faster.

I never really thought of these dips to the edge of sleep as power naps. But looking back, I suppose that's exactly what they must have been. And now I want to find out more about exactly how they helped – and if I should be returning to that habit.

First, I need to be clear on the stages of sleep. There are various reputable sources of information about our sleep cycle out there, but I'll go back to Terman and McMahan, who are clear on the timings for the first cycle after dropping off:

- As we fall asleep, our brain activity shifts from small, fast beta waves to slower alpha waves. This is when you can get those sudden hallucinations and startling jerks.

- Brain activity switches to very slow theta waves. Duration: about five minutes.

- We experience bursts of rapid brain waves among the slower waves. Duration: about twenty minutes.

- Very deep sleep. Delta waves appear. It's this sleep that seems to alleviate built-up sleep pressure. Duration: about half an hour.

- After a brief return to the second stage, we usually move on to REM: rapid-eye movement sleep.

- A complete sleep cycle lasts on average about 90–110 minutes, but as the night wears on, we spend less time in slow-wave sleep, and more time in REM.

A daytime nap has no scientifically defined duration, of course. My dad will happily call a two-hour afternoon retreat to the bedroom a 'nap'. And clearly, how long you spend engaged in a nap will determine which sleep stages you pass through. Bearing that in mind, let's move on to the research findings:

- Naps can boost memory (which I'm not really dealing with here), but

- they can also act as powerful 'emotional balms'.

I've interviewed Robert Stickgold, a professor at Harvard Medical School and one of most preeminent researchers in the field of sleep, on several occasions for features. He once said to me:

> 'I often joke that one of the questions I'd like to answer most in life is: what is it about a ninety-minute nap that turns a psychotic dwarf into a delightful two-year-old? We all know what total emotional dysregulation comes without a nap, but we don't ask the question that should be staring us in the face: what happens to the brain during a nap in that child that makes such a huge difference?'

I already know – from personal experience and the published research – that night-time sleep deprivation makes regulating emotions so much tougher for adults, never mind kids. Matt Walker, at the University of California, Berkeley, thinks REM dreaming is key here. (In fact, he puts emotional regulation at the top of his list of the functions of dreams.)

'I think the evidence is mounting in favour of dream sleep acting as an emotional homeostasis – basically, rebalancing the emotional compass in a good way at the biological level,' he told me.

In one study, Walker found that over the course of the day, both adults and children get more sensitive to angry or fearful faces, and a nap can not only prevent this, it can make you more receptive to happy faces. REM dreaming seems to drive this, so your nap would have to last long enough to get you through those early non-REM stages – so a long Spanish-type siesta, rather than a spa nap experience.

I call an acquaintance who moved to Madrid from London, with her Spanish husband and three young children a few years ago, and ask about her experiences with siestas. She tells me that they don't take any during the week, but generally try to at weekends. She says that while small independent businesses in Madrid still close down between 2 and 5pm, air-conditioned offices have made it less necessary to get time out in the afternoon and weekday siestas are not that common in the city. Even people who work outside in the sun don't take long siesta breaks any more, she says – at least not in Madrid. But I should talk to her twenty-year-old niece, she suggests, because Clara, a student in Madrid, takes a siesta every day.

I call Clara, and this is what she tells me:

'Yes, I take a siesta almost every day. The minimum is twenty minutes, but I can sleep two to three hours. If it gets to that, though, it's not good. I feel dizzy, I don't feel OK. Normally, I set my alarm clock to go off after about forty-five minutes or an hour. If I'm really tired, I go to bed. Otherwise, I lie on the sofa in the living room with my mum, because she takes siesta too.

I notice when it's getting to the time. My classes are between 11am and 3pm. I eat at about 3 or 3.30. Then by 4, my eyes are starting to shut. I go to sleep and afterwards, if it's only for half an hour or one hour, I feel rested – really good. If I have to miss a siesta for some reason, I feel tired and a little bit angry. That lasts for an hour or so, then I feel OK. I go to bed at about 12 or 1 and sleep till 9 or 10.

Most of my friends have siestas. Sometimes I'll have them at my friends' houses. I think when I start work, I won't have time to. Until then, I will have it!'

Clara's just told me she goes to sleep at about 4pm. But if independent shops shut between 2 and 5pm, most people who take siestas must be taking them a little earlier, I assume – closer to the early afternoon.

The reason we *can* nap in the afternoon, Terman explains, is that by this stage, sleep pressure has reached a reasonably high level. Also, the morning cortisol burst has eased off, and the rise in core body temperature, which makes you feel more awake, and keeps you going till bedtime, is only just getting going.

There are plenty of people who believe in 'power naps' – and there is research showing that just a ten-minute nap can boost your alertness. (I know I experienced this, though I'm not sure I ever had ten minutes of actual sleep.) Longer naps may well help with emotional regulation. But Terman warns they can leave you feeling groggy, and Clara's own report is testament to that. After a long nap, it takes a lot longer to get back to full alertness, and you risk relieving your sleep pressure so much it becomes very hard to get to sleep at bedtime.

For many people, of course, this talk of daytime naps is a completely theoretical discussion, up there with: hmm, should I take my next holiday on a private island in the Maldives or the hotel George Clooney got married in? I can imagine many of my friends crying: 'A lunchtime siesta! I don't even get chance to grab a sandwich!'

Still, a ten-minute nap may be more of a possibility than Clara's forty-five minutes to an hour, especially given the rise of home-working, and spa 'nap experiences'. I think perhaps micro-napping is a practice I *should* return to.

Deciding just *when* to have one will be the biggest problem, of course. But I'll set that decision aside, for now. Because I want to tie up loose ends first. I want to know: apart from correcting circadian mistakes, and avoiding too much caffeine or alcohol, is there anything else I can do to make it more likely that I'll actually sleep well at night – and reap the psychological benefits?

How about exercise? Will that help?

Matt Stults-Kohlemainen at Yale and Stacey Young-McCaughan had the same, and surprising (at least, to me) view on this: we *think* that we sleep better after exercise, they said, but we don't actually sleep any longer. Whatever sleep we do get just *feels* more restorative.

Well, I've already resolved to exercise more anyway, so I guess I'll take that. But I'll note that for some people, at least, if you exercise late in the day, it can be harder to fall asleep. The most extreme advice I've seen recommends no exercise within six hours of bedtime. If you do really struggle to get to sleep, this must be worth bearing in mind.

What else?

The American Academy of Sleep Medicine recommends this: 'Do not bring your worries to bed with you.'

Oh, excellent advice. If *only* it were that simple. Perhaps, as I mentioned earlier, mindfulness techniques may help. When I visited the Altrincham Grammar School for Girls (see Chapter One), I spoke to a sixteen-year-old, called Hannah, who told me: 'I find it helps a lot if I can't get to sleep, or if I'm worrying about something that's distracting me from sleep. I've learned to acknowledge what it is that's worrying me – but then to try to ignore it.'

Ana Roslan, the assistant headteacher at AGGS, told me she uses something from the mindfulness-in-schools curriculum called Beditation with her ten-year-old. Beditation involves taking a few long breaths, releasing physical tension and focusing on the feet. Her son 'finds it very difficult to get to sleep,' Roslan told me. 'I used to hold him until he fell asleep. Now I just get him to do Beditation.'

The NHS also has some other tips for if you often find it hard to sleep because you're worrying:

• If you tend to lie there worrying about everything you've got to get done the next day, start making time in the day to write down your plans for tomorrow.

- If you can't sleep for worrying, get up and do something relaxing, and only go back to bed when you feel sleepy again.

These suggestions sound like they're worth trying, too. Because I know I need all the sleep my kids will allow me to get.

I'm clear now that adequate sleep is fundamental for supporting a calm, strong mind. And I'll share a final note on this point from Stacey Young-McCaughan. Soon after our phone conversation, she emailed me a journal paper, which she co-authored. At the end of that paper is a model of 'military resilience'. This model is in the shape of a pyramid.

The broad base layer contains what Young-McCaughan and her team consider to be the main foundations of psychological resilience – the capacity to cope well with stress. They are:

Sleep

Nutrition

Physical fitness

Exactly the factors I've looked at, in fact (minus meditation, of course.)

Young-McCaughan adds a note: efforts within the US Army to build psychological resilience in military personnel are focusing now on these three factors, she tells me. 'For the army it's all about the "performance triad" right now,' she says.

I like this. Unsurprisingly, perhaps, because it's pretty much how I've started – with what I see as the basics – the biggest potential influences on the brain and the mind.

Go up a step on Young-McCaughan's resilience pyramid, and you get to 'psychological factors'. These include 'optimism' and 'hardiness'.

Then, as the pyramid narrows still further, there are factors that relate to military, but not so much to civilian life, like 'understanding of mission'.

The pinnacle of the pyramid is 'positive adaptation within the context of significant adversity'. That is, actually experiencing psychological growth as a result of a stressful experience.

I'm not really too worried about significant adversities (well, I am, but not right here, right now). I am, of course, intensely interested in building the kind of mental strength that can help me to cope better with day-to-day life.

And I think I've arrived now at a reasonable understanding of the mind/brain fundamentals – meditation, diet, exercise, circadian cycles and sleep. But clearly the *contents* of your thoughts can make or break a mood, and can either drive you to climb mountains, metaphorical or otherwise, or keep you huddled at the bottom, too afraid to even attempt an ascent.

So, it's time to tackle thoughts.

First, though, the main lessons from circadian rhythms and sleep.

THE SLEEP CHECKLIST

- Not everyone's sleep needs are the same. While many of us do best on seven or eight hours a night, you might need five. You might need nine. 'How much can you live on, and your family doesn't want to kill you because you're so irritable and crabby?' is one professional recommendation for arriving at a figure.

- Try to spend as much time outside as you can. This will help to align your body's clock with the day. Keep lights dim in the evening, and try to minimise evening exposure to bright, artificial light – like that from a laptop screen. Or a bar. Actually, as far as sleep scientists are concerned, late nights out should not happen.

- If you wake early, but it takes you a long time to feel alert, or you don't feel tired until late into the night, but need an alarm clock to wake you, you might want to consider trying to adjust your sleep/wake cycles using artificial light.

- There are daily patterns in mood and alertness. It varies from person to person, but you're probably at your brightest between around mid-morning and lunchtime, and then between 4pm and 10pm. It might make sense to work with that pattern, rather than to fight it.

- Naps of 90–110 minutes are most effective for improving emotional wellbeing, but may leave you groggy after-wards. Short, ten-minute 'power naps' can help boost alertness. If you are going to nap, the best (and easiest) time to do it is the early afternoon. If you nap any later, you may find it hard to get to sleep at your normal bedtime.

• Try to keep to a regular bedtime and wake time.

CHAPTER FIVE

RETUNE YOUR MIND

I'm standing on the corner of Madison Avenue and E 101st street, a block from Central Park, in East Harlem, New York City. Across the road, public housing blocks loom. Down to my left is a Duane Reade chemist. When I dropped in there, looking for something for a headache, I found it full of people shuffling along in slippers and dressing gowns, others in wheelchairs, breathing tubes in their noses, shopping baskets brimming with packets of pills.

The wheelchairs and the breathing tubes shouldn't really have been too much of a surprise. Because right behind me is Mt Sinai Hospital. Next door is the Icahn School of Medicine, which trains doctors and is home to an array of specialists in everything from emergency medicine to food allergies to stem cells. The dean is a man named Dennis Charney (the Dennis Charney involved in the research on Special Forces soldiers – see Chapter Four) and I'm here to meet him, to talk about his work on psychological resilience.

For the past two decades, Charney has been hunting for clues to why some people cope well or even thrive in tough times, while others crumble. I know from my reading that he's identified 'thinking styles' that help. And while Charney focuses on how to weather and bounce back from trauma, I'm sure he'll have a lot of insights that can be applied to daily life, too. Still, I know that to answer my fundamental questions about thoughts, I'll have to go beyond Charney's work, into philosophy and even social relationships, and to broader psychological research into how to change our minds.

Because my main questions when it comes to thoughts are these:

- If you regularly have unhelpful or even unpleasant thoughts, how do you change them?

- What are the most genuinely *helpful* types of thoughts?

- Are there *ways* of thinking that research shows are most likely to support a strong mind?

But before I go inside to meet Charney, I'd like to take a few steps back – in time, and my own research – and pose a question that I've tried putting to myself.

If I asked you to put this book aside, go somewhere on your own, and sit in silent contemplation for fifteen minutes, would you welcome the chance for a bit of time with your own thoughts? Or would you fear it? Would you find it so unpleasant you'd rather do anything, even zap yourself with electricity, than sit there, reflecting?

One American study explored this exact question. And one quarter of women and two-thirds of men gave themselves an electric shock they'd earlier said they'd pay good money to avoid. I'd like to think that I could get through fifteen minutes alone without *self-harming*. But why did so many people feel differently?

The reason, the researchers suggest, is that we find it very hard to focus our minds on pleasant thoughts. Hence the popularity, they say, of meditation and other 'mind-control' practices (their phrase). 'Without such training,' they write in their paper, 'people prefer doing to thinking, even if what they are doing is so unpleasant that they would normally pay to avoid it. The untutored mind does not like to be alone with itself.'

I'm not entirely sure what might constitute a *tutored* mind. But I think I want one. And if I can't have one, I'd like to understand whatever tricks may be available for directing my thoughts, so that I am master of them, rather than the other way around. I'd like a mind that's self-confident and strong. Not fake-smile positive, but genuinely at ease. A mind that can take me places.

An obvious place to start is with strategies developed to help people with a psychological disorder. I'd like to look at how they might help me, and people like me. People who have up days and down days, who feel anxious in some areas of life, but not so much in others. People who aren't actually living in Hell, but who'd like some tips on how at least to contemplate trying to make their mind a Heav'n.

One thought-centred approach to treating full-blown depression or an anxiety disorder I'm already aware of, because I've written bits and pieces about it over the years. It's called cognitive behavioural therapy (CBT). CBT is designed to change the way you think and behave. And it can be very effective.

Take a woman struggling with depression after a divorce. Perhaps she's come to think of herself as a failure who'll never have another meaningful relationship. A therapist trained in CBT might encourage her rather to accept that many marriages end in divorce, and that it's possible to learn from mistakes, and move on (which might mean starting to go out with friends again, and ultimately even asking someone out on a date). This kind of approach can work well with anxiety disorders, too. A review of 101 studies found that cognitive behavioural therapy is more effective than drugs at treating social phobia – characterised by a strong fear of social situations – and the positive effects last for longer.

CBT isn't a single rule-bound entity, however. It comes in different forms. Over the past decade or so, 'third-wave' cognitive behavioural therapies have emerged.

Mindfulness-based Cognitive Therapy, which Mark Williams at Oxford University co-developed, is one. So too, I read, is something called Compassion-Focused Therapy. Meanwhile, some psychologists seem to be arguing that certain thinking strategies from ancient schools of philosophy should play a bigger role.

I've already looked at mindfulness, which, as I understand it, advocates not *changing* thoughts but rather, noticing them and accepting them for what they are: *thoughts* – and not reality. So now, I'd like to look at compassion therapy (whatever that is), and philosophical (rather than modern psychological) ideas about how to think, as well as another approach that many people seem either to love or hate: positive psychology. Of course, I also want to learn about Dennis Charney's findings from real people who made it through traumatic experiences.

One 'strategy' that I know Charney has identified as supporting psychological resilience is religious or spiritual faith. Clearly, for some people, their religion has a huge influence on how they think about life, and what they tell themselves in bad times as well as good. I have friends who are strongly religious. And I know their beliefs provide them with an enormous amount of psychological succour. Emily, the young Christian teacher I met at Altrincham Grammar School for Girls (see Chapter One), talked to me about how her faith offers practical guidance, encouraging her to turn negative events around – to focus not on the downsides, but rather on what she can learn from the experience, however bad it may feel at the time.

But I'm not going to look here at how religion can influence self-talk, because I think you either have the fundamental beliefs, or you don't. No one's going to become a Christian or a Muslim *because* of any psychological benefits. So I can't really consider 'following a religion' as a recommendation for anyone in search of a stronger mind – including me.

That doesn't mean you can't abstract generally helpful ways of thinking from religions, of course. And various religions have picked and mixed ideas from philosophy. I'm more familiar with Protestant Christianity than any other religion. And, as far as I can tell, there are Protestant attitudes (and even prayers) that stem directly from one school of philosophy, in particular – an approach to life that has a reputation for keeping people psychologically afloat in even the wildest of storms: Stoicism.

An email pops into my inbox:

> 'I am a fan of warm blankets. Place a cup of coffee nearby and a good book in my hand and I will stay cosy as long as possible. Of course, I can't do that 24/7 without my life unravelling. So I have to get up and face the day. I shouldn't complain about this . . . But how am I to prepare my mind for the day ahead? Well, thankfully we Stoics have a means of warming up our mental engines. It's a form of early morning reflection called premeditation.
>
> The longer-form name is the premeditation of evil but I had just mentioned cosy blankets and didn't want to shock your system . . .'

This particular post is titled 'How to Meet the Morning', by Matt Van Natta. In recent weeks, I've siphoned off a stack of others with titles including: 'Stoic Parenting: Praise the Process', 'On the Motivations of the Stoic' and 'Musings of a Stoic Woman: Part Three'.

They've come from Stoicism Today, a group based at the University of Exeter, UK, which formed in 2012 – around 2,300 years after Stoicism was founded, in Athens – to explore what Stoicism still has to offer people, and to provide practical advice on Stoic techniques to build psychological resilience.

My plan is to now go through them, to try to make sense of the ideals. Because my understanding of Stoicism is pretty vague. Like many people, I imagine, I associate it with having a 'stiff upper lip'. With being the originator of the now much-parodied phrase 'Keep Calm and Carry On', no matter what life throws at you.

But what does it *really* mean?

I read through the emails, and get a few hints.

From 'Stoic Parenting': 'A person's ability to make "good use" of their circumstances (including abilities) is worthy of praise . . . otherwise, praise "has no utility".'

From 'On the Motivations of the Stoic': 'Virtue is not something that one merely has, it is something that must be DONE.'

OK . . . interesting. But I'm starting to realise that I really need an expert overview. I contact Donald Robertson, a founder member of Stoicism Today. I ask him to sum up Stoicism in a few sentences. He writes back:

'The Stoics believed that the goal of life is "living in agreement with nature". That means living consistently in agreement with our own rational nature, in harmony with the nature of the universe as a whole, and in concord with the rest of mankind. They also said that the goal is to live in accord with virtue, or to flourish and excel as a human being, and they believed this was fundamentally achieved through a kind of practical wisdom.

The Stoics were renowned for training themselves to remain calm in the face of adversity. However, another connotation of "stoicism" (small s) that differs from Stoicism (big s) is that someone should be emotionless, like a robot, which is not what the ancient Stoics taught. They believe we should master unhealthy or excessive "passions" (a word meaning both desires and emotions), but that there is a place in the philosophical way of life for healthy and rational emotions, like natural affection for our loved ones, which the Stoics believed should be transformed into a more general attitude they called philanthropy, or love of mankind.

Stoicism involved training in self-discipline and psychological strategies that resemble those found in modern psychological therapies, particularly cognitive-behavioural therapy (CBT).'

A Stoic must, I gather, differentiate between things she *does* and *doesn't* have control over. Getting upset or angry about something outside your control is non-virtuous (not to mention futile). So becoming frustrated about a traffic jam or even a spouse convinced of the need to divorce is extremely un-Stoic. (If this sounds familiar, the famous Serenity Prayer used at the start of Alcoholics Anonymous meetings – 'God grant me the serenity to accept the things I cannot change; courage to change the things I can; and wisdom to know the difference . . .' – expounds this idea.)

In fact, I learn, Stoics believe that the *only* things within our control are our reactions and actions – and a good Stoic is in *firm* control.

I quite like the theory. But can anyone really *live* like a Stoic? Donald Robertson:

'I try to follow Stoic principles and practices in my daily life. I've been quite immersed in it for years now, so there are quite a lot of things involved. However, for example, if I feel myself becoming stressed, the first thing I'll normally do is pause, take a step back and observe my attitude, and ask myself whether the things I'm worried about are under my direct control or not. If they're not (and for Stoics nothing is, except our own actions), then I try to patiently imagine things going against what I'd prefer to happen, and what it would be like to respond to such a "setback" like a Stoic, with a certain detachment from the external outcome, and focusing instead on how I cope in response.

Recently, I imagined failing some exams I was sitting, and tried to accept that is always possible no matter how hard I study. For Stoics, it's our actions that matter – that's where virtue resides – and wisdom consists in viewing external events, including the outcome of our efforts, with a special kind of studied "indifference". It's important to explain that doesn't mean complete indifference, as Stoics do prefer certain outcomes over others, and work toward achieving them. However, the way we do things is ultimately more important than whether we succeed or fail, in terms of things in which other factors can intervene – those things we say are "partly in the hands of fate".'

Yes, I *do* quite like this. Why get depressed if you prepare hard for an interview and don't get the job? You might have liked that job, and it was worth pursuing. But it was partly in the 'hands of fate'. How you comported yourself during the preparation and the interview itself – and afterwards – is more important than whether or not you got the nod, and should underpin how you feel about yourself.

I guess there are aspects of Stoicism that seem a *little* on the negative side: imagining failing exams you're about to sit, to prepare yourself for the genuine *possibility* of failure, could not be more different to the 'positive-thinking' approach to life. But I can't help feeling that *not* getting something we'd like or hope for happens quite a bit – surely more often than wild success. So this attitude could lead to less disappointment, and less self-criticism, while not stopping us from *trying* for things we really want.

Preparing for the possibility of failing forthcoming exams is one thing. But Stoicism advises expecting our everyday interactions to be less than perfect. The 'premeditation of evil', mentioned by Matt Van Natta, turns out to be a morning meditation designed to prepare yourself for the likelihood that during the day you'll encounter ill will, ingratitude and disloyalty.

Isn't it hard to live like this – constantly trying to be aware of and in control of your emotions, reactions and actions?

'Yes, it's very hard,' Robertson says. 'The ancient Stoics say it is very much like physical exercise. Of course, it's hard to do press-ups or run until you're out of breath, especially if you're unfit to begin with. It becomes easier with practice. In a sense, it always requires effort to maintain, though. The Stoics said a special kind of inner tension is always required – a sort of vigilance. If we let our attention wander, we can relapse back into unhealthy emotional responses, and they can become bad habits or character traits.' But while it may be hard, especially at first, and requires constant vigilance, so too, I note, do other general approaches to life – like being mindful.

Cognitive behavioural therapy was inspired, in part, by Stoic ideas. But there are some differences, which Robertson spells out to me.

Both approaches agree that the focus should be not on events themselves, but on how we look at them. Divorce isn't 'bad' in and of itself ; it's our view on it – our *thoughts about it* – that determine how we feel and how it affects us. But while Stoicism asks only if what's distressing us is within our control or not, standard CBT asks us to look at thinking 'errors' ('I'm a failure', 'I'll never have another meaningful relationship') and to weigh up the evidence for and against these thoughts, before considering alternative perspectives that might be more helpful, not to mention realistic.

Personally, I'm feeling quite drawn to Stoicism. I understand that mindfulness can help you to accept rather than reject negative thoughts – which can lead you to face them – and to stop equating thoughts with reality. But I also like Stoicism's guiding practical tenet: getting upset or frustrated about something outside your control is destructive. You can *only* control your emotions and your actions. And you *can* control them.

If you want to find out more about Stoicism, the Stoicism Today website has a lot of information. The group also runs an annual Stoic Week. You sign up, download a handbook, and practise living like a Stoic for a week. In fact, you can do it any time, but during the formal week there's more in the way of online and social media support.

I decide to try it – to see if, for one week, I can live as much like a Stoic as possible. Partly because I like the sound of it, and partly because I know Robertson is *far* from the only person who thinks Stoicism can lead to genuinely helpful self-talk, building the kind of psychological strength needed to deal with anything from a child in mid-tantrum to near-certain death.

Former US vice presidential candidate Vice Admiral James Stockdale was a US prisoner of war in Vietnam. He credits his Stoic values with saving his life in the camp. After the jet he was piloting was shot down over Vietnam in 1965, he suffered a fractured bone in his back and severe damage to his leg. He later wrote:

> 'I was alone and crippled; self-reliance was the basis for my daily life. The system of values I carried with me into this realm was to be tested by my captors. The payoff was my self-respect. I would keep it or it would be torn from me and used as leverage against my sense of purpose and stability.'

Where did I read about James Stockdale? In *Resilience*, a book co-authored by Dennis Charney.

Once inside the cavernous lobby of the Icahn School of Medicine, I find the lifts, and soar to the twenty-first floor. A few minutes later, I'm shown into an office with what strikes me as an appropriately commanding view over run-down public housing blocks and glittering skyscrapers – over the extremes of success and struggle and psychological highs and lows that characterise Manhattan, perhaps more than any other place on the planet.

As you might expect, Dennis Charney's expansive office is a scene of success. The signs are everywhere: in framed certificates from elite universities and academies, and in the trophies and awards jostling for space on the overflowing bookcases.

Charney is a big man, with a movie-star presence (I write, having never actually met any movie stars . . . but surely they must radiate a similar force-field of charisma). He wears his greying hair swept back, his moustache and beard neatly trimmed. Smart but casual in a shirt and blue braces, he welcomes me with warmth – and a strong New York accent.

How did you get into all this? I ask him. Do you have a personal interest in psychological resilience?

It didn't start that way, he tells me. 'But my grandparents came from Russia. America was the land of opportunity, but they had to have a certain resilience and confidence to say, "I'm coming to America, I got no money, and I don't speak English" – right? And the portal was New York. Ellis Island. So if you look around New York City, you got Asian populations, Italian, Jewish and so on, who came here. So many of us here have generations of people who taught us resilient behaviour.'

Charney was born in the Bronx. When he was five, he and his family moved out to a solidly middle-class community in Long Island. His own childhood was not difficult. But, later, as a psychiatrist, he encountered a lot of people whose lives were or had been traumatic, and who were suffering.

His research focused on the biology of depression, stress

and post-traumatic stress disorder (PTSD), with the main aim of finding new treatments (like that nasal spray I mentioned earlier – see p. 147). 'Then my group said, maybe we can learn from people who've been stressed, who've been traumatised, but who did not develop PTSD or depression or substance abuse – or if they did, they recovered. We thought maybe we could learn from people who are resilient, and that would help us develop new approaches to help people who have problems. That really started the journey.'

US Special Forces soldiers were among the first groups to be studied by Charney and his colleagues. They've now talked to a wide range of people, including earthquake survivors, men and women afflicted by poverty and physical and sexual abuse in Washington, D.C., people who've lost limbs to land mines, New Yorkers hit hard by the terrorist attacks of 9/11 – and former prisoners of war.

'We identified there was a national prisoner of war institute in Pensacola, Florida, funded by the government, where they get free medical care for the rest of their lives. We explained what we wanted to do, and they put out a communication saying a bunch of psychiatrists are studying resilience, and asking, "Would you be interested in talking to them?" We got a great response. We flew down. We did some brain scans. But the big part was the interviews. These people were amazing, right? They'd been held in prison for six or eight years. They had amazing stories. We started out with a blank slate. We said: tell us how you made it. What were the factors?'

Yes, what *were* the factors? I already know that religious or spiritual faith was one . . .

Having a 'moral compass' – identifying personal core values

and striving to live by them, as James Stockdale strove to live Stoically – is another.

A third is something else I've already looked at: physical exercise. This particular factor has been highlighted by a lot of the team's 'resilient' people. Some (especially former PoWs) even credited staying fit with saving their lives.

But there is a personality type – and a way of thinking – that also seems to be hugely helpful for forging resilience.

This is optimism. 'Not a Pollyanna kind of optimism,' Charney says, referring to the unrelentingly stubborn optimism of the protagonist of the bestselling 1913 novel, but 'realistic optimism': an ability to evaluate current circumstances 'without rose-tinted glasses', as he puts it, but with a deep-seated belief that things will get better.

Of all the personality factors that might influence resilience, optimism really stands out. And so, I decide, it's something I should take a close look at.

✳

First, I try to evaluate myself. At heart, I think, I'm more optimistic than pessimistic. I do believe that if I work hard, I'll succeed. To a degree. In the end. Still, I'm not optimistic about everything.

Put me on a mountainside in full daylight with a map and a compass and I would not be optimistic about my chances of navigating myself back to a checkpoint. I'm not that great with directions.

Put me in a room full of strangers and I wouldn't be that optimistic about making a bunch of new friends. I'm more introvert than extrovert. I have some very close friends, and I love them dearly, but I don't make friends as easily as some people I know.

Then there's this, which I've already recognised as being a problem because I appreciate that it doesn't make sense: unless I'm going to be meeting up with *really* good friends, I don't always look forward to going out – whether that's to a party or to dinner – because I don't feel optimistic that I'll enjoy it. Yet, probably nineteen times out of twenty, I *do* enjoy it. So why the lack of optimism?

And what about all the plans I'm making to change my mind for the better? How optimistic am I that I'll be able to stick them all?

Honestly?

I'm not one hundred per cent sure.

Not because I'm unconvinced that they work or think deep down that they're not really important, because I *fervently* believe that they do, and they are. The problem is, they require sustained effort, and I know I've given up on all kinds of effortful projects in the past. If I said, 'Oh sure, I'll have no trouble at all sticking with the regular exercise and meditation and the new diet', I know I'd be kidding myself. (Though I *am* expecting to get some serious help with all this when I get to the topic of mental toughness – see Chapter Six.)

So . . . optimistic in some areas. Not so much in others.

I wonder, am I suffering unnecessarily? Could I enhance my psychological resilience – and my life, full stop – by somehow encouraging my patchy optimism to bloom?

Dennis Charney thinks so. And the field of positive

psychology is built, in fact, on the idea that you *can* train yourself to become a more optimistic thinker.

At this point, I think I should get a better understanding of just how optimistic a psychologist would say I am. There are all kinds of questionnaires available online. Martin Seligman at the University of Pennsylvania offers an optimism test (as well as many other tests – seriously, you could easily spend days on them). I visit the website (see p. 328), create an account and take the test.

It turns out that I'm 'averagely to moderately' optimistic when it comes to a belief that good events have a permanent cause, and that bad events have a temporary cause. However, I'm 'very pessimistic' when it comes to a (psychologically desirable) belief that good events will enhance everything I do. Instead, I seem to believe firmly that good events are caused by specific factors (that dinner party went really well because I was on good form that night and put a lot of effort into the cooking, rather than 'because I'm a great host'.)

The results page explains that these two dimensions ('permanence' and 'pervasiveness') must be taken together to indicate how hopeful – or optimistic – you are. My final result? I'm 'moderately hopeless'.

This isn't good.

You can only have genuine self-confidence in your ability to win gold – 'your powers' – if you've put in the training, Sebastian Coe pointed out in a discussion during an athletics competition shown on the BBC (having the talent was taken for granted). Realistic optimism *must* be built on something solid. But must it *always*? Can you teach yourself to feel more optimistic, which may help you train – or study, or make friends, or host great parties – which may further boost your optimism, in an ever-uplifting curve?

And if so, how?

I *am* going to come back to my meeting with Dennis Charney. But first, I'd like to jump to a conversation that took place a little later.

I was chatting to my sister, and she mentioned Mark, her banker friend (the one who told me about all the Diet Cokes stacked up on the desks on the trading floor – see p. 100). He'd taught himself to be optimistic, she said.

Intrigued, I asked him about this. He told me:

'I think I'm optimistic about certain things, like: can I climb that mountain? I tend to be optimistic about that kind of stuff. But pessimistic when it comes to people. I think a lot of people are like that: optimistic about some things, pessimistic about others, and that's based on your history, I think – what's worked out and what hasn't.

I work with money. It's all quite high risk. It's challenging and stressful. But I noticed I was being unduly pessimistic about all kinds of things. I wouldn't make certain decisions, because I only saw the negatives. I highlighted these, and I talked about them. For a few reasons, that's bad. One, it's just miserable. Two, it's illogical to be pessimistic in situations where the outcome doesn't matter. In areas where there are major implications, though, there are reasons to be cautious. I decided to figure out the areas where there would be consequences, and areas where there wouldn't.'

You mean, at home or with friends, versus work?

'Everything. I've learned that if I find myself feeling negative about something to apply that test: will the outcome *really matter*?'

What prompted you to try to change your outlook?

'I guess a few people pointed out to me that I'm pessimistic by nature. That was one trigger. But also I came to the realisation that because of things that have happened in your past, you can have predispositions. I don't like having predispositions. Not without properly understanding them, anyway.'

So how did you go about becoming more optimistic?

'I read a book called *Learned Optimism* [by Martin Seligman]. It was quite interesting, but it didn't really give me any useful tools. So it's been a case of trial and error.'

What's worked?

'A few things have worked. What worked the best – and I've shared this with friends – is when you're interacting with someone, assume they are thinking the best, rather than the worst. For me, a lot of that is to do with meetings with clients. I might have thought in the past, *Are they thinking about what I'm saying, or are they just not interested, or is their company about to go bust?* I was trying to read signals. But it's amazing how just changing your view on what it is they're thinking and saying makes you more positively disposed towards them, and it can make the conversations a lot better.'

Anything else?

'I have a young child. It's easy to let things go – like social events or going to the rock-climbing gym. An optimistic person would say to themselves, "It's going to be good." I've noticed that optimistic people tend to do more stuff because they *expect* things to go well. I've been trying to do that. It works really well.'

Is there anything you've tried, and it hasn't worked?

'I still struggle with conflict stress. I really dislike it. It affects me for hours afterwards. I've worked with people who have been arguing with other people for years. As a rule, they don't look well. You can see conflict as something that might help you to get a better commercial outcome. But I think we underestimate the effects it has on us. When I'm in a confrontation – and this happens for me once a week, or every few weeks – I haven't found a method for dealing with that in an optimistic way. It doesn't feel like optimism is the right tool.'

It's good to talk to someone who's recognised problems with their general outlook, done some research and come up with potential fixes. Before we say goodbye, I tell Mark a little about how some people use meditation and exercise to help dampen the effects of conflict stress – though a Stoic approach could be useful in that kind of situation, too – and I hope at least that's something for him to think about, as his observations are for me. In fact, I go away from our conversation with plenty to consider.

Mark's perception that more optimistic people 'do more stuff' because they expect it'll be good sticks with me. If the reason I don't rush ecstatically to a party or try new things – and I don't, and I *do* want to – is down to general pessimism, this is something I have to change.

And I know that Dennis Charney is far from the only researcher to identify optimism as a crucial strut in constructing psychological resilience. Martin Seligman – sometimes called the modern father of positive psychology – has taken this message into schools all over the US, and abroad, as well as into the US Army. What he calls *learned optimism* can stop people developing the sorts of helpless self-focused thoughts that can lead to depression, he argues.

Martin Seligman stresses the importance of consciously deciding to build a more positive outlook on events and interactions – to *become* more hopeful/optimistic.

This process can be encouraged in cognitive behavioural therapy. You can be taught to notice an automatically negative thought, and to replace it with more a more positive way of thinking. But Seligman would like to encourage us to develop a broad suite of positivity techniques.

One of his suggestions is to write down, every evening, 'What Went Well': to identify three things that went well in the day, and why.

It's only 11.05am right now, but I guess if I had to write something, I'd start with: the kids and I walked to school – we all got exercise, and *no one got upset*. Why? Because I made an effort to be encouraging, and tried to get them to focus on 'fun' things about walking, rather than driving, like seeing cats and patting passing dogs.

I feel a little awkward, because writing down something that's gone well is not the kind of thing I usually do, but I find I quite like it. It isn't mindless pep-talking, like: 'You're an amazing person! You're going to be so super-successful today!' It's based on reality. And perhaps because I'm 'moderately hopeless', it can be easy to focus on the negatives in the day, rather than the positives.

Another of Martin Seligman's key recommendations is to try to avoid 'catastrophising' – exaggerating the negatives of a situation.

Say you ask a colleague on a date, and he gives you the brush off. You might think: *I must be repulsive. I'll never find a boyfriend.* But Seligman advocates trying to put a thought like that 'into perspective'. First, think of the 'worst-case' scenario, then the 'most likely', then the 'best'. Worst-case: I *am* repulsive. I'll never find a boyfriend. Most likely: he's an unpleasant, arrogant man, and I will find the right man in the end. Best: he's got serious problems, because I should really be a model slash TV presenter.

Once you've identified the 'most likely' situation, you develop a plan for dealing with it. You might decide to try online dating, and wait for someone to approach you, at least until you feel strong enough to ask a real, live human out again.

I don't know though . . . is that really the route to *reality*? Why should the 'most likely' case be right? You might like to believe it is, but that doesn't make it always so. I'm put a little in mind of something my sister told me recently in an email about her three-year-old, Idris:

When we were away, he got a small toy bat. It got lost within a couple of days but Idris didn't say anything to us. It was Bea who told us it was lost, and that Idris said it was invisible. When I asked him he said he didn't like to think about his toys being lost, so he prefers to think of them as having turned invisible.

Yeah, sure, he prefers it. And that's great. He's three. I'm a grown woman.

With the dating example, I'd probably decide: so maybe option two is the 'most likely' interpretation, and he could well be arrogant and unpleasant. I might also never find a boyfriend. I guess the professional response would be: you're thinking that way because you're pessimistic. If you want to feel better, and be more realistic, you *have* to try the tricks. And I'm starting to feel that a mix of tricks might work best for me:

Mindfulness for helping me to pay attention to persistent, self-destructive thoughts – because of course if you don't face them, you can't deal with them. Stoicism for warning me that unless I'm worrying about my own reactions and actions, worrying is pointless. And learned optimism, in moderation, for helping me to steer my thoughts – and reactions – in a more reasonable, less pessimistic direction.

But there is another approach to addressing negative self-talk that I haven't looked at yet. It's one of those 'third-wave' strategies I referred to earlier. And it centres on compassion.

At the Yale Stress Center, Karyn Gunnet-Shoval runs self-compassion classes for clients. Whenever they're feeling low and self-critical, they're encouraged to consider what a friend would say to them, and write it down.

This makes sense, I think. When you're catastrophising or focusing on your failures, aren't friends the ones who can provide at least the 'most likely' picture?

Using compassion – not necessarily to make yourself feel more positive, but certainly to give yourself a break, and to relieve the pressure of self-criticism, as a friend might – is something I want to investigate. And I get the chance to learn more while I'm in New York. While idly checking out event listings for Manhattan, my attention is grabbed.

Tibet House, West 15th Street, 7pm.

I'm in a large gallery, hung with works of paint and silk. About 200 people dressed variously in business suits and jeans, with coiffured hair and intricate tattoos, are sitting expectantly. We're waiting for a young, pop-star-styled woman with dark, bouncy curls and immaculate make-up to begin her talk on The Science of Compassion.

Elizabeth Pyjov trained at the Stanford Center for Compassion and Altruism Research at Stanford University, California. She promises to tell us about some of the centre's research findings. But first, she explains, as background, that she's previously run a series of sold-out, eight-week-long evening courses on compassion at Stanford. Tonight, she's hoping to sign up the first-ever group of New Yorkers. This talk then will be part explanation, part pitch.

'My goal is your health and your happiness,' she tells us, and the evening will be 'experiential – you'll be trying it out.'

In fact, we move straight into a gentle introduction. She

197

asks us to roll our shoulders, close our eyes and 'bring awareness to our foreheads'. She wants us to relax . . . to relax the
muscles around our eyes, to let our cheeks release, to notice
the breath in our bellies. 'See if you can feel a little bit of
gratitude for the body that has brought you here today,' she
says.

After putting up a few quotes on a big screen (among
others, 'The highest realms of thought are impossible to
reach without first attaining an understanding of compassion' – Socrates), Pyjov talks about how our brains regularly
generate anxiety, stress, confusion and anger, 'and one way
to change that – these seeds of stress – is compassion'.
Compassion, she says, can help us to break out of the cycle
of rumination.

Self-criticism is associated with under-achievement and
procrastination, she goes on, but 'self-compassion allows us
to persevere toward our goals and even take risks. It takes
that self-critical voice away. If you remove that inner criticism,
it becomes easier to try the hard things – even if you fail.'

I'm thinking: *an example*? And that's what she provides:

'You can go to the gym thinking: I'm lazy, I'm fat. I haven't
been for three weeks. Or you can go thinking: I want to do
a lot of things that are important to me, and my body is
important to me. As a gift to myself, as a gift to this body,
I'm going to the gym.'

You'll get to the same place – the gym – but one psychological route there will make you feel bad, she points out,
while the other will make you feel good.

I'm not sure I could think about giving a 'gift to my body'.
Maybe I'm too British. I just couldn't. But I like the

fundamental concept. I know, in the past, I'd be likely to think, while dragging on my gym kit on a Monday evening: *I haven't exercised in ages; I'm rubbish at sticking to a gym routine. Why didn't I go on Sunday? It'll be so much harder now.*

Giving myself a break and just feeling good about the fact that I'm actually going simply wouldn't have occurred to me. I think it would have made me feel weak. *There's no excuse for poor behaviour*, etc. But this isn't about excuses. It's about turning away from the negative, towards the positive. It doesn't change anything about yourself or the reality of what you're doing. But it makes you *feel* better, and so, I suspect, more motivated. So why not?

Pyjov talks about the impact on volunteers' brains of the eight-week compassion programme developed at Stanford, which she's now proposing to teach in NYC. It triggered changes to regions 'involved in perception, memory and problem-solving', she explains. Being more compassionate doesn't just make you feel better, she argues – it results in helpful changes to your brain.

Painful experiences are pretty much unavoidable, she goes on. Compassion is a 'non-stress response to suffering'. She quotes Viktor Frankl, who wrote about his experiences in Nazi concentration camps in World War II in his book *Man's Search for Meaning*. He wrote: 'Between stimulus and response there is a space. In that space our freedom lies.'

We can choose how we react to a situation or a thought, she stresses. (A freedom emphasised by Stoicism as well as Buddhism.) And we can learn to *choose* for that to be a compassionate response.

Then Pyjov asks us to close our eyes . . .

'Remember a time when somebody was compassionate and truly kind and caring to you, maybe for no apparent reason. Play that scene vividly in your mind. What kind of day it was . . . How it made you feel . . . Now think of a time when you were able to feel compassion for another person. What was that like? What were the sensations involved? How did that make you feel? How do you recognise compassion when you are giving or receiving it?

Next, she asks us to open our eyes. She wants to hear 'some words'. There's no shortage of suggestions from the floor. *No judgement. Collective. Selflessness. Kindness. Generosity. Empathy. Safety. Love.*

Compassion to others, even if only in thoughts, can bring some of the benefits that stem from actually being with someone, she says. 'Imagining being with a person and thinking well towards them has many of the same benefits as being with that person.'

And compassion, she says, can be learned – and developed. How?

Mindfulness training is useful, says Pyjov, because it helps with the recognition of judgements and assumptions. But there is another type of meditation that she teaches in her classes. It's called 'compassion meditation'. And this is how it goes:

'Choose a person or a pet you truly adore. Close your eyes and imagine them being right in front of you. Imagine them truly happy. Let that person be the happiest you've ever seen them. Keeping that image in mind, bring awareness to your heart. Imagine there's lots of warmth there and as you breathe out, imagine there's a warm, golden light that stretches out, that carries your love to that being. Imagine it touching that loved one, bringing happiness and peace . . . Stay with the image, on every exhale bringing joy to your loved one . . .

Repeat these phrases, imagining your loved one . . . wish: "May you be happy. May that person feel safe and be safe. May they be healthy. May they be happy, healthy, may they feel peace. May this person live with ease in this moment and in all moments . . ." Notice how you feel as you send these wishes. May this person feel joy, no matter what else is happening. May they feel happiness and spread it to others . . . Notice any sensations around your heart as you send these wishes . . . On every exhale, you send these wishes from the centre of your heart and they touch your loved one and bring them happiness . . . See yourself next to the loved one, and wish: "May we both be happy, may we both be strong. May both of us feel joy in every moment and share that joy with others. May we live with ease. May we live with peace in our hearts . . ."

Coming back to the body, relax any tension that came up in your forehead or your eyes. Release any tension in your chest, your shoulders, feel your feet rooted on the ground.'

Pyjov asks: 'Who did a compassion meditation for the first time?' Most hands go up. 'This grows your ability to have compassion in the future,' she promises.

The meditation finished, she winds down her talk. She tells

us how excited she is to be teaching compassion in NYC. If we want more details, she can email them. She passes around a clipboard. I fill in my address, feeling just a little sceptical (yes, she studied at Stanford University, which has an impeccable academic reputation, but still, all this talk of wishes touching your loved one, and so on, makes me feel slightly uncomfortable). The next day, I get an email with, as promised, journal papers relating to her various claims. At the end of the email, she signs off:

'Feel free to ask me any questions that you have about compassion, self-compassion, the research or the class. Together, let's make New York an even more beautiful and compassionate city.

Wishing you well,

Elizabeth'

I check out the papers she's emailed over, as well as work in the field in general. Some highly reputable academic work has been done. Richard Davidson, Professor of Psychiatry and Psychology at the University of Wisconsin-Madison and his group have found that novices who practised compassion meditation for half an hour a day for two weeks behaved more altruistically (in a lab test). These people also showed changes in brain regions involved in emotion regulation and positive emotions. Could compassion training help combat bullying in schools? The team would like to investigate.

While compassion entails being moved by suffering, there's a closely related Buddhist concept, called loving-kindness, which involves wishing happiness for yourself and others.

After witnessing Pyjov's compassion meditation and talking to someone trained in loving-kindness meditation, it seems to me that there's a lot of overlap in the styles. Both involve sending kind wishes and hopes for happiness towards others, and ourselves.

Barbara Fredrickson at the University of North Carolina has found that loving-kindness meditation improves heart-rate variability – that measure I had tested back at the Yale Stress Center. 'Good' heart-rate variability reflects a well-functioning vagal nerve. This major nerve connects the brain to the heart, lungs, eyes, digestive tract and genitals. It's the core component of the parasympathetic nervous system, which helps us to calm down after a stressful event. Good 'vagal tone' doesn't only make us less vulnerable to feeling chronically stressed, it also helps with emotion control and is linked to more empathy, sociability and self-esteem. Poor vagal tone has even been identified as a risk factor for depression – and vagal nerve stimulation is sometimes used as a treatment for people for whom anti-depressant drugs don't work.

I already know that regular meditation can help with controlling emotions and stress. But loving-kindness and compassion meditations don't involve clearing the mind of everyday thoughts, as Herbert Benson recommends (see Chapter One). So how might they work?

One theory is that it's because the vagus nerve is linked to other nerves involved in your ability to make eye contact, as well as your facial expressivity and your ability to tune into the frequency of the human voice, all of which are important for effective social interactions, which can, in turn, be crucial for psychological wellbeing.

Fredrickson and her colleagues taught loving-kindness meditation to a group of adults, and encouraged them to meditate daily at home. Every day, they reported on their emotions (whether positive or negative) and rated their social interactions. The meditation led to more positive emotions *and* better vagal tone. 'Vagal tone seems to be both a predictor of having a high positive emotion yield from "wellness behaviour", like interacting with people and being socially active, and learning loving-kindness meditation improves vagal tone. You've got this reciprocal causality,' Fredrickson tells me.

It seems, then, that loving-kindness or compassion meditation may 'work' at least in part because they encourage better relationships with other people.

Which leads me on . . .

Why does Fredrickson call social activity a 'wellness behaviour'?

There's a lot of research on this. Loneliness hikes the risk of depression, and one now-famous study found that having a low level of 'social connectedness' has as big an influence on a person's chances of dying (during a given period) as smoking, drinking too much alcohol, obesity and physical inactivity.

A tragically huge number of people have no close social contacts. One quarter of adults in the US fall into this category, according to one survey. And a 2014 study estimated that nearly ninety per cent of British adults have a spouse, close friend or relative they can turn to for support or advice about a personal matter – but that also means that almost *five million* adults have no one. Even for those of us who do feel connected to other people, is it, I wonder, a case of the more friends, the better? And when it comes to interactions, does it matter if we talk via email or the phone rather than in the flesh? What does an ideal social network look like? Is there even such a thing? If I want a stronger mind, should I be enhancing my own network of close friends or acquaintances – or improving the quality of my social interactions – and if so, how?

As I said earlier, I'm more introvert than extrovert. I've also moved around a lot, as have almost all my friends, which doesn't help. Take my four closest friends from school: until recently, we each lived on a different continent. Today, I'm the only one living in Britain.

Of course, I've made good friends since then. They're mostly in London and Sydney. And now Singapore. And Queensland. And France. Because, like me, almost everyone I know well seems to move with regularity. When I came to Sheffield, I had no friends locally. At least, none that didn't come with James. I do have some of my own now. A few.

But then, *what about* James? His family's roots in Sheffield are generations deep. He's surrounded by people he's known since he was born. There's a local football team named after the family, for heaven's sake. (The original members of Handsworth Parramore FC were men who laboured at the now defunct F. Parramore & Sons cast-iron works.) Every year – excepting the seven he spent in Sydney – James goes salmon fishing for a week with mostly male family and friends to one particular spot on the River Thursoe in Scotland. He's been doing this since he was five. There's a Parramore Pool on the Thursoe, named in honour of his grandfather, who fished there for fifty years.

This degree of belonging to place – and to people – is completely alien to me. I know that James derives a lot of psychological support from it. But am I a completely hopeless case in comparison?

How do you define what level of social contact is best, or even 'enough'?

There are a lot of researchers working in this area. One of the most eminent is John Cacciopo, Director of the Center for Cognitive and Social Neuroscience at the University of Chicago. He's been working in this field for decades, and he led the development of a social-wellbeing module for Martin Seligman's US Army resilience programme.

I take a look through some of Cacciopo's key findings, keeping an eye out for a psychologically 'magic' number of people you should class as friends. I vaguely recall research reporting a consistency in the number of people most of us can reasonably maintain as 'friends'. I expect that whatever that number is will be Cacciopo's recommendation.

And it isn't.

Of all his fascinating findings (and there are plenty of them, but sadly not enough space to go into them all here) I think this is the most crucial:

What matters, in terms of your psychological and physical health, isn't *how many* friends you have, but how socially connected you *feel*.

You could have a spouse, decent colleagues, people you get on with, including some you could reasonably call friends, but you may still feel lonely – and it's that feeling of loneliness that's linked to a poorer health outlook.

The flipside, of course, is that if you have only one good friend or perhaps even, in rarer cases, none, if you don't *feel* lonely, you're OK. And being alone, even for long stretches of time, perhaps at a meditative retreat, or while working on a book or a scientific theory, or on a solo journey, doesn't necessarily make someone feel lonely, Cacciopo adds.

He does point out that we all feel lonely from time to time. It's when this settles into an ongoing state, creating negative thoughts, leading to a level of social awkwardness that could stop you securing the one thing you most need – connections with other people – that it's a problem. And then, as the data shows, it's a serious one. Being 'not lonely' is like being 'not thirsty', Cacciopo says. It's just the way we evolved to need to be.

Personally, I find this reassuring. I might not have as many friends locally as James. But I don't *feel* lonely. If you do, Cacciopo's book, *Loneliness* (see References, p. 343), is full of helpful, evidence-based advice. Here's just one of his recommended strategies for building more and closer friendships: Cacciopo has found that making an effort to *think more kindly* about people – concentrating on their strengths rather than their flaws – is a more effective way to build meaningful social connections than simply meeting more people, more often. This is something I'm determined to bear in mind.

And now, before I leave the area of social relationships, there's one more finding I'd like to highlight, because it really struck me. It concerns not friends, but casual interactions. I used to avoid them at virtually all costs. Now I find myself actually chatting to cashiers in Tesco and getting into conversations with strangers in the park. And I realise I quite like it. None of these people will become friends – at least, I don't *expect* they will (perhaps because I'm naturally pessimistic; after all, I only know Sunny, one of my dearest friends, because our husbands met in a queue to buy concert tickets and hit it off) – but these brief moments of human contact do seem to give me a slight psychological lift. This surprises me, because I'm not an extrovert. But then I spot an interesting study . . .

Rail commuters in Chicago were asked to imagine behaving as they normally would during their journey – whatever that might be. They were also asked to imagine two defined situations. 1. Sitting in silence during the journey. 2. Striking up a conversation with a stranger. They were asked to rate how much they'd enjoy each. Talking to a stranger came last. Why? Not because the commuters didn't want to talk to someone else, it emerged, but because they thought other people wouldn't want to talk to them.

Next, the researchers asked volunteers to try three different things on actual journeys: to do whatever they normally did, to determinedly sit in silence and to strike up conversations. This time, striking up a conversation was rated as the most *pleasant* of the three. And this was true for introverts, as well as extroverts.

Not a single stranger, the team noted, refused to enter into conversation. The reason we ignore each other in places like plains and trains (at the very least in Chicago), they say, is that we mistakenly assume that nobody else wants to talk.

And now, back at last to Dennis Charney. Social support is one of the top ten contributory factors to psychological resilience revealed by his work. In fact, I realise I've now mentioned five of those factors: physical exercise, optimism, religion and spirituality, social support and having a moral compass and a set of ethics.

Having good role models has also emerged as being important, as has having meaning in your life. (Perhaps looking after your family gives your life meaning; perhaps it's feeling that the work you do really matters). That's seven.

Then there's what Charney calls 'cognitive and emotional flexibility'. As a concept, this is a little more amorphous than some of the others. It means being flexible in the way you think about challenges and respond to stress. It might involve using an emotion like anger to fuel courage, or searching for opportunity in adversity. That's eight.

'Brain fitness' – keeping your brain challenged – is nine.

So there's a final, tenth factor left.

Towards the end of our conversation in his office, I ask Dennis Charney to tell me a bit about how he uses what he's learned in his own life, at work or at home. He says that when he's recruiting new staff, he looks out for (realistically) optimistic people. Then he tells me about how he's used the remaining tenth factor to try to help his own children.

He has five kids, four daughters and a son. As a direct result of a particular resilience-building intervention, one of his daughters told him, he recalls (able to smile about it now), that 'out *of her soul*, she *despised me*'.

I think this is fascinating. And I could go right on into it. But it's shifting into another area related to psychological strength. And I know it's a big one, with lots of research to explore. So I'm going to keep Dennis Charney, and this particular factor, on the line, as it were. I'll come back to him in the next section, on mental toughness.

Before we go there though, here are the main lessons I've learned from looking into how to approach my thoughts, to make my mind stronger.

THE THOUGHTS CHECKLIST

- If you regularly think destructively negative thoughts, there are strategies that can help. Mindful awareness without judgement is one. A 'cognitive approach' – based on evaluating the evidence for that thought, deciding how reasonable it really is and changing it, if necessary – can work well.

- More optimistic people are more psychologically resilient. Try adopting a simple optimism 'trick' – like 'imagine the person you're talking to is thinking the best, not the worst'.

- Self-compassion can help with negative self-talk. Try writing down what a friend might say to you if you voiced your thoughts.

- Write down, every evening, 'What Went Well': identify three things that went well in the day, and why.

- Compassion meditation and a more generalised 'loving-kindness' meditation (thinking nice thoughts about other people and yourself) can help to build meaningful social relationships and reduce stress.

PS Near the start of this chapter, I referred to a journal paper that talked about an 'untutored mind', and I wondered what might constitute a tutored version. I found the paper. There at the top is a now-familiar quote I mentioned earlier: 'The mind is its own place, and in itself/Can make a Heav'n of Hell, a Hell of Heav'n' (John Milton, *Paradise Lost*). A 'tutored mind', the authors go on to explain, is one that understands the techniques of meditation, including mindfulness and loving-kindness and compassion meditation, as well as appreciating the usefulness of finding a balance between mindfulness and mind-wandering. OK . . . So, I wouldn't say I have a tutored mind *just* yet. But I do at least have a grasp on the strategies available to help me to achieve one.

CHAPTER SIX

TOUGHEN YOUR MIND

I pull into a car park and stop by a single-storey building with a Union Jack flapping out front. To my right, there's a row of pebble-dashed terraces. To the left, blocks of flats give way to views of open countryside. It's just before one o'clock on a Friday, and there are only a couple of other cars here. I'm hoping one belongs to Gary Roberts. Or maybe he's run here. He doesn't live that far away. I've just dropped my kids with his fiancée, Niki, and now I'm here, as arranged, at Sheffield's Powers Martial Arts Centre, to talk about mental toughness.

Gary, you might remember (I mentioned him briefly in Chapter Four), used to be a corporal in the British Army. After he left, he went back to Iraq and then on to the Gulf of Aden, to work in private security. When he's on leave from the boats – as he is this week – he likes to get in some kick-boxing training. He's offered to meet me after today's session.

We've talked before about sleep, but now I'm ready to look at mental toughness, I can't help thinking it will be useful to go back to him. What did the army teach him, I wonder, about how to keep going – to achieve a goal, rather than flaking out and giving up? And what has he learned since?

I have, I realise, quite a few friends who surely class as being mentally tough. There's George, a teacher, who recently ran a twenty-four-hour race over the forty-two highest peaks in the Lake District. Oh, and Paul, our vet friend, who let slip the other day that he's completed an Ironman triathlon. (That's a 3.8km swim, immediately followed by a 180km bike ride and a 42.2km run.) Then there's Ed Douglas, who goes off every year to find *new* climbing routes in the Himalayas, and who has faced near-certain death more than once.

Ed recalls a formative trip with a friend to Alaska in his twenties. Out on a glacier, days from civilisation, they ran out of food. His clothes got wet, he was freezing and he started to hallucinate from exhaustion. At one point, he was sure he was going to die. But they managed to walk back to safety. 'One of the great things about that experience was that I learned how far you can push your body,' he tells me. 'We could probably have gone on for two or three days more than we did. Most people have no conception of what their bodies can do. I had a glimpse through a door.'

I'm glad for Ed. Honestly, I am. But I don't intend to find myself peering through that particular door any time soon. Clearly, there are lessons to be drawn from life-or-death situations. But as Ed spells out, if you think you're going to die, you'll do *anything*. You have no choice. Finish that work project or spend time on Facebook? Go to the gym or read a magazine for an hour? Eat an apple or a slice of chocolate cake? It sounds facetious – and I have every respect for Ed – but *those* are choices. And they're the sort I need help with. Right now, in fact, more than ever.

A couple of weeks ago, I got a letter from my doctor, asking me to phone in about the results of a blood-glucose test.

While pregnant with Lucas, I developed something called gestational diabetes. It's a kind of diabetes (a problem with regulating blood-sugar levels) that usually goes away after giving birth, as happened to me. Because of that history, though, I was advised to get another test every year. So far, they've been normal. This time, when I ring the surgery, the receptionist tells me my result is 10.4, on a scale where below 7.8 is normal, anything between 7.8 and 11 is prediabetic, and anything above 11 is diabetic. So, I'm right at the top end of the prediabetic range. And I know enough about the disease to panic.

Being prediabetic doesn't mean you're fine. It's a serious condition, with many of the health risks of full-on diabetes. It means I'm more likely to suffer a stroke and heart disease, as well as something else that worries me even more: there's a theory that Alzheimer's disease is (or can be) late-stage type-2 diabetes – 'diabetes in the brain'. I'd rather have heart disease than Alzheimer's. And I'd rather not have heart disease. I'm not technically overweight, and while I eat biscuits and cake, I don't gorge myself on them. My diabetes is probably more to do with bad genes than a poor lifestyle, which means I may not be able to do much to try to reverse it. My GP, when I see her, tells me blithely that I'll 'just' have to watch my diet. I can't have anything sweet. Well, I can have sugary foods, but only 'on high days and holidays'. Where's she from? The 1940s?

And now what am I going to do?

First, I guess, I should accept the sliver of good news: high blood-sugar levels could be the cause of my brain fogs and bouts of obliterative fatigue. If I stick to a diabetic diet, which is designed to keep those levels in a more normal range, perhaps they'll stop.

I've followed the diet before, so I know what it entails – or what it entails in Australia, because there are different guidelines in different countries. No simple sugars, like caster sugar or those in honey. (So, no sweets. No cake. No biscuits. No pastry. No ice cream. No chocolate – though when I was testing my blood, I found that a square of dark chocolate made little difference to my readings.) No white or wholemeal bread – only super-seeded because all the fibre helps. I'll have to eat only relatively low-GI (glycaemic-index) carbs, like potatoes and pasta, in strict moderation. Fat is bad, because it slows the absorption of glucose from the blood. (So no chips. No Yorkshire puddings. No cream. Not even nuts, apart from almonds.) Protein is all right. Non-starchy vegetables, like broccoli and cabbage, are good. Fruit in moderation is acceptable. And exercise is crucial, because exercise helps draw glucose out of the blood.

I know I've resolved to do more exercise and to eat a healthier diet. And I managed to stick pretty well to the diabetic diet for four months, to protect Lucas. But for the rest of my life?

Seriously?

While Ed may have walked to safety across an Alaskan

glacier, freezing and starving, anyone who sticks to a diet or an exercise programme in the long term – who resists the temptation of the moment, moment after moment, month after month after month – is also pretty mentally tough in my opinion.

That's *my* opinion. But what do the experts say?

As far as I can tell from my initial reading, psychologists don't agree on exactly what 'mental toughness' means. Some seem to view it as the ability to bounce back from a difficult experience – which others call resilience. I'm not sure that resilience encompasses what mental toughness means to me. And if even the experts can't agree, I feel I'm entitled to devise my own definition.

So this is what I'm taking it to mean: the ability to get through less-than-desirable circumstances to achieve a goal, whether that's to complete a work project in the evenings, rather than watching TV, or to cut out cake to lose weight, or to follow an exercise programme to get fit, or even, yes, to walk across a remote glacier without food or dry clothes to survive – and not whinge about it.

Not whinge? Yeah, I really do need help.

The lights are switched off. The half-hearted Yorkshire sun isn't exactly streaming through the windows, so the place is dim. Pumping music is playing. The dominant smell is of sweat. I realise I'm feeling slightly apprehensive. I think of Sheffield as being pretty soft as cities go, but still, I've never been inside a martial-arts centre before.

I take a few more steps and notice a couple of aphorisms printed in big letters on the wall:

'Better to be a tiger for a day than a sheep for a thousand years.'

'If you are loyal and respectful you will receive loyalty and respect.'

I'm a little intimidated. Have I ever been a tiger for a minute, let alone a day? I'm really not sure I have.

There's a gym to my right, and two rings to the left. The first is roped. The walls of the farthest are padded with mats.

A towering, lean man steps from the shadows. He asks if I'm all right.

'I'm here to see Gary Roberts,' I tell him, and he nods to the far ring. I'm a few minutes early. Gary's still in his session.

Gary is olive-skinned, slim but solid, with tattoos on his arms. He's wearing a black T-shirt, black shorts and boxing gloves. Bare-headed and bare-footed, he thwacks his fists onto pads mounted on the forearms of the young trainer, who calls out, 'Cross, hook, cross!' Then, 'Ten straights!'

Gary hits the pads hard with alternate fists. 'C'mon, kick!' the trainer tells him. 'Twenty and you're done!' Gary whacks the forearm pads with the front of his shins. Sweat trickles down his face. Eighteen, nineteen, twenty . . .

And he's done. He notices me. He comes over, breathing hard. He pulls out his mouthguard.

'How long have you been training?' I ask him.

'An hour,' he says, panting.

The trainer jerks his head at Gary and grins at me. 'He's a machine, him,' he says.

Gary asks after my kids, and if he can have a couple of

minutes before we sit down to talk. While he goes off to catch his breath, I head back to the reception area. As I go, I hear the trainer, whose name I later discover is Shaun, advising a client who's preparing to go into the ring: 'Rather than getting frustrated, think: "What can I do to stop it?" Don't get in a frustration bubble. You've got to burst it.'

Yes, but *how*? I find myself thinking. Because I know exactly what Shaun means by a 'frustration bubble'. I get into them with the kids. They grow and grow. And of course, they're a problem if your goal is to be mentally tough. But perhaps I'll find out soon. Because Gary's already heading over. We sit down on a leather sofa, and to the background sound of shins thwacking pads and upbeat music from the radio, I ask him to tell me anything he can about mental toughness.

Gary joined the army at eighteen, straight from school:

'To be honest, the baptism of fire in joining the army is not basic training. You leave a platoon of thirty boys, and join a battalion of 600 men. When I left basic training, I was in Belfast within a week. That's where I grew up fast.'

Did you learn anything useful about mental toughness in basic training?

'You learn about giving up, and not giving up. If you do a march and you're ten or fifteen miles away from camp, your instructor will tell you you're marching back whether you like it or not, so you might as well just *like* it. You might as well get on board with it mentally. Thinking about it isn't going to help you.

I think, *OK. If you have to do something, tell yourself you might as well like it. Maybe that would help.*

Did you have that kind of attitude before you joined up?

'I think I'm reasonably mentally robust. I'm not a whinger. I don't complain about things I'm going to do anyway.'

Did other recruits whinge?

'Yeah. Most people that fail basic training, it's not the army that's failed them. They've failed themselves, really. They miss their mum's food and shit like that. Just being away from home for the first time . . . They're the people who give up and fail themselves.'

So, say you're on a fifteen-mile march, and you're feeling tired, were there things you'd say to yourself to keep you going?

'Well, I'm quite competitive, so I'd always look at someone else and think, *If he can do it, I can do it.* I'd think: *I won't quit now. I'll quit later, but not before he does.*'

I think: *that sounds like a good strategy in a run, or if you're in a class of students or colleagues up against the same challenge. But it's difficult to be competitive about dieting – unless you're in a dieting club, of course.*

Can you think of any particular experiences in your life that helped to make you mentally tough?

'I wasn't neglected or anything, but I taught myself everything when I was growing up. I made my own way to school, right across Sheffield and back every day. I just came and went from my house as I pleased.'

Gary has two children, Daniel, who's seven, and big-eyed Georgia, who's the same age as Lucas. I ask him if, knowing what fending for himself did for him, he'll expect the same of Daniel. He smiles. 'I'll be, "No: you can't go on a bus on your own!" Then again, you've got to, haven't you?'

Basic training in the army involves building you up, he tells me. Pushing and building. Like Ed in Alaska, pushed by necessity, you learn you can do more than you think you can. On active duty, Gary says, he realised the truth of this. 'Your brain's just like an early-warning system. When you're cold, you can always get colder. When you're tired, you can get more tired.'

He uses this knowledge in pushing himself – on a run, for example. 'There aren't many people who get to the point where they really can't take another step. I've felt like it. But I've always been able to. Everyone can take one more step. Unless they actually lose consciousness.'

I know that one of the problems I've had in the past with exercise is that I've set out with great intentions, but then I've felt really tired, and I've thought, *Well if I run for fifteen minutes instead of twenty, does it really matter*? Clearly, this is not the attitude of a mentally tough person. I ask Gary how *he* thinks about going for a run.

'I always plan what route I'm going to run before I run it. If I've just come home from the boat, it might be five miles. Then I'll be: by Friday, I'm going to run twelve miles. And that'll be it. I'll do it.'

Do you ever worry you won't actually just *do it*? Can you remember a time where you thought, *I can't do this*? 'Not really,' he says. (I know, Gary does seem unremittingly unflappable). He goes on:

'I remember a time I was about to jump out of a plane. I was on the ground, and I thought, *I don't fancy this.* But I thought: *I'm gonna do it* because *I don't fancy it.* So I did.'

What about on active duty? There must have been times when your mental composure was challenged?

'I remember the first ambush in Iraq. There were only four of us in two vehicles. I was in the second vehicle. Then I saw the soil next to the vehicle in front getting stitched up into the air. I called on the radio: "Ambush. Contact. Contact." He took a lot of bullets in his vehicle, I took a lot in mine. We had armoured vehicles so we were all right, but his engine was trashed.'

Were you scared? What were you thinking?

'I wasn't scared. I wasn't thinking about feelings. I was thinking about practical stuff: *If this vehicle goes down, I'm going to take cover behind that rock. He's down, so I'm going to pull up on the left side, get ready for a cross-dec* – to cross everybody into the vehicle that isn't immobilised. If both vehicles go down, you're on foot, so where are you gonna go, what equipment are you going to take or leave?'

I guess that's what military training helps you to do: to avoid getting emotional and focus on the immediate challenges?

Gary looks thoughtful. 'You might think I'm mentally tough, but it's all in context. I wouldn't like to do brain surgery on a child. I couldn't deal with that. Policemen who have to sit through hours of child porn – that would destroy me.'

And he's right, of course. There are different ways to demonstrate mental toughness. I have a friend who works on a child cancer ward. (She has a daughter in Jakob's class.) I couldn't do her job. And the truth is, I've never even asked her how she copes – how she achieves what she needs to achieve without lying awake all night, thinking about those families or worrying about her own child. Because I'm wary of even recognising the fact that children get cancer. Clearly, we can't all be tough at everything. But I admire her. And I know I'd settle for a tenth of Gary's particular brand.

He gets up. He has to leave for another appointment, and I'm set to go away, to think more about what he's told me, and to work out what I can use. But then he asks if I saw Alex on the way in. *Alex?* It turns out he means the towering, lean man.

'He's kickboxing world champion,' he tells me. 'You should talk to him about mental toughness.'

World champion? What, *here?* Then I think: *this is Sheffield.* Sporting world champions seem to reside around every corner. I really shouldn't be surprised. 'Yeah, that'd be great,' I say. 'I'd love to.'

And Alex does give me some very useful insights. But I think it might help at this point if I back up a little, and try to get to get a clearer idea of the factors psychologists think contribute to 'mental toughness', and the strategies they've created to foster it.

This being Sheffield, and given the evident link to sporting performance, there's just the right academic around to help.

At Sheffield Hallam University, literally a five-minute walk from my front door, is Professor Ian Maynard, Director of the Centre for Sports and Exercise Science, and a sports psychologist who has worked with Team GB at two Olympic Games. According to his online bio, he's researched mental toughness, and he teaches it. He's exactly the kind of person I want to talk to.

*

Sport, as I mentioned in the chapter on exercise, isn't exactly my 'thing'. So while I don't instantly recognise the people in the signed photographs that line Ian Maynard's office, I'm more than willing to be impressed.

Near the door, there's a photo of an immaculately muscled young man, standing at the edge of a diving board, a super-sized close-up of his face projected on the vast screen immediately behind him. 'Ian, thank you for helping me to achieve my ultimate goal!' is scrawled at the top in black pen. Next to this is a framed blown-up photo of what looks to be a football referee, inscribed with the words, 'Ian, thanks for believing'.

The muscled young man turns out to be Leon Taylor, a British former competitive diver, and a judge on the ITV celebrity diving show *Splash!* The picture was taken at the Sydney Olympics, moments after Taylor had used one of Maynard's techniques – which I'll come to in a minute. The football referee is called Howard Webb. The photo, Maynard informs me, was snapped ten seconds before the start of the World Cup final that Webb refereed in South Africa in 2010. 'That was his biggest moment,' he adds, with a snatch of shared pride. Maynard, and his colleagues, are still working with elite English football referees, he tells me, to develop their mental toughness.

Maynard himself has a long history in sport. He played rugby union and cricket to county level. Then he trained as a sports psychologist. For twenty years, he worked with British Sailing. At the Barcelona and Athens Olympics, he was a psychologist on the British team. He's worked as a consultant at the World Championships of eight different sports. Perhaps because of this background, he isn't your stereotypical professor. Yes, he's in his fifties. Yes, he has grey hair. But it's military-grade close cut and he's physically solid, with a more weather-beaten face than you'd expect of your average academic. He also has a surprisingly high, catchy laugh.

So, I say, as we sit down – mental toughness – what can you tell me?

For a start, he says, it's a relatively new concept. 'We've been doing sports psychology now for forty or fifty years, but we've only dabbled in mental toughness for about the past fifteen years. Unfortunately, we spent about five or six years trying to define it. And that went on in circles – and still does to some extent.'

To get a better idea of what *he* means by mental toughness, I ask for his favourite example. Surprisingly (to me), it involves a sportsman I've actually heard of: Ben Ainslie, the most successful sailor in Olympic history. Maynard tells me he's worked with Ainslie, 'but I wouldn't say *closely*, because Ben had it – he's mentally tough.'

Ainslie's demonstration of outstanding mental toughness consisted of the completion of literally hundreds of smart manoeuvres to keep his closest competitor down the field, to secure a gold medal in the Sydney Olympics. But there are hundreds of other examples in sport, Maynard says. 'Anything where it's an S or B manoeuvre, as they say.' S or B? He smiles, looking a little embarrassed, 'Shit or bust. Anything where the whole of your future almost hangs on one decision or action. Or not just one – often it's sustained over a period.'

Yes, there are two facets of mental toughness, Maynard explains:

1. Being tough in the moment (saying *no* to that proffered slice of chocolate cake).

2. Having a generally mentally tough attitude – being the kind of person who is consistently mentally tough in all areas of life, and who perseveres with long-term challenges.

Psychologists aren't sure to what degree these two aspects are determined by genes and early formative experiences, and to what extent they can be changed later in life, says Maynard. But he believes both are important, and that, at both, we can all improve.

Perhaps I'm genetically incapable of the feats of someone like the endurance artist David Blaine, who once stood, unharnessed, on the 0.56m-wide top of a 30m-high pillar in New York's Bryant Park for thirty-five hours (actually, there's no perhaps about it). But maybe, with help, I *can* stick to the diabetic diet and my exercise programme, and embark on and accomplish all kinds of new projects.

So how can Maynard help?

Mental toughness is based on four core elements, he tells me: 'We reckon mentally tough people are strong at all these things.' They are:

- motivation

- confidence

- concentration/focus

- self-talk

This seems like a useful framework to work with. I ask Maynard how willpower and self-control fit in, because I think they have to be crucial for mental toughness. He says he thinks self-control, and emotional regulation, cross over the four core elements, as well as playing a role in the over-arching question: are you basically a positive or a negative person? Because, he says, mentally tough people are invariably *positive*.

'Willpower, I'm sure, would be a component that I think most people would identify – whether you call it willpower, or determination or drive,' he says. 'It's like my frog there.' He points to a line drawing tacked to a noticeboard by my chair. It shows a frog wedged deep inside the mouth of a large stork, its legs dangling. Underneath is printed: 'Don't EVER give up!!!'

So, a psychologist trying to build mental toughness would focus on the four main elements. 'But,' he says, 'there is something else apart from those that makes the difference

. . . If I knew what it was, I would have written the book and I'd be on a beach in Barbados.' He laughs. 'The truth is we don't know exactly what it is.'

OK, so there's a mystery factor X involved in creating mental toughness. That intriguing caveat noted, I ask him for more detail on the four factors psychologists *have* identified.

SELF-TALK

I'll start with this because it's something I've already looked into.

As I described in the last chapter, there are different approaches to addressing problematic self-talk. Maynard's seems to involve 'cognitive restructuring' – learning techniques to evaluate exaggeratedly negative statements (like 'I'm rubbish, I'll never be able to stick to a diet, I never stick at anything), to help you *change* your thoughts – and general positive psychology. Because mentally tough people do have an optimistic attitude, he stresses. They 'are definitely glass-half-full type of people.'

What about the other three factors?

CONFIDENCE

There's a fine line between positive confidence (which is definitely desirable) and arrogance, Maynard says. 'But I don't mind my elite sports people being arrogant,' he adds. 'To some extent, we say: pressure is your friend, not your enemy. For a mentally tough person, something like the Olympics is a chance to go out there and show everyone just how good you are under pressure. They'd be saying: "I want the pressure! Bring it on!"'

So how do you go about building confidence?

There are two approaches, he says. And they come from diametrically opposed positions.

1. You create 'manageable adversity'. By giving people challenges, and teaching them that they can overcome them, you build up their confidence.

2. You focus on people's strengths, which makes them feel good, and builds confidence.

Creating psychological strength through adversity is a well-documented concept. Basic military training involves setting challenges that recruits can just about manage, then moving the goalposts, to stretch them further and further away from their starting point and towards their full potential.

How can you create useful levels of adversity in civilian life? With athletes, of course, coaches can push them in training or impose penalties if they don't win. What about the rest of us?

Now, I'm going to bring Dennis Charney back in here, because he told me something that relates directly to this.

Back in his office at the Icahn School of Medicine at Mt Sinai in New York, Charney said that, based on his research, he's a big believer in what he calls 'stress inoculation' for building psychological strength in normal people, as well as sports stars or soldiers.

'The idea is that you get exposed to experiences that are a little outside of your comfort zone, and you learn how to manage them. You develop techniques to handle challenges. You do it in doses, and you increase the dose, until before long, you've got a psychological toolbox to handle the challenges we all face.'

If you accept this, there are implications for how you raise your children, he says. 'You don't want to raise your kids in a stress-free environment, because then they're not prepared. Cos stuff happens. If you're playing little-league sports, everybody wins, everybody gets a trophy. That's not the real world. You've got to learn from failure, right? You learn from disappointment. You *don't* quit. You get up again.'

Regular sports and outdoor adventures that may be a little risky can be good sources of manageable levels of stress for non-athlete civilians, he thinks. And he's used this with his own kids. In fact, it was an episode of stress inoculation that led to his daughter telling him she despised him.

'Every year, I do a kind of adventure with them. They're now aged twenty-eight to thirty-five, so it's not exactly the same as when they were younger. But every summer, we used to take them on adventure trips and kind of push the envelope a bit. When one of my daughters was about thirteen, we were going on a hike, climbing a mountain, and got a little lost. She was scared. And she said she despised me. *Out of her soul*, she despised me. She was somebody who always took a little while to get used to things. So you could take the tack of taking her out of anything that made her a little bit anxious. Or you could take the tack of telling her, 'You're going to be all right', and just keeping moving from one thing to the next. Which is what I did. And a couple of winters ago she actually went off to Yellowstone National Park with her husband. The idea is it's not traumatising. It's just a little out of your comfort zone, but you can do it. So you get satisfaction and self-esteem out of doing it, and you keep moving on.'

And if you try something, and you *don't* quite manage it? Your side *does* lose. You *do* get lost. Then you need to try to view the failure as an opportunity to learn to get better.

Ian Maynard agrees with this: 'Ultimately, putting failure in people's way is one of the best ways of building mental toughness,' he insists.

I try to take all this on board. And I'll certainly bear it in mind when it comes to my own kids. What about me though? I guess I could sign up for an exercise boot camp. I'd see that as an experience involving adversity, if not all-out torture. But are there other ways to use the meta-phorical stick to build general confidence in my capabilities, and so my mental toughness?

'PLEASE, GOD, DON'T LET ME DIE'

Tuesday, 8 August 1978. A young American film-maker called Carl Boenish hikes with four friends up El Capitan, the 900-metre high monolithic rock forma-tion that forms one of the most stunning sights of California's Yosemite National Park. The group tries to keep their presence low key. They're worried that if a park ranger spots them and demands to inspect their bulky gear, they'll be ordered back down, and even barred from the park.

Boenish has already reconnoitred the route along the Tamarack Trail, to the edge of the summit. While he sets up his cameras a local man called Kent Lane makes his final preparations. Lane straps on his parachute, walks to the edge of the rock face and jumps. With that leap – equal parts courage and faith – the sport of modern BASE jumping is born.

Given all the various things that could possibly go wrong in a BASE jump – loss of control of your body before you get chance to deploy the parachute, parachute malfunction, the presence of obstacles (Carl Boenish was killed in 1984 while jumping off a cliff in Norway, apparently after hitting an outcropping rock) – the sport is notoriously dangerous. According to one study, for every sixty people who do a BASE jump each year, one will die.

I'd always thought of BASE jumpers and other extreme sports enthusiasts as being made of different stuff. I assumed they didn't feel fear like the rest of us, and that jumping off a cliff is simply a lot less scary for them than it would be for me. But when a team of British psychologists actually sat down with fifteen men and women who regularly participate in extreme sports and talked to them about their attitudes, this isn't what they found. When asked what was going through his mind when he leaped from a cliff, one BASE-jumper replied, 'Please God, don't let me die'.

All the participants in the study said that they felt fear – they felt it acutely – but they had learned to face it and control it, and the psychological pay-offs were immense. Experiencing, controlling and pushing past intense fear left them positively charged and 'better equipped to deal with the tribulations of everyday life'. Mentally stronger. Fear doesn't have to be physically related, the researchers commented: 'By facing our greatest "true" fears, whether they be death, uncertainty or something else and taking action despite these fears, we transcend our own limitations and invite new possibilities into our lives.'

The ability to face fear – which can be developed through stress inoculation – is the last of Dennis Charney's ten factors underpinning resilience. And this is certainly something to think about.

But before I pick a terrifying experience with which to improve my mental toughness (I really can't wait . . .), let me move on to Ian Maynard's second strategy for confidence-building – focusing on people's strengths – because this one, I have to say, sounds a lot more appealing.

Let's say you have an amazing tennis backhand; your forehand is average, but that backhand is incredible. Or maybe you're pretty lazy, but you're really kind. Or you have a pessimistic outlook, but you're conscientious.

Ian Maynard calls your positive qualities 'super strengths'. Martin Seligman calls them 'signature strengths'. Whatever you call them, try forgetting your weaknesses for the moment and think about what you're good at – or at least, better at than average.

'Because of human nature, often we work on our weaknesses,' says Maynard. 'Unfortunately, too many people work *only* on their weaknesses. In sailing, for the last three months before a championship, we'd *just* play to our strengths, because ultimately that's what underpins confidence. You can only feel confident if you feel good about yourself.'

Seligman would advise you to think hard about what you're good at, and maybe even write these things down. Then, when times are tough, and you're losing confidence, you can refer to that list, and think: *Yeah, I might not be good at making presentations, but I'm passionate, and I'm considerate – I'm really not that bad.* When facing a challenging situation, you might think about how you could use your signature/super strengths to help you through. If you're working hard to achieve a goal, and you're banging your head against a wall, and losing confidence, perhaps you should just *stop*, and go and do something you know you're good at for a while.

Maynard likes to use both adversity *and* playing to strengths to build confidence. But the idea of even just *sometimes* focusing on strengths seems really appealing to me. I think so few of us (narcissists aside) generally do it. And it leads me into the next of the four elements on Maynard's list.

MOTIVATION

I'm sitting here in my attic office, alone, unmonitored, writing and reading. I could slip out, and no one would know (bar the dog). I could drive into town, and go shopping. Winter's coming, and I really do need a new pair of boots. There's a beautiful Victorian day spa here in Sheffield. I could slip into the steam room and spend the afternoon in blissful, warm relaxation. Or, if that would take too long, and make me feel too guilty, I could ring a friend who's just got back from her daughter's wedding in Bali, or check out the YouTube video of a baby panda sneezing that I recently learned I'm virtually the only person on the planet not to have seen . . . I could do any of these things. But I don't. I sit and write, and read, and write.

When it comes to sitting down and working, I'm pretty good at *just doing it*, as Gary said earlier about runs and marches. (Perhaps I should remember that if I find myself struggling to stick to my new diet. I'm not mentally weak at *everything*.) But why should we be reasonably tough in some areas, and not in others?

Self-control is important for staying on-target, of course. To some extent, I've learned self-control in relation to work over time – and I do want to investigate self-control as a concept, and the research on how to improve it. But there's another crucial factor at play.

My motivation to work is very strong. I love what I do. So I have a strong drive to do it. The truth is that, right at this moment, there's just no place I'd rather be than at my desk. No, not even the spa. I'm forced to accept, therefore, that writing these words requires very little self-control, and no real mental toughness. I don't drag myself to my desk every morning. I don't need to. I just do it, because I want to.

That kind of core motivation makes achieving a long-term goal relatively easy – or it means, at least, that there's a strong force acting against the will to give up. It helps to give me, when it comes to this project and this book at least, something that a psychologist might call *grit*.

Angela Duckworth, a former maths teacher who now works alongside Martin Seligman at the University of Pennsylvania, has pioneered the modern study of 'grit', as she calls it. She's developed a simple three-minute test, which you can take online. It asks you to rate yourself on a series of statements, like 'I finish whatever I begin' and 'I often set a goal but later choose to pursue a different one'.

People who are gritty (and I really wouldn't place myself in this category, except perhaps when it comes to work), are, on average, more self-controlled – but not always. Grit involves 'sustaining interest in and effort toward very long-term goals' – the kind of goals that take months, years or even decades to accomplish. According to Duckworth's definition, the gritty person 'approaches achievement as a marathon; his or her advantage is stamina'. Duckworth has studied a wide range of groups, including cadets at the United States Military Academy, West Point; National Spelling Bee contestants; rookie teachers, and salespeople. The best predictor of success in all these fields was not social intelligence or IQ (or physical fitness, for the military cadets). It was grit.

Really wanting something can help to make you gritty. Duckworth found this with the successful West Point cadets.

Their motivation was so strong, it was virtually unconquerable. Contrast that with me and my attitude to cake (or me and cake before I was told about the diabetes). *What harm can one piece of chocolate cake really do? Does it really matter if I don't shift the stone I've put on since having kids? Do I really care that much?* My answers: *none really, not really and no.* A gritty approach? Not exactly.

Alex McKenzie, the world champion kickboxer I met at the Powers Martial Arts Centre in Sheffield, gave me an example of the importance of *really wanting* a difficult goal, to give you the kind of motivation that makes failure simply not an option. Alex has had twenty-five fights. He's won twenty-two and lost only three. He told me about one particular fight that he won – but only just.

'I fought not this Christmas but the one before against a French lad. That year, I lost my mum. And my mum was well into it. She supported me one hundred per cent. She loved it. Losing her really knocked me back. But this opportunity came up for the European title. I knew how much my mum would have wanted me to do it. So I trained as hard as ever and I got into what I thought were reasonable shape. I did everything right. But it were just the hardest thing that I've ever done in my life. After two rounds, I were saying, "I an't got it in me". I had to dig deep.'

Shaun, the trainer, is sitting with us. He puts in: 'Anyone that knows Alex – that's not him.'

'Me knee got wiped in the third round and I were hobbling on one leg. I managed to find something. And it got me through. And I managed to win. I got the European [title]. But it was the hardest thing I've ever done. *Ever.*'

What did he learn about mental toughness from that fight? 'The only thing I can say to you is you've got to solely want to do it yourself. You can't do it for anyone else. I really did that fight for my mum. That was the main purpose. And I did my best for my mum and she got me through it. But in hindsight you can't do that. *You've* got to want it.'

You have to want it. *You* have to have the motivation. Without it, you won't have the grit. But can you build grit?

Duckworth thinks you can. Optimists are grittier than pessimists, she's observed, so if you can build optimism, grit may follow. (Yet another finding, I note, in support of learning to be more optimistic.)

To work very hard at something goes against the instinct to be idle, she points out. 'Those of us who carry the burden of hard work more lightly may do so because our life experiences have led us to pair effort, whose primary association is negative, with a secondary association that is positive. We learn to "love the burn",' she writes. Some people also have more energy than others, meaning they can expend more before burning out, she says – so if doing more physical exercise, sleeping better, and eating a healthier diet can all help with energy, they may help with grit, too.

But if you're facing a challenge that you don't feel a core motivation to accomplish – if your desire to diet or run up that hill or work towards a promotion or study for a degree isn't that strong, yet still, you want it – there are strategies to help.

During my visit to the Yale Stress Center (see Chapter Two), James, the student psychologist, told me about how he tries to motivate clients by encouraging them to really appreciate the discrepancy between where they are now and where they could be. And Gary talked about ignoring how you're *feeling* – and just 'doing' something you've put your mind to.

I ask George, who recently completed that twenty-four-hour, sixty-six-mile race, how he coped.

Adequate preparation was crucial, obviously. But in the third leg of the race, with one more to go, he says he started to feel weak. 'I wasn't hurting. I just felt a bit fed up.' What did you tell yourself? 'Just to keep going. I switched off a little bit. That's an experience thing.' (He's run many long races.) 'You just have to accept it and not question it and not fight it. Not analyse it too much. Just keep going.'

That sounds quite mindful, I think. If what you're thinking isn't helping you, step outside it. I can see how this could help with an immediate challenge.

But for longer-term goals, Ian Maynard points to another motivational strategy. 'It's the easiest one to understand,' he says, 'but it's the hardest to *do*.'

He gives me an arch smile. 'If you were a good goal-setter, you'd have had at least three things you wanted to get out of this interview.'

I realise that to Maynard, it must seem as though I've dropped by for a general chat, rather than to achieve anything specific. The fact is, I've done so many interviews now, I'm fairly confident about the process, and that I'll remember what I want to ask without needing constantly to refer to a list of questions. But I always have one, if only to check through at the end to make sure I haven't forgotten anything. I pull my sheet of questions from beneath my pad and wave it at him. 'I have all these!'

He grins. 'OK. Well, ultimately, everything you do should have goals that relate to each other. So today's goals relate to the goals for the month, which relate to the goals for the year, which relate to me winning an Olympic medal.' The same in general life? 'Absolutely. Some people have no problem with this because they like the structure. Other people hate it. But I think everybody needs a little bit of structure.'

So setting yourself manageable goals – breaking down what may seem an impossible end point (like 'being fit') into achievable steps, and tackling each in turn – is a documented way of building success, and preserving and building motivation.

I'll note, though, that some psychologists recommend not daily, but monthly, goal-planning. This allows some flexibility. If you have a goal for the day, and you miss it, you might feel bad, and lose confidence. Monthly planning helps keep you on track, without exposing yourself to the risk of over-expectation and confidence-denting failure, argue Roy Baumeister and John Tierney in their book, *Willpower: Why self-control is the secret to success*.

Echoing what Alex McKenzie told me, it's crucial, Maynard says, that *you* set the goals for yourself. They shouldn't come from a friend, an instructor, a family member or even a book. 'It's got to come from within.' With athletes, he's learned, 'If they're not engaging in the process, we're basically wasting our time'.

At the Yale Stress Center, Matt Stults-Kohlemainen engages his clients in his exercise prescriptions in part by getting them to rate how confident they are that they can manage the goals he generates with them. Anything less than an eight out of ten for confidence, and he knows he has to change something – either the goal, or how his client is thinking about it.

For someone reporting a six, say, he'd help that client map out their day in detail, down to the minute, to break down the barriers to achievement. The final plan, as I mentioned in Chapter Two, on exercise, might include what time to go to bed, what time to wake up, what time to eat breakfast, what time to put on the gym kit and even when to get the swimming costume from the drawer. 'Sometimes, I'll say, where exactly will your gym shorts be? What pair will you wear? What's the colour? It seems like over-planning in some sense. But some people really benefit from that kind of planning – from visualising the process.' This usually helps boost confidence ratings, which builds motivation. Also, as Matt says, 'weekly goals can more easily become routines'.

And if you set yourself a goal – even a mini-goal on the way to a major goal – and you accomplish it? Reward yourself. Roy Baumeister, who researches willpower, believes this to be important. Whatever the reward is, make it something that means something to *you*. At the end of every leg of that twenty-four-hour fell-running race, George rewarded himself with a can of Coke. 'Everybody has bits of the race they don't like – bits they like to get out of the way,' he says. 'At the end of every leg, I had a can of Coke waiting, which I really looked forward to. It was a treat, to reward myself.'

A can of Coke . . . I might have had a gorgeous dress, which I'd then allow myself to keep, or a pair of shoes. But whatever works for you.

CONCENTRATION/FOCUS

The Sydney Olympics. Leon Taylor is standing at the back of the diving board, in the final. There he is, in the photo on Maynard's wall. And he really doesn't want to be there.

'He was ill,' Maynard says. 'He had flu. This was something he'd been training for for *eight years*. And at that point, on the ten-metre platform, he didn't want to be there. But he'd learned a technique. He knew how to get himself *up*. How to focus himself using lots of sharp, short inhalations to really create tension in his chest and in his mind, which became arousal.' (That's in the general physiological meaning of the term – a faster heart rate, and so on.)

This technique, which Maynard taught Taylor, helps create energy and focus when you're feeling slow. For many of us, though, the biggest threat to our ability to focus and stay mentally tough in a stressful situation is not being *under*-hyped, but the reverse. And indeed the trick of breathing fast and for longer on the inhalation than the exhalation is the reverse of the method Maynard more commonly teaches for improving focus – something called 'applied relaxation'.

Clients start by learning progressive muscle relaxation. The main aim at this point is to help them to understand what being tense and being relaxed actually *feel* like, Maynard explains. They then move on to breathing – learning to associate relaxation with breathing out and tension with breathing in. At stage four of the six-stage programme, they're practising ratio breathing (counting to four on the in-breath and eight on the out-breath) for 'rapid relaxation', and Maynard gives them twenty coloured dot stickers to put on things they encounter every day – like the kettle, the loo handle, the steering wheel and the bedroom light switch. 'Every time they see a spot, they practise the breathing exercise for maybe two minutes.'

To complete the final stage, clients must master a ten-second exercise. It has to take five to ten seconds *max*, Maynard says, because that's the most time you'll get to refocus on a football pitch, or in a tennis match. Or, of course, when faced with a child on the brink of a tantrum.

This is what it involves: 'Just a couple of breaths, where you're associating the inhalation with tension, but more importantly the exhalation with relaxation. I also integrate a refocusing word or phrase with that.'

What kind of phrase?

It varies, he says, depending on the client. For Leon Taylor, practising applied relaxation as he prepared to leap into a particular dive, it was often a relevant instructional phrase, like 'tuck tight'. For me, and my goal of staying calmer when confronted with fighting children, I suppose it might be, 'don't yell'.

Does the technique really work? 'Absolutely,' Maynard says.

I remember Matt Stults-Kohlemainen telling me the only reliable (drug-free) way of rapidly calming someone in a stressed-out state is to get them to regulate their breathing.

Different experts seem to favour slightly different regimens. Stults-Kohlemainen's advice if you feel yourself starting to panic – just before an interview, perhaps, or a date – is to slow your breathing to around five breaths per minute. That's six seconds in and six seconds out. Stults-Kohlemainen uses a timer on his smartphone to do this. It takes only a few minutes for clear physiological calming effects to become clear, he told me.

Maynard likes the addition of a word or a phrase in regulated breathing for refocusing. 'My thinking is that if you have a key word in your head, it doesn't allow a negative thought to come in. If you've got a neutral mind – which mindfulness advocates – I always think there's a space for that negative thought to pop in.'

But while we're talking stress triage, there is a relevant mindfulness technique that I really have to pass on. It came up in conversation with a lot of the girls I spoke to at the Altrincham Grammar School for Girls. They'd talk about how if they went into an exam and encountered a question they couldn't immediately answer, they'd stop and 'do .bs' (pronounced dot-bees) and that would help.

Jill Cinan, the vice-principal at Melland High School, was at that particular meeting, too, with a couple of pupils who need specialist support. At one point, I asked Jill how the mindfulness had helped. She looked over at fourteen-year-old Sarah. 'Can we talk about you and your anger?' she asked.

'Yesterday, there was this boy,' Sarah said. 'He'd threatened me. I was going to go up to him, but I stopped and did the .b and it helped really good.'

Cinan asked what would have happened a few months ago.

Sarah shrugged. 'I would have punched him,' she said, matter-of-factly.

I think a .b sounds pretty incredible. *What* is it?

It turns out to be – as it *must* be, for something to work in the heat of the moment – very simple. It's a two-step process. And this is how it's done:

Sink your mental focus to your feet, then immediately anchor it on your breathing.

Body-scanning meditations help you learn how to move your focus around your body. Being focused on your feet simply means being aware of how they *feel* (are they warm or cold, relaxed or pressed by tight shoes?) Being focused on your breath means being aware of the physical sensations inside your mouth and throat as you breathe in and out.

So if you feel stress building, to do a .b, you suddenly force yourself to focus on your feet (and, if you can imagine *dropping* that focus down from your head to your feet, it really helps), and then concentrate your conscious awareness on the sensations in your mouth and throat as you breathe in and out.

I'm going to report on my experiences with the various techniques that I describe in this book at the end. But if there's just *one* you try now, today, or at least next time you feel your anger rising or your stress level soaring, it should be this one. It's that good. Or at least, it is for me. There's something about just sinking my attention that pops the kind of stress/frustration bubbles that Shaun the trainer referred to back at the Powers Martial Centre. Try it – and hopefully you'll see what I mean.

So . . . Positive self-talk. Confidence. Motivation. Concentration/focus. Those are Maynard's four crucial factors for mental toughness.

But though he says that he thinks willpower – or

self-control, or self-regulation, different terms for essentially the same thing – works across those factors, I can't help feeling that willpower deserves a category to itself. In part, because of all the relevant research that scientists have conducted since the 1980s, and specifically because of the finding that self-control, along with grit, is a crucial predictor of success in life.

Roy Baumeister at Florida State University, whom I've already mentioned, has done a lot of work in this area. His book (see p. 239) is packed with detail and relevant interviews. It's well worth reading, if you want the full picture of his ideas and findings in the field. But if you can live with a *highly* abbreviated and selective summary, with a few personal observations thrown in, here it is:

As adults we spend about a fifth of our waking hours resisting desires – like the desire to eat, take a nap, watch TV or look at websites (according to German research). The stronger our willpower, the better able we are to resist those desires, and stick to the task in hand (like working).

Baumeister argues that we each have a limited reservoir of willpower, and if you draw on it, you deplete it. Use a lot of willpower in one area of your life – in sticking to a diet, for example – and you're left with less for other areas, like keeping your house tidy or completing a tricky work assignment. For this reason, he argues, you should focus on one big project at a time, or you risk spreading your self-control too thin, and making mistakes. Above all, he counsels, don't make a list of New Year's resolutions. Because no one has enough willpower to cope at once with *all* the changes so many of us resolve to make – to spend less money *and* do more exercise *and* eat less chocolate *and* work harder *and* be more romantic and so on . . .

Hmm. Isn't that what I'm doing right now? Effectively drawing up for myself a New-Year's-resolution-type list of mind-improving strategies too extensive for any normal person's stock of willpower?

But, as I read on, I get to research implying that if all these things are bothering you – you *are* spending too much and exercising too little and eating too much sugar, etc. – you *must* address them, if only because they're a psycho-logical drain. And a very effective step towards dealing with nagging tasks or problems, it seems, is to make a proper plan for *how* to deal with them. A plan allows your worried, exhausted subconscious to relax. *Finally*, it'll sigh, you've taken charge!

And that's what I'm doing, I realise. Acknowledging these drains on my mental energy, which ironically enough, consist of concerns that my mind isn't strong enough, and coming up with a plan. Executing the plan can come in stages, if necessary. And the greater my willpower, the better I'll be able to manage it.

So how can I improve my willpower? Among Baumeister's observations are these:

1. Willpower is like a muscle. While it's temporarily weakened through use, the more you use it over time, the stronger it gets.

2. Having a high-level, abstract focus – wanting to 'be good', say, whether that's defined by religious or secular

moral beliefs – supports the willpower you need to stick at some difficult challenges.

3. Being 'observed' helps – whether that means literally being observed, or knowing that your actions will be made known to other people, including family and friends. As *Willpower* points out, if you waste a lot of time looking at non-work-related websites, there's software out there that will track your website-viewing and mail a list of the sites you visit to someone else, like your boss. The book also points to companies that allow you to choose a goal (like losing weight) and also a penalty to be imposed if you don't meet that goal. The penalty might entail emails pointing out your failure to friends, or even enemies.

Now, let me get back to Ian Maynard. I'm checking over my list of questions, and I realise there's one – an obvious one – that isn't on there, but which I really should put to him. It relates specifically to me. But you could substitute any challenge of your own.

I'm thinking about my prediabetes and the diabetic diet. I'm planning to go back through everything he's told me, and use what I can. But I really should take the opportunity to ask him for some specific advice. How would he help me develop the mental toughness needed to stick to my diet?

'First, I'd work on your ability to turn around the situation,' he says. "Instead of looking at diabetes as a negative thing, you could say, "Well, if I stick to the diet, think how sylph-like I'll become".' He looks a little embarrassed, evidently worried he's just insulted me. 'I mean, um, like you are already!' It's all right, I tell him. I understand what he's saying. I need to consider how I *think* about the challenge.

'I'd also work on some breathing techniques,' he goes on. 'Because there are going to be times when you'll want to eat cake.' So, I should try to stop myself with a rapid relaxation? 'Exactly.' In theory, he says, that should give me space to refocus on my goals. (He favours rapid relaxation, but a .b could be used in the same circumstances.)

'I'd probably also work on your confidence quite a bit. We'd go back to the things that get forgotten. Things you're good at. Things you've attempted in the past that have been successful. Why you're good at what you do. Then you can go back to those things when you need to.'

With any goal, it's also important to avoid a focus on winning, he adds. In my case, that would mean being successfully 'on' the diet. 'Thinking about winning creates anxiety,' he says. 'So you want to think about the *processes*, not the outcome. What do I have to *do today* that means I'm going to perform to my potential? Because ultimately that's all we can ask of anybody – whether that's the coach or the husband or whoever.'

For me, I suppose focusing on the processes could involve thinking not about being 'on a diet', but on practical strategies: what I'm going to do if I'm at a friend's house, and they get out a tin of biscuits. Or I'm at the shops, and I'm feeling hungry. And this would feed into goal-setting.

'Goal-setting would be important,' Maynard goes on. "Putting structure around eating habits would reduce the likelihood you'd get caught in a situation where you had low blood sugar – so maybe you'd want to make sure you had a little snack at 10.30. But for me,' he says, 'probably the most important aspect would be to deal with the negative thoughts.'

To be mentally tough, then I'll have to focus on the *positives* of being prediabetic. I *will* lose weight, if I stick to my diet. I *will* shift that stone I've put on since having children. I'll *have* to do more exercise, which will have benefits for my psychological strength and wellbeing, as well as my body.

And you know what, as I think about all this, I do feel my motivation levels starting to rise. Suddenly, I'm not focusing on what I'm losing – the homemade chocolate fudge cake at the cafe in the park, fish and chips for a hung-over lunch, the perfect naan from the Indian across the road – but what I'll be gaining.

I'll be slimmer, and fitter. And if I *can* get a reward from that, perhaps I'll learn to enjoy the burn of abstinence. I might actually get grittier. And what about my self-control? If I do manage to stick to my in-the-moment goals, my will-power 'muscle' will have enjoyed so much exertion, it'll be stronger than ever before. Maybe it'll be strong enough for me finally to learn French. And perhaps to play the guitar, because I've always quite liked the idea of it. Or really to engage in the kinds of adversity-focused adventures that would build my mental toughness even further. After talking to Ian Maynard, I can see so much more of the silver lining, and so much less of the cloud.

I walk home, thinking, *That was a really useful meeting. I learned a lot.* Then something hits me. I realise I've previously interviewed someone who must know through personal experience a huge amount about this topic, and I asked him not a single question about it.

I'm thinking of Matt Stults-Kohlemainen – the Yale Stress Center's exercise specialist and former United States Marine. In the past, I've read a bit about the recruit selection process. About Hell Week and the final fifty-four-hour-long 'Crucible', during which recruits get a *total* of eight hours sleep and are put through some of the toughest physical and mental challenges that a human can endure. I have to go back to Matt. And I do. I could weave bits and pieces of what he tells me into the pages you've just read, but I found *everything* he had to tell me interesting. It would be a shame, I think, to chop it up and cut it. So I'm going to reproduce that interview here as a standalone section:

MENTAL TOUGHNESS IN THE US MARINES

How did you come to sign up?

'I dropped out of college my senior year (much to my parents' concern). I was bored with life, essentially – burned out on studies and my other obligations. Some of my life goals were not playing out as I planned, and I wasn't as good an athlete as I hoped I would be. I was looking for something new. I actually clicked on a Marine Corps officer training link on the Internet and entered some information. The only recruiter in the town I lived in at the time was for the enlisted ranks, however. He contacted me and that was that.'

How did you feel about your chances of making it through boot camp?

'Like most recruits, I was extremely anxious. I went to a series of pre-boot camp events with my recruiter. I was fairly convinced that I was as prepared as most others, at least physically. I did feel somewhat out of place, given the fact that I was leaving college just before my senior year. Most recruits in the enlisted ranks join just out of high school.'

I've heard that the 'Crucible' at the end of the recruit training period is the toughest part. Was it?

'The Crucible starts about two weeks from the end. It is absolutely gruelling. The sleep-deprivation alone really stretches you to your maximum. I also recall completing an eighteen-mile forced march with a very heavy backpack. There were considerable challenges in terms of completing obstacle courses, etc., but these were nothing compared to the utter exhaustion.'

How did you prepare yourself mentally?

'My recruiter gave me an exercise routine which I completed nightly. I also recall reading lots of materials on the Marines and a few books that I purchased. Lots of quiet reflection. My mother gave me the rosary my father took to Vietnam – and that was comforting.'

Did you know much about theories on mental toughness beforehand?

'I didn't know anything! The whole point of boot camp was to develop mental toughness.'

Were you explicitly taught about mental toughness during training?

'The Marines offer little in terms of guidance or advice. It's more of a "Do-it-or-else" mentality. Sink or swim.

251

'I recall many moments when I simply could not allow myself to think any more to cope with the stress of various activities. When we used pugil sticks to practise hand-to-hand combat, I recall specifically telling myself to "just do it", to be clichéd. I had to get in touch with my more primordial and aggressive self. Dwelling on morals, civilian standards for conduct and so on isn't very useful. It's about forgetting who you are and focusing on what you're supposed to be – a United States Marine Corps recruit and aspiring Marine.

'The Marines are big on history and tradition. I remember many instances in which we watched videos and heard stories about the valour and heroism of Marines of the past. The stories about the Marines at Inchon in Korea, or the survivors of the Corrigidor death march, or the Marines who defended Wake Island.

'What the Marines do not offer is canned "positive psychology", which everyone seems to want these days.'

For you, what was the toughest bit of training? And how did you cope?

'Quite honestly, the Crucible was not the toughest part of boot camp.

'The Sundays of "rest" were the toughest for me . . . because your hope of finding some relaxation never (or rarely) materialised and sometimes you simply were trying not to think about the week ahead. If we were actively doing something ("close-order drill", for instance) and I could "turn off my mind", I was OK, but having moments of reflection on Sundays were the toughest. After a while you grow accustomed to adversity, and my own experience was that "letting up" was unbearable. You start to think of home and everything you're missing.'

How did your fellow recruits cope?

'Several recruits had a hard time handling the stress and dropped out for a variety of reasons. One recruit (my bunk mate, actually), on a particularly stressful day, started hitting his head on the metal bunk so hard that he started bleeding quite badly. Some don't have toughness!'

And when you made it – you actually became a Marine – what happened?

'One important aspect of Hell week: I don't remember any big "Congratulations, you did it" at the end. It was simply our duty and what we had to accomplish to earn the title "Marine". I don't think my drill instructors wanted us to feel any sense of elation. That came with graduation many days later, when we got to see our families.'

Do you feel you learned useful lessons about mental toughness from that training?

'To this very day I am absolutely astonished at what I accomplished. Climbing ropes and holding my body up at the top for what seemed like twenty minutes, clutching as hard as I could until my hands were bleeding. Jumping from high decks into huge pools with all of my gear and backpack on, rapelling down towers and zip-lining down cords when I was terribly afraid of heights.

'I tried my best to always just focus on the moment

and not think too far ahead. I remember lots of "doing" and not "thinking" – or "feeling", for that matter. Marine Corps training is designed to promote readiness for battle, which means carrying out orders unquestioningly. I think I often felt like a robot or an automaton. In fact, my senior drill instructor used this metaphor quite often – that it was better to operate like a machine and less like a human. I think that is what happened. There is not a good analogue in the outside world. We don't operate like this in civilian life.

'The whole experience was designed to be super-focused. We didn't have watches or newspapers or music or anything to distract us. I never knew the time, or date.

'My twenty-first birthday was during boot camp and I remember it being like any other day. I do recall receiving a letter from my mother reminding me about my birthday, but I gave it the smallest nod in my mind. It came and went and no one ever knew.

'In civilian life there are many freedoms and distractions.'

Thinking back over your time in the Marines, what was the biggest lesson you learned about mental toughness?

'Only this: you can do anything if you put your mind to it. I don't tend to question my ability any more on anything. I make a decision to do something and I do it. The hardest part is making the decision.'

THE MENTAL TOUGHNESS CHECKLIST

- Develop an optimistic attitude – mentally tough people are 'invariably optimistic'.

- Break a big challenge into small parts, and reward yourself each step of the way.

- Concentrate on the process – on the *present*, and what you have to do next (rather than thinking about ultimate 'success' or 'failure', or how you're feeling).

- If you've made your mind up to do something, tell yourself you're going to like it.

- Develop strategies for coping with suddenly rising anxiety or anger – like the .b or breathing techniques.

- If you're losing confidence, remember that concentrating on (and playing to) your strengths rather than your weaknesses is an effective way to build it back up (thinking about past successes can help).

- Stress inoculation – facing challenges and learning you can overcome them – can build mental toughness.

- To strengthen your willpower, you have to *use* it (and when you do use it in a specific area, you're building a general strength).

- If you're contemplating a tough challenge, make sure *you* really want to do it – and that you set your own goals for achieving it.

CHAPTER SEVEN

KEEP YOUR SENSES IN MIND

It's a grey, damp day, and I'm coming back from the shops with a packet of cold and flu pills in my pocket. I turn the key in the lock, and as I open the front door, I hear 'Happy' by Pharrell Williams. In the living room, I find Jakob and Lucas dancing as only young kids can, jumping and twisting, grinning from ear to ear. James is on the sofa, smiling at them. And I smile too. Not just because the boys are having fun, but because of the song. I expect you've heard it. Maybe you hate it. Even if you do, the emotional 'up' is unmistakable. It's there in the harmony, the danceable beat and the lyrics.

And I think: I've looked at meditation, diet, exercise, sleep, self-talk and mental toughness. I've learned a lot. I've made plans to change. And I'm pleased with them. But they all require effort. What I haven't looked at yet is whether there are any effortless routes to greater psychological strength.

What about music? And scents? Or even the colour I choose for the walls of my study? How can I use input from my senses to calm me down, or improve my energy and motivation?

At this point, I don't know much about the theory. I vaguely remember reading that red makes people aggressive. And I know fast-paced music can get your body pumping in the gym. Lavender's meant to help you sleep. Sweet tastes can help us feel good . . . That's pretty much it.

The sense to focus on first, I decide, is hearing – with the emphasis on music. Surely everyone enjoys music of one sort or another, whether you're like James, who constantly listens to new songs, or more like my dad, who prefers the music of his later youth (Bruce Springsteen and . . . well, mostly Bruce Springsteen, though there was that dubious Foreigner period; and he did once buy an Enya CD).

As for me, thanks almost entirely to James, I've largely escaped the pull of the past, and I'll often put on new stuff. Though sometimes I'll play something from my teens. More often than not, that'll mean a song by The Smiths.

Vicky, James's sister, is firmly convinced that listening to The Smiths makes you depressed. Yes, so there are lyrics about a bus crashing into you, and dying. Not to mention being on your own, and going home alone, crying and wanting to die. 'Sit around listening to that all day, and you'd want to top yourself, wouldn't you?' she said the last time she was exposed to my musical choices.

But I clearly remember discovering The Smiths, at fifteen. The lyrics didn't make me feel depressed, and they still don't. Looking back, I think perhaps the songs allowed me safely to explore the emotionally darker side of teenage experience, one that I was drawn to – or at least, more than I was to peppy pop songs.

I wasn't unhappy, or any more unhappy than most teenagers. But *should* I have been listening to peppy pop songs? Would they have made me feel more positive? And what should I be listening to now if I want to feel calm, or energised, less stressed, or more motivated? Are there even objective answers to those questions?

I email one of the world's leading experts on music and the brain, and he agrees to talk. The following week, I call him up on Skype. A former professor of cognitive neuroscience here in the UK, Larry Parsons is now affiliated with the Centre de Neuroscience Cognitive in Bron, France. He talks to me from his ridiculously romantic-looking sixteenth-century apartment building, a poster from a Tiepolo exhibition beside his head.

I ask why he moved to France. 'Ah.' He smiles. 'I came here on a sabbatical. And I met a girl . . .'

They're now married, with a four-year-old daughter who's at school part time.

Over three mornings, we Skype in the time between me getting home from dropping off the boys and him needing to leave to collect his daughter.

One of the biggest joys of my job – and this project – is that I get to talk to smart, interesting people with fascinating brains to pick. And Larry Parsons', it turns out, is packed with everything I could need to know about music and emotion.

'Sex, Drugs & Rock 'n' Roll: Dopamine is the Common Bond'

I love this subhead. It's from a journal paper that Parsons sent to me, and it's a classic example of scientists taking a popular concept and providing their very un-rock'n'roll academic explanation.

Sex. Drugs (by which they mean drugs of abuse – like alcohol and cocaine). Music. What we all know at an essential level – that listening to music can make us *feel great* – was only demonstrated in terms of observable effects on the brain's so-called 'reward pathway' in 2011.

In the wonderfully dry dialect of academic papers, the Canadian team point out in their introduction that 'most people agree that music is an especially potent pleasurable stimulus that is frequently used to affect emotional states'.

They then report the first direct evidence that listening to music you like (whether that's Mozart or heavy metal) triggers the reward pathway. This pathway, which involves several parts of the brain, is evolutionarily old. A behaviour crucial for our survival, or the survival of our genes – like eating or having sex – activates it. As a result, dopamine, a 'motivational' brain chemical, is released. So too are are the body's feel-good endorphins. We are encouraged, then, to go on eating and having sex. And *listening to music*?

Animals don't respond to music, at least not in the way we do. Neither do they dance (cute YouTube videos of trained creatures aside). You'll often hear that the reason we humans love music so much is a mystery because it isn't vital for survival. But there are all kinds of reasons why music – and being emotionally vulnerable to certain types – could have helped our ancestors to survive, Larry Parsons says.

There are the individual ones: music can increase your pain

threshold, and music and dance can help to shape the growing brain at the highly sensitive time of puberty. But we're also social creatures – we evolved to rely on each other – and music can help us to interact positively with others in our group.

In ancient times, music might have helped group bonding before a battle or a hunt; today, you'll hear it in the stadium before a football match or a political rally. And if members of a group of warriors, say, are singing the same song, and, even better, also dancing the same dance, this signals to outsiders that they are a bonded group, so they'd better beware (this makes me think of the Haka, used today most famously by the New Zealand rugby union team, just before kick-off). 'If somebody says, well, it's easy to see why language, say, is adaptive, you can equally show a whole range of possible ideas for music,' Parsons says.

OK, so I can understand now *why* listening to music should trigger the brain's ancient reward pathway, and have a powerful impact on how we feel. But how can we best use music to influence our emotional state?

There are a few different ways of looking at this, Parsons says.

You may have strong memories associated with particular pieces of music. The first song at your wedding reception. The album an ex-boyfriend played to death. The first track you ever bought. They can make you feel good or bad, irrespective of the tune or lyrics.

Then there's the group-identity factor. Maybe you listen to a certain genre of music not because you love the harmonies or the lyrics (or at least, not at first) but because you want to be the sort of person who listens to that type of music.

But then there's the evidence that music can make an elemental kind of contact with our emotional brain.

Parsons sends me research papers, including some of his own, showing that a piece of music can connect with brain regions crucial for emotion, whether we're familiar with the song or not. And while the music that we *like* varies hugely between people, the way a tune is *constructed* can reliably make most of us feel happy or sad.

In fact, according to one analysis, music can influence not only how happy or sad we feel, but our sense of wonder (feeling amazed, or moved or simply happy), transcendence (feeling awed, and having the sense of spirituality), tenderness (feeling love, affection or sensual), nostalgia (making us feel sentimental or dreamy), peacefulness (feeling calm and relaxed), power (involving feelings of energy or triumph) and also something dubbed joyful activation (feeling stimulated, animated and simply joyful).

A piece of music makes you feel how you feel, so perhaps you don't need or want a scientist to explain the technicalities of how it exerts its effects. If you're not particularly interested, please do skip down a few paragraphs.

I'll focus on 'happy', 'sad', 'scary' and 'relaxing' music:

- Happy music generally has a medium rhythm, according to Parsons. 'It's danceable', he says, 'and the pace is regular – it tends not to be chaotic'. It also tends to be in a major key.

- Sad music is likely to have a slow pace, slow chord changes and to use minor keys.

- 'Music that's fast-paced, with fast chord changes is usually considered angry or strident or scary,' says Parsons.

- Relaxing music tends to be slower-paced, but can be 'happy' or 'sad'.

There's an aesthetic theory linking these observations to how we behave in different emotional states. 'Someone who's angry might be pounding on a table,' Parsons tells me. So perhaps that's why a fast beat can seem angry. 'If someone is moving slowly, perhaps it's because there's been a death in the family.' So a slow pace can seem sad.

However, there's also work suggesting that the beat of a piece of music can influence the pace of the firing of neurons in the brain stem. The brain stem regulates breathing and heart rate (among other things). So fast-paced music may trigger physiological changes that make us feel more alert, and the reverse would apply for a slow pace.

It's important, Parsons stresses, to separate the *pleasurableness* of a piece of music from its emotional impact. Both happy and sad music can stimulate the reward pathway, and give us a pleasure hit. But the same tunes won't necessarily do this for everyone, underscoring the importance of ignoring what your friends or family might say and listening to what makes *you* feel good, no matter what it is. (Even Enya. And yes, even The Smiths.) As one researcher in this field told Canada's CBC news: 'Rather than the doctor saying, "Oh, you've got depression – take two Joni Mitchells and call me in the morning," I think what we need to have is a recognition that people need to have control over what they are listening to.'

Still, there's a theory for why many of us can agree on which tunes are enjoyable, or at least impressive, and which are dull.

'There's this theory that pleasurable music is cleverly organised to build up a set of expectations about how the chords and the melody should change over the course of the passage,' Parsons explains. 'By cleverly manipulating these expectations, the composer or performer can influence the emotional experience. If you prolong the delay until the last expected chord change, you can make the emotional experience more intense. The music can wind you up. It can tease you, in a sense. It gets close to resolution, then backs away. Finally, it resolves as you expect, and the experience of being correct about that resolution, and having predicted it accurately, is a reward.'

The classic 'pleasurable song' of the lab is Pachelbel's Canon. But as Parsons talks, I'm thinking of The Killers' 'All These Things That I Have Done'. This was the first song at our wedding reception, chosen simply because it was the one we most liked to dance around the house to at the time. If you know the song, you'll know that interlude about having soul but not being a soldier. I'm not at all musical, but if that's not a teasing delay, making the predicted resolution even more pleasurable, I'm not sure what is.

I find this really interesting. Teasing delays before a predictable resolution are pleasurable in all sorts of other ways, of course. *I'm thinking books and films.* There's an idea, apparently, that we have a kind of instinctive understanding of the 'grammar of music', just as we do of the 'grammar of story'.

Now I realise I'm getting a little off-track. So, I ask Larry, which tunes reliably make people feel happy or sad or relaxed?

Much of the scientific research has been done with classical-style music (whether old or modern). So I'll give you examples from this genre.

Top tunes for feeling happy:

• Joseph Haydn's Symphony No. 70, D Major

• Johann Strauss II's *Tausendundeine Nacht*

• Georges Bizet's *Carmen* Suite No. 1, 2nd movement: 'Aragonaise, Allegro vivo'

Top tunes for feeling relaxed:

• Mozart's Andante for flute and orchestra, C major, KV 315

• Mozart's Piano Concerto, No. 21, C major, KV 467

• Max Bruch's Concerto for violin, No. 1, 2nd movement: 'AdagioBirdsong'

Top tunes for feeling sad:

• Albinoni's Adagio in G Minor

- Franz Schubert's String Quartet No. 14, D minor

- Mendelssohn's *Songs Without Words*, Op. 30, no 6 in F

You might be wondering why I'm listing tunes for feeling sad. Isn't this book at least partly about being more positive than negative? The thing, of course, is that if you're feeling low, sad music can help. One recent survey – the first comprehensive survey of music-evoked sadness – concluded that listening to sad music can have emotional benefits, helping to regulate negative emotions, and providing consolation. No doubt this is why another survey, organised by BBC Radio, which asked listeners to vote for the best way to relieve depressive symptoms musically, found that 'I Know It's Over' by The Smiths came out top. One respondent described the song as being 'like a giant pair of arms coming out of the speakers to hug me'.

'I Know It's Over' does, I note, have lyrics about the knife wanting to slit you, and soil closing over your head. And I start to wonder about the relative importance of lyrics versus the tune for how the listener *feels*.

Parsons sends me a journal paper that explores exactly this question. Happy music without lyrics produced more powerfully positive emotions than happy music with lyrics, while lyrics made sad music seem sadder. Still, I decide not to worry too much about listening only to classical 'happy' stuff. Most popular songs have lyrics, of course. And songs, lyrics and all, *can* make you feel great, Parsons points out: 'You find your song of the summer, and you feel *golden*.'

What with the Apple Watch and other devices that monitor

your heart rate and sweat (indicators of anxiety or relaxation) and talk to your smartphone, it surely won't be long, Parsons says, before there are apps that can detect if you're starting to feel stressed or anxious, or slow and lazy, and that can prompt your phone to play music to put you in a more helpful state of mind. By the time you read these words, they may well be available.

But I'm already thinking that perhaps I should use music in the morning, the peak stress point in my day. I'm not sure, however, that 'relaxing' would cut it. Could the dawn chorus or a little flute adagio really counteract the psychological impact of Lucas trying to steal Jakob's Lego Bat-copter instead of getting dressed, and Jakob spotting him and tearing towards him, arm raised, instead of finishing his breakfast? I suppose it's worth trying. And I will. Though I might also try 'happy' music.

In fact, I might try to play more 'happy' music, in general. Because there's research finding that not only is happy music likely to make listeners *feel* happier, but they're more likely to think other people *look* happier. A similar effect holds for sad music. I can't help concluding that if you listen to sad music (even sad but beautiful music) on a regular basis, this might skew how you feel not only about yourself but others. And if positivity is so important for psychological strength – as study after study has shown it to be – I really should bear this in mind.

I ask Larry Parsons how he uses music in his life. He was a 'bit of a musician' as a teenager, and in his early days at college, he says. Back then, he learned to play jazz songs by imitation. So he developed a fairly sophisticated understanding of music. 'My parents were the same. They weren't musicians, but they listened widely. I listen very widely. My wife only listens to a few things. She won't listen to country and western. Or blues. Or opera. I could go on . . . If I'm by myself, walking in the street, I'm listening to music. If I'm cooking – and I'm the main cook in the house – I'm listening to music. Often, I'll listen to the same song on repeat.'

The *same* song? For how long?

'If I'm walking across town to do the shopping and back, it could be forty-five minutes. Do you know "Idioteque" by Radiohead?'

I confess that I don't.

He plays it to me.

My first impression is that it's an odd song.

He says, 'I don't know what your reactions are, but you can see it's an interestingly structured song.' (Oh, yes, *that's* what I meant.) 'There's that sad vocal falsetto, the background is very simple, the rhythm is interesting and insistent, a bit like a march, but not really a march. I stumbled on it. I didn't know anybody else liked it. I thought, *Wow*. Then I went to see them in the south of France. They played their whole concert, then did their encore, and the very last song was "Idioteque". And that's when I realised that everybody else who liked that kind of music also thought it was the peak achievement of the band. I realised it wasn't just me. There was something very ancient that the band had hit upon.'

He'll play 'Idioteque' over and over and over, he tells me. 'There's something really contained about it, and pleasantly stimulating. I put it on repeat, and I listen. Then I start to do something else – email or work. But it's still there, influencing me. I might leave it on while I burrow into work for a couple of hours.'

I've never really been able to work with background music. But then I've never put the same song on repeat. The idea of using what becomes, as you stop actively listening, a subconscious positive musical influence seems like a brilliant one. I'll have to experiment, and for me, I think it might make sense to start with something simple, and without lyrics. Perhaps birdsong.

During my final conversation with Larry, I also make another resolution.

He's talking about how people evolved with music and dance. 'Music and dance is an evolutionarily critical thing that allows members of a group to co-exist in such a way that the group is functional and harmonious. In a traditional society, hunters would come back, and they'd tell an intense story about the activities of the day. There'd be a sort of theatrical dance, which other members of the group would join in with. The youngest members would be playing a simple rhythm, the older ones would be acting in it. But over thousands of years of specialisation and industrialisation, now people think they can't sing, and they can't play an instrument; they can only have music on their iPod, and they can only dance at a concert.'

It's obvious that he thinks this is pretty sad. Not to mention a waste of an easy, free (or cheap) way to bond with the people around us, and simply to *feel good*.

Having young kids does give you a bit of a pass on behaving like a grown-up at times. And so I decide to try to keep it that way. We will still dance around the living room.

Jakob's just started to learn to play the guitar. James has, too. As soon as Lucas is old enough, I *will* learn with him. We'll make music together, with no regard for how good or bad we are, just as our ancestors would have done.

✳

Next up in my exploration of the senses is touch.

It's a blustery day in central London. The clouds are hurrying faster than the people along the pavements. But here, in a treatment room at the spa of the luxurious Intercontinental Hotel on Park Lane, the atmosphere, as you'd expect, is one of enveloping calm.

I'm lying on my front. Pearl, the therapist, is using the long, sweeping strokes of Swedish massage all along my back.

Once my muscles have warmed up, she grabs a clacking handful of rocks from the hot caddy in the corner. These volcanic stones, warmed to between 100 and 140°C, feel searingly hot as she places them on my skin, and uses them to work her way deeper into my muscles. But when people talk about 'feeling the burn', *this* is the type I like.

The heat, as well as the reassuring pressure, is intensely pleasurable. With stroke after stroke, the tension that's been building since early this morning – since I had to hurry the kids to school and race for my train, then work on a tight deadline all the way to London, before tackling the crowds in the Tube – all that tension is melting away.

Of course, you can buy massage devices. A flight to the US is not complete, I feel, without a thorough perusal of all the scalp-massaging shampoo brushes and electronic glove hand massagers on offer in the *SkyMall* magazine. But I wonder, is there something special about the touch of another person? And just how special is it?

Our closest relatives use touch all the time in social situations. Grooming keeps the fur clean, but it also plays a crucial role in bonding, in reconciliation and even in resolving conflicts. When it comes to people, the 'laying on of hands' was once a technique for healing. Hippocrates, the so-called 'father of medicine' was a proponent of gentle massage to relax the body.

We all know how good a hug from a partner or a friend can feel. Some companies even offer 'therapeutic cuddling'. But when it comes to touch, it's *massage* that really gets the credit cards across the counters. It's a multi-billion-pound industry. So when we hand over the equivalent of a pizza night out with the family in return for an hour of kneading, is that money well spent? Can massage justifiably be called medicine for the mind?

There's an awful lot of research on massage out there.

Much of it, as far as I can tell, is pretty flaky. Conducted by people who believe massage works, so are biased. Done without proper controls, so you can't really be sure of the effect. Based entirely on self-reports – which certainly count for something, but not everything. I want to know what *biological* impact massage might have. What does it do to stress hormones, like cortisol? And how long do any effects last?

The scientist best placed to answer those questions with authority is Mark Rapaport, Chairman of the Department of Psychiatry and Behavioural Sciences at Emory University School of Medicine in Atlanta.

Rapaport and his team have done the most scientifically rigorous work on massage to date. They've focused on Swedish massage because that's the most common type in the US (not to mention the UK and the rest of Europe). And, importantly for me, they've looked at normal people, without diagnosed depression or an anxiety disorder. I call him up, to ask about their discoveries.

This is what they found:

- A single, one-off forty-five-minute session of Swedish massage improves measures of stress-related hormones and has positive effects on the immune system.

- The biggest ongoing effects of one session of Swedish massage per week are improvements in immune functioning (especially the type of immune response involved in allergies).

- Two sessions of Swedish massage per week have somewhat different effects: the biggest ongoing improvements are in levels of stress-related hormones.

The team compared people who got massages with people whose bodies were touched in the same places, for the same length of time, but not massaged. *Touch alone* did improve levels of hormones related to stress and anxiety, like cortisol, and oxytocin, the so-called 'cuddle hormone', which can relieve stress and promote positive feelings about other people, but the volunteers who got the twice-weekly massage had bigger improvements. The work clearly shows that 'both touch and massage have active biological properties', Rapaport says.

I ask him if these findings changed his opinion on massage at all. 'Yeah. I'm scientifically usually very sceptical of everything. I'd had only about four massages in my life when we began this work. But I was impressed by what I saw. I began to get more massages. I've actually found them to be very helpful in terms of relieving stress. I truly went into this area completely sceptical. I'm a lot less sceptical now.'

Of course, there's another powerful way to reduce stress through touch, and that's sex. As with exercise, sex causes an immediate rise in stress hormones, but leads to lower overall levels in the long term and less anxiety. Regular sex can apparently combat normal age-related reductions in the formation of new brain cells, and improve brain functioning in middle-aged rats (acting as models for people). For many of us, sex, like exercise – and unlike massage – is free. And massage not only costs, it's downright *expensive*. So is it really worth it?

Rapaport says he thinks there's room – and a need – for a wide variety of strategies to combat stress. 'I exercise every day. It's clear that exercise is very effective at decreasing stress and decreasing the signs and symptoms of depression. There's increasing data that meditation is effective at decreasing stress, and may have palliative effects on both anxiety disorders and depression. Also I believe it's quite possible that other forms of somatic [body] therapies, whether it's massage or some type of acupuncture, may also have benefits. But we do need to do the research to demonstrate that.'

So – more research is needed on massage, and on other therapies that involve touch, to get a better grip on their potential. But then Rapaport tells me he also uses another technique for stress relief: 'I sing. One of the greatest stress relievers in my life is singing. I can go from being very preoccupied to feeling joyful and relaxed by singing for an hour.'

Really? What do you like to sing?

'Show tunes. Old traditional folk songs. Things like "The River is Wide".'

I tell him I've just been talking to a cognitive neuroscientist who thinks many of us don't take enough advantage of the positive psychological effects of making music – whether that's singing or playing as instrument (or dancing to it). 'Yeah, I think it's actually very, very powerful,' Rapaport says. 'I'm a big believer in it.'

I thank him for his help, and we say goodbye. Then I realise there's another touch-related area I haven't looked into. I benefit from it – or I feel that I do – multiple times a day . . .

. . . at 6.30am, when Jakob comes through to our room, and she comes in with him, leaps onto our bed and snuggles in, her head resting on my neck; in snatched minutes on the sofa, when she jumps on my knee and foils my attempts to meditate by licking my face; in the evening, when she stretches out on top of James and me and rolls onto her back for a stomach stroke. Dottie is half toy poodle, half King Charles spaniel and a *lot* like a living teddy bear. Stroking her certainly feels good. And, of course, there's plenty of research out there to show that stroking a pet *is* relaxing.

In fact, the benefits of 'human–animal interactions', to use the scientific terminology, are many. Time with a pet seems to boost levels of the hormone oxytocin, which both reduces stress and makes us look at other people more favourably. And of all the pet-related findings that I come across, this, on, I quote, 'normal' families, is probably my favourite: one month after getting a dog, the families took part in more leisure activities together and their children were more often visited by friends. Yeah, so maybe the children developed better friendships because they had higher levels of oxytocin *or* other children wanted to visit more often because of the *dog*, but whatever the reasons, more time with friends is clearly a good thing.

And, since there's no obvious single spot in this book to note all the ways I think Dottie makes me feel better, let me make a few brief notes here. Because if you are able to look after a dog, and you've always thought perhaps you'd like one but weren't sure (what about going away for the weekend, and all the walks?), all I can say is, I have no regrets, only joy.

For a start, she's just *there*, a comforting presence, especially when, as now, she's curled up on my feet while I work in an otherwise empty house. She loves to cuddle. She's the only member of the household who never gets cross or sulks or whinges, and she's always on the lookout for fun. She's a constant reminder of the virtues of positivity, trust, kindness and a disregard of wealth or physical attractiveness. And she makes me exercise. As I'd expected, I can't work through the day any more. I *have* to take her out.

I could take her down the high street. But I don't. Every lunchtime, we head to the Botanical Gardens. And to my surprise (because I love the sunshine, hate the cold and don't much like the countryside), I don't seem to mind even when it's wet. The silent mists in the bare trees and on the empty lawns on a damp late autumn afternoon, are, I have to concede, a powerfully peaceful draw.

I know there's some evidence that we might feel more relaxed in natural settings because our brains, which evolved before cities, find these scenes easier to process. And now I want to find out all I can about how sensory influences via a third sense – vision – can affect my mood.

✳

Certain images can trigger powerful responses, of course. Pictures of war-maimed children vs ultrasound scans of our perfect unborn babies. But it's the scenes with less obviously emotive information that I'm more interested in. To what extent does the decor in my house or the road I choose to walk along affect my psychological state? Can I make better use of what I *see* to improve how I feel?

I'm on a two-hour train journey to London, with what looks to be the perfect accompaniment: *The Architecture of Happiness*, by Alain de Botton.

It's an elegantly written and persuasive book. De Botton argues that architecture can influence our happiness (used in this case to mean more than an upbeat feeling, but also a sense of satisfaction, contentment and belonging). The influence may be subtle. As he puts it: 'The noblest architecture can sometimes do less for us than a siesta or an aspirin . . .' But there *is* an influence, and it's worth exploring. 'An ugly room can coagulate any loose suspicions as to the incompleteness of life, while a sun-lit one set with honey-coloured limestone tiles can lend support to whatever is most hopeful with us,' he writes.

De Botton goes on to make these arguments for why, as individuals or sometimes as societies, we prefer certain styles of architecture or decor over others:

1. The way we decorate our home can remind us of who we are, at heart or at our best.

2. The style of our surroundings can reflect values that we feel are important and that may be missing from our lives.

For example, you may work all hours with money or technology and rarely eat around a table with your partner and kids, but a farmhouse-style kitchen might give you a sense of a simpler, more family-connected kind of life.

Later that day, I find myself in the West End with an hour and a half to spare before a meeting. I start to follow a familiar route, up through the bustle of Charing Cross Road, zigzagging into the calm of Museum Street and emerging in front of the British Museum.

For twenty years, I've been coming here whenever I can. When I first moved to London, I worked just off Trafalgar Square as an office temp to save money to pay for a post-grad journalism course, and I used to walk here most lunchtimes. That I'd have perhaps only ten minutes inside was irrelevant. After a morning of typing memos and water-cooler gossip, it was a balm, and a motivator. I realise – with the benefit of hindsight and de Botton's book – that it reminded me of other worlds, and other possibilities. It spoke to me of adventure and knowledge – things I wanted but couldn't easily have, at least not then.

To me today, as to my twenty-year-old self, the Classical building suggests serenity and solidity, qualities that I was certainly missing all those years ago. The modern spaceport-style glass roof over the Great Court, built several years after I first began to visit, talks to me now, as a middle-aged woman, of a twist to the tale. A second chance. The possibility of reinvention, rather than stagnation or gradual decrepitude. De Botton's book has helped me to understand why I like what I like – and I start to think about my home.

If the question is: 'Bohemian cluttered styling versus modern Zen simplicity – which is best for psychological well-being?' there's no simple answer. Because it depends on who you are.

If you crave a calmer, simpler life, or you value restraint and order, then perhaps Zen simplicity is the style that will work best for you. There are times I think I'd like a Zen-style house. I don't have one. Not even close. But if a home can help to make you to feel psychologically strong if it reflects your values and reinforces your sense of who you are or how you'd like to be, then, I think, my home does a reasonable job. The bits and pieces from when I lived in Cairo in my mid-twenties, and from our journeys around the world, and the packed bookcases, remind me that though I may be watching *The X Factor* right now, and our last holiday was in the Algarve, and the one before that was on the Costa del Sol, and the one before *that* was on the Costa del Sol, I do value adventure and literature. It all helps to remind me of *me* – who I was, before children changed everything, and who I still am.

If my home wasn't like this, after reading de Botton's book, I'd be doing my best to make it this way. And it gives me a fresh resolution to avoid the generic, where I can, and to try to avoid falling for a decor argument well-made by someone else, but which means nothing to me.

That's the case for an individualistic approach. But there do seem to be a few universals when it comes to the psychological impact of our surroundings. These are not from de Botton's book. I'm going back now to the scientific research:

- Try to keep your surroundings tidy. People in a messy room demonstrate less willpower (Roy Baumeister's work).

- If you can see yourself in a mirror, you'll be more honest and behave more ethically (Roy Bauemeister again).

What about the millennia-old concept that *colours* can affect our mood and psychological health?

In the East, the idea goes back a long way, and in the first half of the last century, it seems to have become popular in parts of Europe and north America. After World War I, for example, a Colour Cure ward, painted spring-green, and sunshine-yellow, with a firmament-blue ceiling was developed, with the aim of treating soldiers with shell-shock.

Did it work? Does it work? Would a sunshine-yellow office encourage me to feel more positive and motivated? Would staring at a piece of card coloured firmament-blue help me to stay calm in the face of screaming children?

The fact is, there's a mountain of pseudoscience in 'colour medicine' or 'colour therapy', as it's sometimes called. You don't have to delve far into the research before coming across papers that talk about your body's inner vibrations, or how swallowing pigments dissolved in water, oil or milk can cure various diseases. This kind of thing makes me want to run from the very idea that colour may influence wellbeing. But it *is* intuitively appealing. So I drag myself back.

If you just stick to the reputable science, effects have been found. But they're often contradictory.

There's a fair amount of evidence when it comes to the colour red, for example. Women are rated as more attractive by men when they're wearing red (the so-called 'red-dress effect' – *and* women are more likely to wear red or pink when they're ovulating). Red-coloured pills are reported as being more effective stimulants and painkillers than blue pills (when only placebos with no active ingredients are given to volunteers). Sportspeople who wear red are also more likely to win (levels of skill being equal).

But what about the colour itself – alone, on a bit of card or on a wall? Yes, you'll often hear that red is stimulating (while blue is calming). And there is research finding that red can sharpen memory (while blue and green may improve creativity). But there's also work finding that red can *reduce* people's scores on IQ tests. And where's the rigorous research showing that a blue room reduces heart rate or blood pressure or stress hormone levels more effectively than a red room or a black room? I can't find any.

If you ask British people who are feeling anxious or depressed to match their mood to a colour, they mostly choose grey, while people who are feeling more positive pick yellow. Of course, we *do* associate our moods with colours. But this doesn't mean that if you paint your walls yellow, you'll feel better. I once lived in a rented house with sunshine-yellow walls. I found the colour oppressively intrusive. My dad's old study was painted black. To me, it was a cosy, cave-like place to work. Grey colour schemes are popular today. I've been in plenty of restaurants done out in everything from dove grey to dark slate, and I haven't noticed any of my fellow diners looking tempted to use the cutlery to cut their wrists, rather than their steak.

So, when it comes to colour, with so much contradictory research and so much that's unclear, I can't see the need for me to repaint my house any time soon.

And I think I'll leave vision there.

That's three senses down. Two to go. But I can't find a huge amount to say about the influence of taste on our psychological wellbeing. At least, not that doesn't involve another sense – smell, which I'll look at next.

Snow-soft white light saturates my eyes. It dims and slowly brightens . . . Dims and brightens . . . Every time the light intensity from the LEDs mounted in my goggles starts to rise, a sweet lemon scent drifts past my nose. The scent fades with the light, then returns. Fades, and returns . . . It's hypnotic. At first, it felt slightly odd to have my senses of sight and smell so hijacked in this way, but now I'm used to it, I like it. There's something reassuring about the light, and the scent is . . . pleasant.

If I were to let the Aromalux run a full cycle, I'd be sitting like this for fifteen minutes. But I'm conscious of the time, and I'm also feeling a little awkward, because I'm not alone. I'm in the lab of Tim Jacob, a professor of physiology at the University of Cardiff, and an expert on smell and the mind/brain. This device is his prototype for a piece of kit he thinks could boost mood in healthy people, and, he hopes, perhaps even treat depression.

The light aspect I understand. Full-spectrum white light, which the goggles provide, can ease depression, as Michael Terman, Director of the Center for Light Treatment and Biological Rhythms at Columbia University Medical Center, has described in Chapter Four on sleep. But what about the scent component?

The goggles are held in place by a headband. At the back of the headband there's a little plastic pack containing a battery and a pad, onto which a smelly oil can be dripped, as well as a fan, to blow the scent molecules towards your nose. For my try-out today, Jacob's chosen lemon oil. But in theory you could use anything. If the device does go to market, he plans to create blends that are 'relaxing' or 'energising', or that lift a user's spirits.

So – what's the justification for this? Where's the research to show that scents really can influence your psychological state?

First, Jacob goes back to basics.

An odour molecule enters a nostril. It binds with a receptor in the lining of the nostril. A nerve signal travels to a site within the limbic system of the brain.

The limbic system is evolutionarily old. A sparrow has one.

A gecko has one. It's made up of parts that developed before the bits that allow you to think. Your limbic system handles the 'fight-or-flight' response. It deals with your memories and emotions and impulses – to run away from something scary, perhaps, or to gorge yourself on chocolate cake, or to have sex with that good-looking stranger. It's also home to the 'reward pathway' – which makes us feel good when we do escape death, eat cake or have sex (though the thinking cortex may well then decide that sex with that stranger was *an even worse* idea than all that cake). The limbic system can prompt us to feel terrified or miserable, ecstatic, relaxed or hyper-motivated and everything in between.

There's quite a bit of overlap between the limbic structures involved in processing smells and emotions – and scents can influence our emotions subconsciously as well as consciously, Jacob says. He points to a now-famous finding that sleeping people who inhaled the scent of roses later reported having more pleasant dreams, while the smell of rotting eggs provoked unpleasant ones. The people didn't report smelling or tasting anything in the dreams. Rather, the scents influenced the emotional tone of their unconscious experiences.

We can even smell emotions from sweat. At least, humans can tell, by sniffing, the difference between cloths that have been rubbed into the armpits of people who were petrified (watching the horror movie *Candyman*, for example) and cloths from people who'd been watching an innocuous documentary. Women can smell happiness in a similar sort of way – though not as accurately as they can smell fear, Jacob tells me. (Any way you look at it, women are better at smelling than men, he adds.)

No one knows exactly which chemicals we're detecting when we smell fear or happiness. But there is work showing that specific, known scents can influence our moods, Jacob says.

He's investigated this in his own lab, using a helmet-type device, which emitted only scent and not light. His volunteers completed questionnaires designed to evaluate these five mood factors: anger/hostility, confusion/bewilderment, dejection/depression, fatigue/inertia and tension/anxiety before and after exposure to various scents. After a single ten-minute exposure, he says this is what he's found, in as yet unpublished work (so research that I should note hasn't yet been subjected to the scrutiny of his academic peers):

- Vanillin has a 'very significant' overall impact on mood. Specifically, it improves ratings of dejection/depression, fatigue/inertia and tension/anxiety.

- Lemon improves ratings on dejection/depression.

These findings are supported by some other work. There's research suggesting, for example, that lemon oil is an effective anti-depressant (at least in rats), possibly because it influences levels of serotonin, which is affected by Prozac and similar drugs. Other teams have also found that vanillin helps general mood and calmness.

Lavender has been shown to have an impact on the brain. It seems the main smelly ingredient in lavender, called linalool, has anaesthetic effects. 'It's one of the few aroma chemicals for which there is a really good sound physiological, phar-macological basis for its activity,' Jacob says.

Jacob has also investigated rosemary, and he wants to look at it more, because there are some suggestions from the research that it may act as a stimulant. The same may be true for peppermint. 'There is quite good evidence that peppermint is alerting,' he says.

Exactly how vanillin might influence mood isn't clear, though there are hints of some kind of biological action, since it does bind to certain receptors in the nervous system. But Jacob thinks that memories probably also have an important role to play. At least, for people who grew up in countries where vanilla is used in puddings: 'Vanilla was in all those treats we received as kids. Ice cream. Cakes. Biscuits. All those nice things. So it's a reward and it activates positive memories,' he says.

For the first commercial Aromalux mix – if it gets that far – Jacob says he'll probably use a blend of lemon and lavender (because there's published research finding impacts on mood) and something else, probably peppermint. But of course you don't *need* a device like this to expose yourself to scents. Along with his prototype, Jacob has a variety of scent disseminators in his office, ranging from an old-fashioned oil burner to an electric device that blasts air through oil-soaked pads.

Bottles of perfume are also dotted around the office. There are fragrances from Hugo Boss, Christina Aguilera and Dolce & Gabbana ('people give me all sorts'), plus an atomiser with a lab-type text-only label on the front. 'That's from Procter & Gamble,' he tells me. (The company manufactures various perfumes.) 'We were doing some experiments and they gave us all these bottles with numbers on. We don't know what they are. Am I going to throw them all away now? No! *This one* has a really nice smell.'

He sprays a little on a pad, and gives it to me. It does smell . . . pleasant. (I think I need to work on my scent description skills.)

'I decided to use this one to perfume the office,' he tells me. 'I spray it in the air. I like to play with scent.'

Do you?

'Yes, all the time. Absolutely! I always spray my handkerchief – which is what they used to do in past centuries – with things I can't go around wearing. There's a new Chanel. It's in a black bottle. It's for women. It's very feminine – though I don't like the masculine/feminine distinction – it's a *smell*. I don't think my wife likes me smelling of perfume. But I like it.'

I ask him if he has favourite scents. 'Well, I often come back to the woody scents. But I do like to try new things.'

I'm prompted to remember what Larry Parsons said about music: we've become stuck in ruts in terms of how we feel able to use music in our lives – and perhaps the same is true for scents, too. I don't really use smell at all. Well, I wear perfume if I'm going out. I quite like *some* scented candles. But the only time I've really tried to use smell, it didn't work out that well. For reasons that seem pretty obvious now.

When I think of Sydney, a city I love, I think of my senses. The burning heat of the sun. The diamond-rippling harbour. The *food* – all that Asian spice and rich Italian gelati. The calls of the fruit bats flying through a rose and gold pre-dusk sky. And the *scents* – and, of all the scents that assail you in Sydney in summer, the star jasmine. I remember one particular afternoon, walking home after lunch with James and a few good friends past bush after bush of the stuff in full flower. The air was overwhelmingly sweet and intoxicating.

Fast forward now to B&Q, Sheffield. There, in the plant section, I spot a little pot of star jasmine. I *have* to take it home. I put it on the windowsill in the kitchen. And every time I catch the scent, it brings back intense memories of past happiness – an experience so bittersweet it makes me want to cry.

So. Not entirely successful. But I guess I could try pairing scents with happy moments *now* – moments I know I can have in the future, too – and use those scents to help to put me in a good mood at other times.

I ask Jacob if he thinks we don't make the most of smell's ability to influence us. Are we too restrictive?

'Oh my God, yes! Men don't necessarily like scent. They think it smells effeminate. Where did that come from? It's ridiculous. We could do so much more with smell.'

And I resolve to.

And, though I did warn Jacob at the start of our conversation that while I was keen to try the Aromalux, I wouldn't be going off to write, 'Oh, you *must* try it, it's amazing', I have to say . . . I did like it. There was something very relaxing and almost meditative about the rise and fall of the light and the scent (designed to allow our scent receptors to recover in between bouts of stimulation, to maximise the effects).

I can't help thinking, in fact, that a device like this might help me with meditation. Fifteen minutes of meditation plus light therapy plus smell therapy. It could be a pretty pleasant form of multi-tasking. I mention this to Jacob.

'Ah,' he says. 'You know, I think the experience of the Aromalux is very similar to meditation.'

Are you interested in meditation?

'Yes, very much so.'

Jacob *is* a scientist (and while meditation is much more accepted than it used to be, I suspect you wouldn't find most scientists embracing it). But this isn't a huge surprise. There have been hints. The wooden bead bracelets I noticed around one wrist. The interest in new ways of addressing emotional and mental health. The friendly, warm demeanour. OK, yes, even the floppy hair.

'I'm a meditator,' Jacob says. 'My mother taught TM. I've been doing TM since I was fifteen. With TM you use a mantra. The purpose of a mantra is to remove thought. You replace thoughts as they arise with the mantra. With *this*, it does have a way of distracting you from whatever you're thinking about – taking you back to focusing on the light. My daughter had been doing mindfulness, and she said, "It's a bit like mindfulness meditation". That was never the intention. It's just something I've noticed. With hindsight, I think it's a mechanical way of inducing the same state.'

A reputable scientist *and* a TM practitioner. I have to ask him about some of the things that have bothered me about TM since I learned about it back in New York.

How do you, as a scientist, feel about the claims of layers of consciousness and influencing crime – and even yogic flying? Can you do TM, but not buy into the whole package of beliefs?

'Too right! I've been meditating for a long time. But I have determinedly stayed in the real world. It really is not mystic.

The mechanism by which it works is pretty well understood now.'

Herbert Benson's Relaxation Response?

'Yes! I think Benson's right.'

What he hopes, he tells me, is to use scent and light, like meditation, to improve psychological health: 'Depression is a huge problem. And nobody really knows how to treat it. I think it's really about mental and physical health, and somehow we seem to have lost the capacity for managing our own health. We turn automatically to drugs.'

At the moment, I explain, I'm focusing on psychological strength. But I know there's a growing body of reputable research that suggests we can use our minds to influence our physical health as well. I say to him: at least the idea is being increasingly recognised by scientists.

He looks incredulous. 'Not by any scientists that I know! I've had to keep very quiet about this.' He waves a hand towards his Aromalux.

Have you?

'Yeah! Absolutely! I'm a physiologist. I'm a member of The Physiological Society. I've done all the right things in terms of doing science. But I'm interested in taking science out of its strait-jacket.'

Like Herbert Benson?

He looks thoughtful. 'Yeah.'

The last thing I expected when I got on the train to Cardiff this morning was that I'd be talking to Tim Jacob, a physiologist, about TM and meditation and Herbert Benson.

Here I am, very close now to the end of my journey into investigating how I can tone up my mind – into the *evidence-based* ways of boosting it from the bottom up – and I seem to have come back to where I started.

And this seems, I think, like a good point to stop.

THE SENSES CHECKLIST

- Music that *you* like is most likely to make you feel good. And it doesn't matter if that's Mozart or heavy metal. So there's no need to buy into someone else's idea of 'feel-good' tracks.

- For relaxation, there's evidence that birdsong is better than silence.

- Try to break the music 'rules'. We evolved to play music as well as to listen to it, and to dance. Who cares if you don't have perfect pitch or didn't get past grade one on the piano? Sing anyway. Play something simple. Dance around your living room. That's the professional advice.

- Swedish massage does seem to have physiological stress-relieving effects. Simple touch has similar, though less strong, effects.

- Sex relieves anxiety and improves mood.

- When it comes to home decor, choose a style that reflects who you are at your best and what *you* value for maximum psychological support.

- There is no clear, consistent, universal relationship between wall colour and mood or behaviour. So pick colours that you like for your home.

- Of all the scent–mood relationships that have been investigated, there's most evidence for: lavender for reducing anxiety and promoting relaxation; vanillin for improving mood and calmness; lemon oil for improving general mood.

CHAPTER EIGHT

CHANGE YOUR MIND

Meditation, exercise, diet, sleep, thoughts, mental toughness, use of the senses . . .

Seven factors. Some, like exercise, take a fair amount of time. Some, like changing your thinking style, take less in the way of time, but even more in the way of effort (at least, for me).

Taken together, I think these changes really do promise to do for the mind what so many of us already do for our bodies: toning it up, to build stability and strength.

But . . . Seven factors. Not to mention all the ministrategies that come with each.

That's quite a lot.

Is it reasonable to expect yourself to make simultaneous changes in *all* of them? Would it be better to focus on one or two, introducing others as the first become routine? Or to ditch some of the less appealing or more complicated factors in favour of those that might produce the biggest psychological bang for the time/effort buck?

It's clear that strengthening the mind shares at least one big similarity with physical training: it's not something you can do for a bit and expect the effects to last. You have to keep at it, and *keep at it* (though, like physical training, it does get easier the more you do it).

It'd be crazy to expect something truly significant for nothing. And I don't. But – just how do I take everything that I've learned and produce a manageable, workable, integrated life-changing programme that I'm pretty confident I'll be able to stick to long term? And how do you?

First, I think, it might be useful to identify how easy – or otherwise – it's actually been to follow the recommendations that I've arrived at in each section. And having now tried them out, I think I'm in a position to attempt to be realistic about the kinds of differences they've made to my mind.

On no level, of course, is this a scientific experiment. I'm just one person. No one's evaluated me at the start or at the end – save myself. Though I might argue that I'm probably my own best judge, because if I do feel less stressed, more positive, more mentally energetic and more in control, who's to say otherwise? (My husband, I think, may be the only other person who could reasonably push for a vote.)

Anyway – back to the strategies, beginning in each case with a recap on the recommendations. (For a more complete review of these, see the checklist at the end of each chapter.)

I. MEDITATION

The recommendations?

- Choose a technique that suits you.

- Expect that it will take time to get used to it.

- You don't *need* to meditate for longer than ten to twenty minutes a day (in one session).

- Aim to meditate every day.

I decided to use Herbert Benson's technique: sitting comfortably and quietly, eyes closed, concentrating on a particular word (like 'love' or 'peace') on the out-breath, not worrying if other thoughts come to mind, simply saying, 'Oh, well,' and returning to my focus.

The first time I tried to meditate, it didn't work out that well.

It was the end of a work day, which is 3pm for me. I had fifteen minutes before I had to leave to get the kids. Surely, now would be the ideal time.

I laid down on the sofa, closed my eyes – and my mind was flooded with thoughts about things I hadn't done, or had done badly. *I forgot to add that quote to the feature before sending it off! I should have put Lucas's muddy cat teddy in the washing machine – it'll never be dry by bedtime! I still haven't replied to that email from Jane, telling me she's got a new job!*

It just wasn't working. I was lying there, trying to meditate, and getting more and more anxious about not being able to do it. And time was running out – because I had to get going or I'd be late for the pick-up . . .

Straight after work is, for me, it seems, a *bad* time to try to clear my mind of everyday thoughts. If it's your mind's first release all day, it has a lot of pressing stuff to deal with before it can calm down (at least, that's my experience).

So when can I do it? The mornings are no good, because the kids generally come in any time from six. It'll have to be some time between getting them to bed, at about 7.30pm, and going to sleep myself. The most obvious time seems to be as I go to bed. So I try it that night.

It begins reasonably enough. My mind isn't racing so badly now. At first, I silently say 'Peace' to myself on the in-breath as well as the out-breath, to keep regular thoughts right at bay. Then I experiment with dropping 'Peace' on the in-breath. And I find I can do it. In fact, it doesn't seem that necessary. There's something about breathing in that feels mentally constricting. If my mind starts to flood, it's on the out-breath.

So – I'm breathing evenly. Thoughts wander in on the in-breath, but I'm able gently to push them aside. I'm doing it. *I'm meditating. Now stop thinking that.* Herbert Benson advised not to set a ten-minute alarm but to have a clock near, and to peek at it every now and again, until the time is up. I do this. I've been meditating for three minutes. And then –

I fall asleep.

At least, I must have done, because when Lucas wakes me by tumbling into our bedroom the following morning, I don't remember checking the clock again or thinking my normal thoughts for a minute before opening my eyes, as I was meant to do.

So – the mornings are out. Bedtime is out.

After work will just *have* to be the time. Which means stopping work a little earlier, to give my thoughts a chance to burn off some energy before I ask them to be silent.

I try this. I'm not sleepy at this point, but I'm not hyper, either. I find it hard to *not* think, so I experiment with a multi-syllabic phrase on the out-breath. ('Hotel California' comes to mind, for some reason.) It helps, but soon becomes irritating. So instead I make 'Peace' last as long as my exhalation ('Peeeeeaaaaace'). And this really does work. I find I *can* clear my mind – at first, for only a minute to two, but as I practise it more regularly, for longer and longer.

Many people find that meditation apps or guided audio meditations help, especially at first. And while I had decided to use just Herbert Benson's technique, because I thought it would be simpler to stick to a single style, I find in the end that mixing it up *does* help, and that if I've run out of time, and haven't been able to give my mind a chance to settle first, a guided mindful body-scanning meditation can work really well to keep it focused.

So – I use Benson's method a couple of times a week and guided body scanning the rest. At least, I do during the week. (I know in theory the weekend's meant to be time off, but with young kids, that isn't exactly the case.)

What effects does this regular – if not daily – meditation have? I can't say for sure how I'd feel hour by hour if I hadn't made other changes as well. So I think I'll have to trust the research demonstrating ongoing benefits. But in the short term, it does feel very luxurious. And while I don't always *want* to do it (I've spent so long prioritising everything that comes under the heading of 'tasks' during the week, it can be hard to allow myself to take the time), I *always* feel better afterwards: thanks to the sense of energised peace it provides, I'm more at ease and less mentally exhausted, and so more ready to have fun with my kids.

2. EXERCISE

The recommendations?

- 'Lifestyle'-type exercise (gardening, housework, a stroll to the shops) should take place every day.

- Strength and flexibility training – which includes yoga or lifting weights – should ideally be done at least twice a week.

- One hundred and fifty minutes per week of 'moderate intensity' exercise will provide you with the maximum psychological benefits.

- If you can exercise outdoors, there seem to be psychological benefits.

- There may also be benefits from mindful exercise – but if music helps you, use it.

I drew up plans to walk to school at least a few mornings a week, to join a weekly outdoor adult fitness class and to go to the gym twice a week – once during the week and once at the weekend. We also got Dottie the dog, who, we decided, based on her cross-breed and the garden and walks to school, required a minimum of an additional half-hour run around a park each day.

So how did it all work out?

Remarkably – *incredibly*, to me – relatively easily.

At the outset, I was doing *no* exercise, except that involved in entertaining the kids (so walks in parks, around castles, etc.). I viewed my exercise plan with all the trepidation I'd expect a US Marine recruit to feel embarking on Hell Week. But what I absolutely had not counted on was this: the more exercise I do, the more I *want* to do. What at first looked to be a brutish list of episodes of self-torture has become some-thing I embrace, and have even expanded.

I'm no marathon-runner (I don't go further than about three kilometres on the treadmill at the gym). I haven't taken up mountain-biking or cross-country skiing. But I have realised that exercise makes me feel good. So I want to do it. So it becomes easier. And so more enjoyable. It's been a complete revelation. (And on a physical level, too. I realise now how easy it is for fit people to walk up a hill. They have proper hamstrings. Muscles actually *help* you in daily life. Like I said – a revelation.)

To start with, the gym visits *were* hard. I worked out a plan with a trainer, based on my fitness level and what I wanted to achieve. It consisted of twenty minutes of high-intensity interval training (bouts of sprints interspersed with much longer periods of walking on the treadmill, building up to slow jogging as I got fitter), then ten minutes of squats and arm weights and ten minutes of stomach crunches and more core body work.

Even at first, I didn't mind the weights or the floor exercises too much. It was the treadmill that killed me. Six months on, there are still days when I have to just force myself *not* to stop until I've finished. I do what I have to – focus on the song lyrics, think about what I'm going to eat for dinner – *anything* to ignore the fact my legs are moving. But the hideous days are now a lot less frequent. There's even the odd day when I feel like I'm flying, and the joy of that is hard to convey – especially, as it's so unexpected.

Still, whether or not I've enjoyed the gym session, I *never* regret going. Afterwards, *one hundred per cent of the time*, I feel good. More energised. Clearer-headed. More positive. Less stressed. In fact, the more stressed I am at the start, the better exercise feels (one reason, I think, it always feels better to me in the late afternoon, rather than the morning). To have my heart beating for a physical reason seems to loosen my system up, and I come out of the gym feeling a lot calmer than I did before. But the gym isn't even the best bit.

At first, the weekly outdoor fitness class wasn't pleasant. Especially, as I was easily the least fit of the five or six mothers in the group. But, there was social contact (good), even cama-raderie (good) and after a month or two, I started to notice a positive impact from the exercise itself.

One October morning, cold enough for hoodies, jackets and gloves, there's not much talk as we arrive at the playing field and Cory, the trainer, who also plays scrum half for the Sheffield Eagles rugby league club (yes, that's right, the mums' fitness trainer . . . there are times I think sport stars probably outnumber normal people in Sheffield), sets us off on a couple of warm-up laps. The sky's grey, the grass is rain-sodden and muddy, the view is of houses and an empty playground. It's not inspiring. But as we move into the stations – pushing on through burpees and mountain climbers, Russian twists and squat jumps – the heavens open. The rain pours, and (though I hate the cold and the wet) that's when I start to feel really good. I'm not cold – the exercise has seen to that – so I can face the day with a straight back, instead of hunched shoulders. I normally hibernate at the first sign of rain, but I'm defying the weather, getting on with what I want to do, despite it. By the end, we're smiling and joking, laughing about how the name of one particularly tough trainer – Levi – is an anagram of Evil, complaining good-humouredly about aching necks and painful legs. The woman next to me says: 'I was in a really bad mood this morning. If I'd stayed at home, I'd just have plodded on. This has really snapped me out of it.' And I understand completely. In fact, this feels *better* than an almond croissant and the *New Yorker*.

Then there are the walks to school. I'm forced to accept that I enjoy them. Because we do it not twice a week as I'd planned, but, now Lucas has moved to the pre-school at Jakob's school, four mornings out of five, and if it isn't pouring with rain and/or freezing, we walk home as well. Now they're used to it, the boys don't mind. They like picking flowers from the hedges, gathering conkers, or stomping on frosty leaves. We start the day feeling just a little fresher, our senses alert, instead of dulled by the car.

Finally, there's Dottie. She has broken what was in retrospect my least healthy work habit: sitting down at my desk and not leaving it, except for bathroom breaks or to make a sandwich to take back. Now I take a half-hour walk with her every lunchtime. Before I actually *did this*, I would have viewed those half hours as lost time. Now, I appreciate how much more productive I am in the afternoons. I always take my phone with me, not to check emails or Twitter, but because so many useful thoughts come to mind while I'm walking that I need a note-taker to get them down. I come back to work refreshed, and full of new ideas. It happens at the gym, too. I've lost count of the number of times I've had to dash off the treadmill to write down something I can't afford to forget. (Apologies here to Richard Follett, physiotherapist: judging by the shrinkage of your pile of business cards on the front desk, you no doubt assumed you were about to get a slew of new clients. I'm afraid it was me, taking them to write on the back . . .)

Exercise clears my mind, makes me more insightful, calmer, more energised, more positive and less stressed (not to mention physically healthier and more toned). And I know there's a huge amount of research championing the importance of exercise for mental and emotional wellbeing. Which is why I'm going to place exercise at the top of my mind-changing list – and at the heart of my long-term plan.

3. DIET

The recommendations?

- Ignore faddy diets. Aim for a 'healthy balanced' diet (see the NHS's 'Eat well plate' – http://www.nhs.uk/Livewell/ Goodfood/Pages/eatwell-plate.aspx).

- Try to eat a broad range of fruit and vegetables.

- Sugar, caffeine, alcohol, chocolate and wheat are the foods most often identified as being potential mood-wreckers.

- If you can't honestly say that your diet is 'healthy and balanced', you *may* want to consider taking a multivitamin.

- Be very cautious about taking other nutritional supplements.

Thanks, I suppose, to my prediabetes, I *had* to take a close look at my diet, and make some significant changes. Those changes have led to a diet that's pretty 'healthy and balanced': porridge and grapes for breakfast, banana for a mid-morning snack, chicken or fish and salads for lunch (perhaps with a slice of soy and linseed bread), nuts for an afternoon snack and a dinner low in fat and high-GI carbs (no more pizza, no creamy pasta sauces, no chips), with fruit for pudding. My only guilty pleasure? A square of my favourite dark chocolate, two or three times a day.

At first, I imagined it would be difficult to follow this kind of diet, just from a practical point of view. Lunch used to be a white bread ham or chicken sandwich. It took five seconds to make. Making a tasty and filling salad, I thought, would take *ages*. Until I realised that I don't have to make them. Without naming names, there's a high street food store that sells a variety of delicious salads in little pots. They aren't even that expensive. And, I should emphasise, they're not just leaves. I choose ones with quinoa or couscous because I want carbs, just not the bad ones. Now, at lunchtime, I empty some salad on a plate, chuck on some smoked mackerel or chicken and add half an avocado – and it takes only fractionally longer than making an unhealthy and far less tasty ham sandwich. If I'm out and about, it's harder. I can't eat most sandwiches. But I can eat baked potatoes or salads. Harder, but not impossible.

The potential practical problems were not my biggest concerns, though. No more biscuits. No more cake. How would I do it?

All I can say is that, at first, it was *hard*. Not taking a biscuit when I got some out for the kids was tough. Lining up to buy a coffee in my local cafe and looking at all the brownies and cheesecakes parading themselves in the glass counter right in front of me was *hell*.

In the end, I used a few different strategies to help.

First, I stopped buying the biscuits and other sweet stuff that *I* like. Whereas the kids love Penguin bars and digestive biscuits, I don't find them that appealing.

Second, whenever I felt like eating a biscuit, I forced myself to take a small handful of nuts from the cupboard instead. My hunger (and/or snack habit) satisfied, I no longer craved a cookie. After a while – maybe five or six weeks – it became routine and I honestly no longer find myself even thinking about biscuits.

Third, I tried simply not looking at all the cakes in the coffee shop counters. But they make that virtually impossible, don't they? So I decided that I *would* look at them, but I'd sneer at them as 'weak people's food'. Unreasonable? Maybe. But it worked. I was so determined to be mentally tougher (to decide to do something, and *just do it*), that eventually I found myself able to stare even a chocolate fudge cake in the face. Now, about four months on, cake isn't a problem. I queue up for coffee, and I notice all the sweet stuff almost absent-mindedly. I don't have to fight it any more.

Because I have a problem with regulating sugar, and too much or too little sugar in the blood can seriously affect mental energy and equilibrium, it's not surprising that these dietary changes have made me feel a lot better. I don't get those crushing episodes of overwhelming fatigue any more. That's the biggest difference.

I eat a lot more fruit and vegetables than I did, and less processed meat, and I can't really tell if this makes me feel any more positive or more energetic, but I *know* it's better for me.

And now, after being on my diet for nearly six months, I can tell you there are two other huge upsides:

One: I feel mentally stronger, because I've stuck at it. It turns out that I *can* do something that I think is tough.

Two: I've lost quite a bit of weight. This is no crash diet. It took a while – probably two or three months – before I noticed my clothes had become loose. (We don't have scales in our house. Well, we do, but the kids have trashed both sets by jumping on them.) I'm now a dress size and a half smaller than when I started. And I feel that I eat pretty well. I don't ever feel hungry. I still eat some potatoes and pasta and bread. I just don't eat huge amounts in any one sitting – and I don't eat all that other stuff that piles on the pounds, like battered fish, chips, pizza and cheesecake. At least, most of the time, I don't. I *need* to follow the diet, but I don't want it to cloud my life. So if I'm on holiday, I'll eat dessert if I want to (the three days James and I just spent in Paris would have been so cruel without that clause). And, if we're out for dinner with friends, I won't rule out having some of the pudding. But now, I find my body is so used to my healthy diet that if I eat anything creamy, it revolts. (I was prepared to accept a churning stomach, nausea and therefore sleep loss for the sake of a chestnut and orange panna cotta in one of Paris's hottest restaurants. I find I'm less willing to suffer for a chain-pizza-place tiramisu.) On the whole, the sweet, rich things I used to love are a lot less tempting.

I'm telling you all this, even though you probably don't have prediabetes*, because my diet is a healthy, balanced diet

---

* Or do you? According to Diabetes UK, one in seventy-four people in the UK has undiagnosed prediabetes. This is a 'shocking' statistic, points out the organisation, which urges people to check themselves on the Diabetes Risk Score Test (http://riskscore.diabetes.org.uk/start), and see a GP if they turn out to be a high risk. But let me add my own comment to that. The standard diagnostic test for diabetes is a fasting blood-sugar test. You skip breakfast, and your blood is taken in the morning. If your sugar levels are abnormally high, you'll get a diagnosis of prediabetes or diabetes. My diabetes specialist in Australia made me promise something. She said, in the future, your GP will tell you that a fasting blood test is fine, *but it isn't.* What you really need, she told me, is what's called a fasting glucose-tolerance test. You have the fasting blood sample taken, drink a glucose solution and sit still for two hours, then your blood is taken again. This second test shows how well your body copes with a sugar hit. My fasting levels are in the normal range. But my results after the glucose test are way up the scale. If I'd had only the fasting test, which my GP here indeed tried

– as recommended for emotional as well as physical health. And it's the kind you *can* stick to long term *and* lose weight.

If you do want to change your diet, and cut back on sugar and on 'bad food' generally, my own experience is that while it's tricky at first, after a while – perhaps six weeks – it is, surprisingly, not too bad, and the more you stick at it, the easier it gets. In fact, I've already decided that if (unlikely as it may be) my next diabetes test comes back normal, I'll carry on with the diet anyway. It just feels too good not to do it.

One final note: fasting is not recommended for anyone with diabetes, because of the problems with regulating sugar levels.

4. SLEEP AND CIRCADIAN RHYTHMS

The recommendations?

- Many of us do best on seven or eight hours a night, but you might need more or less than that.

- Spend as much time outside as you can to help to align

---

to convince me was what was required, I'd still be undiagnosed. *That* is also pretty shocking to me. Yes, it takes up more of a nurse's time, and the costs the NHS more to process than a single blood test, and no doubt the regular test does pick up a lot of cases of full-blown diabetes – but what's the cost of leaving people like me undiagnosed? If it weren't for the emphatic advice of my specialist, I'd still be eating cake, suffering debilitating episodes of fatigue and brain fogs and causing who knows what damage to my body and brain. It makes me angry. Justifiably angry. This is just the type of thing, in fact, that it's no good at all to keep calm about.

your body's clock with the day. Keep lights dim in the evening, and minimise evening exposure to bright, artificial light.

- If you wake early, but it takes you a long time to feel alert, or you don't feel tired until late at night but need an alarm clock to wake you, consider adjusting your sleep/wake cycles using artificial light.

- Working with daily patterns in mood and alertness, rather than fighting them might be helpful.

- Naps of 90–110 minutes are most effective for improving emotional wellbeing, but may leave you groggy. Short ten-minute 'power naps' can help boost alertness.

- Try to keep to a regular bed- and wake time.

I'm a 'hummingbird', the most common circadian type. I generally feel sleepy about 11pm (or I would, if I hadn't been woken by kids or the dog in the night and consequently fallen asleep on the sofa at 8pm) and wake at about 7am. I don't feel too groggy in the morning, so I don't think there's any need for me to try to tweak my circadian patterns.

The only sleep-related changes I've been able to make are dietary. Though I was kind of aware that drinking more than a glass of wine in an evening affected my sleep, I've forced myself now to recognise this, and to make a conscious effort to remember it. I also find that restricting myself to a single square of dark chocolate in the evening does mean I'm now a lot less likely to wake in the night.

Still, given my young kids, I'm not exactly a great model for change when it comes to sleep and circadian rhythms. I think the main message – and the one I'll try to remember in the future – is this: if you're trying to get by on what's 'too little' sleep *for you*, and you can rectify this, the impact on your mental and emotional wellbeing could be huge.

5. THOUGHTS

The recommendations?

- Mindfulness without judgement can help if you regularly think destructively negative thoughts, as can a cognitive approach.

- More optimistic people are more psychologically resilient.

- Self-compassion can help with negative thoughts.

- Compassion meditation and a more generalised loving-kindness meditation can help to build meaningful social relationships and reduce stress.

I have pointless, destructive, negative thoughts. I'm sure most of us do. The hardest thing for me has been to recognise that they're pointless. I'm used to thinking of my thoughts as being useful – that if I'm ruminating on something, it's got to be worthwhile, because surely I'm gleaning a deeper understanding of what makes me feel fulfilled, or perhaps there are some lessons in regard to life or myself that I'll be able to extract if I can only analyse my feelings and my situation more thoroughly.

What I've had to accept is that you don't *find* calmness or contentment by striving to identify external factors that could generate these feelings – you *create* them. And you create them within your own mind. I'm not sure I've completely assimilated that idea. But I recognise it on an intellectual level.

I also realise now that on days when I felt low, I used to look (pointlessly) for thought-related explanations: if *this* is how I'm feeling, I must be unfulfilled, or exhausted, or bored, or otherwise dissatisfied with life. This mood must, I reasoned, be reflecting a problem. And then, I'd start to look for reasons for why I might feel unfulfilled, or bored, or dissatisfied. And of course you can always find some, if you look. So a vague awareness of a negative feeling led to negative thoughts, which spun off into other negative thoughts, which made my mood sink still further. And all of that might have been avoided if I'd been doing regular exercise or meditation, or just slept better over the past week, making that original seed of a negative mood far less likely to sprout.

When I do now find myself starting to think negative thoughts, I ask myself, as a Stoic would: *Do you have any control over what you're worrying about?* If the answer's 'No', I try to move on. If I find that difficult, I use the mindful technique of 'stepping back'. I try to see that line of thought as a bus I don't need to get on. Both work for me, to some extent. Actually, I find the Stoic approach more satisfying, but sometimes it's the bus-avoidance that really gets me out of a rut.

I also get a lot out of the self-compassionate approach. The idea that it's fine to give yourself a break – that this can be positive and useful, in fact, rather than weak – is just so appealing. It seems common among many of my friends and acquaintances (especially, but not solely, the women) to have a negative self-attitude: to publicly put themselves down, belittle successes and despair over failings. Yes, of course, it's healthy to be wary of arrogance, immodesty and naive positivity, but tipping the scale so heavily the other way surely isn't the answer.

If I find myself thinking, *Why am I so rash and impulsive?* I take the compassionate tack, and try to think of what a friend might say. Yes, I've left or turned down some wonderful jobs. But if I hadn't, I'd never have lived in Cairo with a couple of school friends, which was an incredible experience; I'd never have written those five books of fiction (something I'd always wanted to do); I wouldn't have met James again, and Jakob and Lucas wouldn't exist. I didn't think I was mad when I made all those decisions when I was younger, and I really shouldn't criticise myself for them now.

The other thought-related area I decided to work on was optimism. There's so much work finding that optimistic people cope better with stress, and are mentally tougher, and so more capable of setting and achieving goals. The truth is, this is something I haven't got to yet. I've been focusing on trying to counteract overly negative thinking. My next challenge will be to try to become more optimistic.

6. MENTAL TOUGHNESS

The recommendations?

- Develop an optimistic attitude.

- Break a challenge into small parts, and reward yourself each step of the way.

- Concentrate on the process – on the *present,* and what you have to *do* next.

- If you've made your mind up to do something, tell yourself you're going to like it.

- Develop strategies for coping with suddenly rising anxiety or anger.

- If you're losing confidence, focus on (and play to) your strengths.

- Stress inoculation can build mental toughness.

- To strengthen your self-control, you have to *use* it.

- When contemplating a tough challenge, make sure *you*

really want to do it – and set your own goals for achieving it.

I had to develop my mental toughness to cope with my diet. And I did use some of the techniques I learned from Ian Maynard, the psychologist, as well as Matt Stults-Kohlemainen (the former US Marine) and others. I remembered that I'd been pretty successful at sticking to the diet while pregnant with Lucas. That gave me a degree of optimism that I'd be able to do it. I did force myself to concentrate on the moment (*not* taking a proffered biscuit or crisp) rather than thinking about 'sticking to the diet'. Looking at cakes as being 'weak people's food' helped me decide to like the challenge, which, in turn, made it seem a whole lot more achievable.

I haven't found that breathing exercises or .bs (sinking your focus to your feet and then to the breath – see p. 243) really work for me when it comes to resisting sweet things. But .bs do help me hugely in another area – keeping my temper. In fact, of all the techniques I've learned for being calmer and more in control, this is the one I've shared most with friends. It's so simple and so quick, and it really does work for me in a way that 'take a deep breath' or 'count to ten' never did.

'Stress inoculation' is something else I've considered. It's natural, for most of us, to shy away from scary experiences. Not safe-scary ones, like going on a rollercoaster, but experiences that genuinely could leave you worse off. Like speaking in public. This has never been something I've thrown myself at. It could, I decide, justifiably count as something that I fear. And I know it's not just me. Psychologists seeking to generate anxiety in lab volunteers find that public speaking reliably does the trick.

So, when I'm asked to talk in the school assembly (I know, it's hardly the United Nations, but still), I say yes. While I'm not terrified, I am nervous. It's the senior school assembly. They're teenagers. If they're bored, they'll show it. If I forget what I'm meant to be talking about, I'll look a fool in front of hundreds of people, including teachers that I'll see again and again. On the morning of my talk, as the headmaster introduces me, I sit beside the packed rows of chairs thinking, *why* did I ever say yes? But of course it's too late now to back out. So I stand up, and I talk.

As soon as I start, I feel a lot less nervous. I find I can remember everything I meant to say. When, at one point, a fourteen- or fifteen-year-old boy smirks, I find I'm able to address his scepticism, making him look bad, I think, rather than me. (Victory over a child! I'm clearly still far from perfect . . .) All in all, though, it goes pretty well. And afterwards, I *do* feel good. When was the last time I did something I was scared of? I honestly can't remember. And while I didn't just ski down Everest or do anything that would count as tough in most people's books, I felt nervous, and I did it — and I'd do it again, and would be less nervous next time. This was not the kind of transformative life experience beloved of Hollywood. But I *do* feel stronger. Not hugely, but noticeably. And I'll take that.

7. THE SENSES

The recommendations?

- Music that *you* like is most likely to make you feel good.

- For relaxation, birdsong may be better than silence.

- Try to break the music 'rules' – sing or play an instrument regardless of how good you are at it.

- Swedish massage has physiological stress-relieving effects. Simple touch has similar, though less strong, effects.

- Sex relieves anxiety and improves mood.

- Choose a style of decor that reflects who you are at your best and what *you* value.

- There is no clear relationship between wall colour and mood or behaviour.

- Of all the scents investigated there's most evidence to suggest a relationship with mood for lavender, vanillin and lemon oil.

I decide to have a massage twice a week . . . in my dreams. If I could afford it, maybe I would, but I can't. No, the changes I adopt – and that I feel make a real difference – involve music and scent.

First, as I said, I decide to use music at the peak stress point in my day: in the morning, when I'm trying to get the kids ready to leave on time. Not relaxing music, but upbeat, positive music – a mix of songs they like, and stuff we all like – because I'm thinking it might help to stop me getting cross and to keep the mood upbeat. And it *does* really help. I don't know what the neighbours think about 'Lightning Bolt' by Jake Bugg (Lucas's number-one choice) booming through the walls at 7am, but I suspect they'll take that over screeches.

As far as scent is concerned, I get a simple oil burner and use it in my office. While I know there's research suggesting that lavender, vanillin and lemon oil can all promote a good mood, personally I find vanillin and lemon oil a little sweet, so (though I know it has anaesthetic properties) I go with lavender. There's the smell itself, but also the pleasant memories that go with it (childhood summer holidays in the south of France; a gorgeous lavender farm in the Hunter Valley near Sydney . . .). And I find I like the fact that my sense of smell is being stimulated. It adds a layer of experience to sitting at a desk in the silence (I tried working with a song on repeat, and found it hard) with nothing to look at but my monitor and the Velux window vista of rain-spattered grey.

If I was going to choose just one sense-related factor to focus more on, though, it would have to be music. Many people naturally self-medicate with music. I've realised I wasn't using it enough – and the more I do use it, the better I feel. And so does the family. The kids will dance to anything – the electric toy guitar, some random song in the middle of a *Scooby-Doo*. And now, instead of just watching them, I persuade myself to get up and dance too.

So how do I feel now?

The answer is: an awful lot better than when I started out.

Looking back at everything I've learned, and all the fascinating people I've met – from Anne Dutton, the ageless American yoga expert, to Gary Roberts, the former soldier, people from such different backgrounds, but with something in common: they've reflected on what gives them psychological strength, and were willing to share their insights with me – my overwhelming sense is simply of gladness that I embarked on all this. I just can't imagine being without those experiences, and this knowledge. It seems a little crazy that I didn't seek it sooner. But as that thought strikes, I rebuff it with self-compassion: *I've made the effort. I should be pleased I've done it now.*

And now I have, I feel, a pretty good understanding of the top factors for forging a strong mind, which makes a big difference just in itself. But, even better, I know how to use them.

If I start to get dragged down by negative thoughts, I have a couple of go-to strategies to help. If I feel my stress level soaring, I can do a .b, and burst the bubble. If I fail to meet my expectations, I know it can help to give myself a break (while not losing sight of my goals). But I've been most surprised by what a difference exercise makes. If I could go back to my late teenage self, and argue for just *one* change, it would be this: to do more exercise for the sake of my mind, if not my body.

Now back to the issue I raised at the start of this chapter: the sheer number of recommendations.

If I had to rank them, I'd put exercise top. Sleep and nutrition would have to come joint second, with meditation right behind. For me, these are the fundamentals. They all act to prevent low mood and stress and anxiety, as well as to treat those problems. Who knows, if you get the fundamentals right, maybe you'll feel so much better, you won't need to work at trying to become more optimistic or to re-appraise your thoughts.

Does that still seem like a lot to change in one go?

While some of my suggestions are quite demanding, a lot don't have to take much time or effort. Little bits of change *can* go a long way.

If I'm early for the school pick-up, I might spend five minutes thinking nice thoughts about other people. If I'm starting to feel lethargic at my desk, I might run up and down the stairs a couple of times. With something like optimism, deciding to be optimistic about just one thing in the day, or just one conversation, can only help.

There's quite a lot to think about, but if you're feeling apprehensive, push your concerns to one side, and draw up your own list *now*, before you think of reasons to prevaricate. As the mental-toughness experts advocate, *just do it*. And then make a start – even if to begin with, it's just in one area.

I remember once having to read *The 7 Habits of Highly Effective People* by Stephen Covey. (I write 'having to' because it was related to something I was working on, and wasn't the kind of book I'd have chosen for myself.) I'd expected business-type jargon and waffle. But it wasn't like that at all. It made a lot of sense. For a while, I became practically evangelical about some of the techniques. My friend Michelle had just moved from Damascus to Philadelphia, and was finding it hard to adapt and to manage everything she wanted to get done during the day, I told her about the '7 habits'. Her response was: '*Seven*? How am I going to manage *seven*?' (Fair enough.) I remember saying: 'Well, you don't have to be *highly* effective. A *bit more* effective would be good?' And she went with that. One or two habits. A bit more effective.

Surely if I'm thinking now of psychological strength, being *quite* strong is so much better than not feeling strong at all? Still, if you can integrate several strategies, you should stand a better chance of feeling a lot stronger, a lot faster. And that's it. My ultimate recommendation.

I'm aware this isn't exactly the single shining secret so commonly offered in self-help. I know there are all kinds of books out there that claim to hold The Answer to everything that's wrong with your life. *That* kind of book I'd call the killer heels. Attractive. Confident. Apparently strong. Fundamentally weak. At the risk of sounding like one of those trite-but-true slogans (like '*If it doesn't challenge you, it doesn't change you*', which is printed on the wall of my gym), I can't help feeling it's this – the sensible shoes – that'll take you on a real journey. I'm not sure exactly where I'll end up. But I've come quite a way.

Take yesterday. It held, I appreciate, only a small, domestic challenge – but I was never good with them, and that always bothered me.

It's the kids' bedtime, the other peak stress point in my day, because we're all tired, and they invariably try to argue that they're still hungry and need to stay downstairs to eat more post-banana Cheerios, and why can't they just have one more *Scooby-Doo*, and why am I the meanest parent in the world? To my shame, I often used to bully them upstairs: 'If you're not up there before I count to three . . .' But while I'm tired tonight, I don't feel as shattered as I used to. I find I have the energy to ask if they want to ride a dragon to bed.

Giggling, they take it in turns to climb on my back. I jump up the stairs (I have hamstrings now!), pretending to be a wild dragon, and as I drop them in the bathroom, they're still giggling. The good humour carries us through the teeth-brushing. James is away, so I take them both into Lucas's room for stories. They get to choose one each. In the past, I'd often have been harrying: 'Come on, choose one! It's so late!' and while I love to cuddle them, I'd rush through the text, one eye on the clock. Tonight, I'm mindful of being *here,* present with my kids, the most precious things in my world.

Stories done, Jakob goes to wait on the landing while I sing Lucas's regulation three songs before kissing him good night. Sometimes, Jakob waits quietly. Often, he doesn't. Tonight, just as I'm finishing 'Twinkle Twinkle', a remote-controlled car comes zooming into the room and Lucas jerks upright. My first instinct, still, is to yell: 'Jakob!' But I do a .be. And it gives me the space I need to calm down enough not to yell.

I give Lucas a stroke, go out and tell Jakob firmly but calmly to put the remote control down and wait in his room, then I go back to give Lucas his regulation three kisses and three cuddles (only the dog is a bigger stickler for routine). Lucas tucked in, I move on to Jakob, and while only a minute ago, I felt mad with him, I'm now completely calm. In the past, the irritation would have festered. I'd have felt it for a long time afterwards, as tension in my chest. This evening, my body and mind became stressed, but recovered almost instantly.

So, yes, I didn't just climb Everest or discuss my opinions on all seven volumes of *Remembrance of Things Past* in French . . . but I *do* feel that I've come quite a way.

And now at last, I like where I'm going.

ACKNOWLEDGEMENTS

Thanks, of course, to everyone who spared the time to offer their insights and knowledge, but special thanks to Matt Stults-Kohlemainen and Larry Parsons, for all your efforts, and to Kate and Ed Douglas, not just for being willing to subject yourselves to my 'cooking' but for reading some of the text, and making helpful suggestions.

I first approached some of my interviewees (Richard Hammersley, Michael Terman, Stacey Young-McCaughan, Barbara Fredrickson, Mark Mattson, Herbert Benson, Manoj Bhasin) for features for *New Scientist*, and others (Mark Williams, everyone at Altrincham Grammar School for Girls, Dennis Charney) for a story on strategies to enhance resilience in schoolchildren for the online science magazine, *Mosaic*. Thanks again to Kate Douglas at *New Scientist*, and to Mun-Keat Looi at *Mosaic* – both wonderful editors.

Thank you to Karolina Sutton, my first-class agent at Curtis

Brown – and to Norah Perkins for much-appreciated support in some of those early meetings.

Thank you, too, to Liz Gough, my editor at Yellow Kite. This book is significantly better for your suggestions, Liz. Thanks also to Anne Newman, Emily Robertson and Becca Mundy.

Thanks to Gaia Vince and Jo Marchant for your advice, and 'just' for being there to talk to.

Finally, biggest thanks to James for all your support, always.

GLOSSARY

Amygdala Your brain's 'alarm bell'; the bit that fires in response to something emotionally charged, like a hostile boss striding towards your desk.

BDNF (Brain-Derived Neurotrophic Factor) A protein that keeps brain cells healthy and stimulates new ones to grow. Dubbed by brain/exercise specialist John Ratey, 'Miracle-Gro for the brain'.

Body scanning A style of meditation. It involves shifting awareness around your body.

CBT (cognitive behavioural therapy) An evidence-based therapy designed to change the way you think and behave. Used most commonly to treat anxiety and depression.

Circadian rhythms Daily cycles in attention, alertness, energy and mood, regulated by the body's own internal clock.

Compassion meditation Meditations centring on the wish to relieve others' suffering (Buddhist origin).

Cortisol A long-acting stress hormone. It helps the body 'gear up' to deal with a demand, which could be just facing the morning or coping with high expectations at work.

Dopamine A neurotransmitter (brain-signalling chemical) involved in motivation and feelings of pleasure.

Flavonols A sub-group of **polyphenols** (see over). Found in cocoa, for example.

GABA (gamma aminobutyric acid) A neurotransmitter (brain-signalling chemical), low levels of which are associated with anxiety. Many anti-anxiety drugs target GABA.

GI (glycaemic index) High-GI foods (like pies and cakes) produce a bigger rise in blood sugar levels.

Grit 'Sustaining interest in and effort toward very long-term goals.'

Hippocampus The brain region where memories are organised and stored.

HPA (hypothalamic-pituitary-adrenal axis) A brain-signalling route that plays a crucial role in the response to stress.

Hypothalamus A tiny control centre in the brain, responsible for regulating many key processes, including heart rate and body temperature.

Limbic system An evolutionary old set of brain regions. The limbic system deals with memories, emotions and impulses, and handles the 'fight-or-flight' response.

Loving-kindness meditation Meditation centred on the wish for happiness for others (Buddhist origin).

Mantra A sound reputed in the Hindu Vedic tradition to allow entrance to a deep state of meditation. 'Om' is a famous one.

Mindfulness Directing attention to what is happening *right now*, with curiosity and acceptance.

Phenolics A sub-group of 'polyphenols' (see below).

Polyphenols A group of chemicals found in many fruits, vegetables and cereals, as well as tea, coffee, chocolate and olive oil (and, thanks to the grape skins, in red wine). Eating polyphenols may be healthy because they reduce inflammation in the body. (Exactly why they are healthy is still debated, as I mention in the diet chapter.)

Prebiotics Foods that can change the bacterial composition of the gut.

Probiotics Microbes that are ingested to improve gut health.

Prefrontal cortex The 'thinking' part of the brain, which can overrule impulses – say, to shout at your kids, eat an entire chocolate cake or have sex with a handsome stranger.

Relaxation Response A state of physiological relaxation – the opposite of the fight-or-flight response.

Serotonin A neurotransmitter (brain-signalling chemical) involved in mood. Some anti-depressants work by altering levels of serotonin in the brain.

FURTHER READING AND RESOURCES

The Relaxation Response, Herbert Benson with Miriam Z. Klipper (HarperTorch 2000); www.relaxationresponse.org

The Architecture of Happiness, Alain de Botton (Penguin, 2007)

Plants and the Human Brain, Dr David Kennedy (Oxford University Press, 2014)

Cure: A journey into the science of mind over body, Jo Marchant (Canongate, to be published January 2016)

Spark!: How exercise will improve the performance of your brain, Dr John J. Ratey and Eric Hagerman (Quercus, 2010)

The Philosophy of Cognitive-Behavioural Therapy: Stoic Philosophy as Rational and Cognitive Psychotherapy, Donald Robertson (Karnac, 2010)

Flourish: A New Understanding of Happiness and Well-being – and How to Achieve Them, Martin Seligman (Nicholas Brealey Publishing, 2011)

Resilience: The Science of Mastering Life's Greatest Challenges, Steven M. Southwick and Dennis S. Charney (Cambridge University Press, 2012)

Chronotherapy: Resetting Your Inner Clock to Boost Mood, Alertness, and Quality Sleep, Michael Terman and Ian McMahan (Avery, 2012)

Mindfulness: A Practical Guide to Finding Peace in a Frantic World, Professor Mark Williams and Dr Danny Penman (Piatkus, 2011); franticworld.com

A list from the US Food and Drug Administration of companies found guilty of 'health fraud' for making, among other things, unsubstantiated claims for nutritional supplements: http://www.fda.gov/ForConsumers/ProtectYourself/HealthFraud/ucm255474.htm

'Brain Basics, Understanding Sleep': http://www.ninds.nih.gov/disorders/brain_basics/understanding_sleep.htm

'Circadian Rhythms Fact Sheet', National Institute of General Medical Sciences: http://www.nigms.nih.gov/Education/Pages/Factsheet_CircadianRhythms.aspx

Guided self-compassion meditations: http://www.self-compassion.org/guided-self-compassion-meditations-mp3.html

Stoicism today: http://blogs.exeter.ac.uk/stoicismtoday/

'Stoic Week 2014 handbook': http://philosophy-of-cbt.com/2014/11/22/stoic-week-2014-handbook-pdf-and-mp3-files/

Transcendental Meditation: uk.tm.org (UK); tm.org (US)

For information on regimens and dawn/dusk simulators, visit Michael Terman's website: www.cet.org.

For Martin Seligman's optimism test, visit: https://www.authentichappiness.sas.upenn.edu/testcenter

There are also a lot of apps designed to help with meditation, exercise and healthy diet programmes. A web search will return plenty of reviews of the various options. I'm not being lazy here. I just can't justifiably single any out for special mention.

REFERENCES

INTRODUCTION: I KNEW I HAD A PROBLEM . . .

Hype in media health coverage Sumner, B., et al., The association between exaggeration in health-related science news and academic press releases: retrospective observational study, *BMJ* 2014;349:g7015 (doi: http://dx.doi.org/10.1136/bmj.g7015).

Experts and pet theories see Yatz, Dr David, Yale University, quoted in Hamblin, J., 'This is Your Brain on Gluten', *The Atlantic*, 20 December 2013. (http://www.theatlantic.com/health/archive/2013/12/this-is-your-brain-on-gluten/282550/)

Negative consequences of seeking happiness Kenrick, D. T., *Psychology Today*, November 2011, https://www.psychologytoday.com/blog/sex-murder-and-the-meaning-life/201211/if-you-pursue-happiness-you-may-find-loneliness.

CHAPTER ONE: CLEAR YOUR MIND

The Relaxation Response Benson, H., et al., 'The Relaxation Response: Psychophysiologic Aspects and Clinical Applications', *Psychiatry in Medicine*, 6 (1975), pp. 87–98 and Benson, H., *The Relaxation Response* (HarperTorch, 2000).

William Hague and TM Hughes, Colin, 'Profile: William Hague', *Guardian*, Saturday, 4 July 1998.

TM and crime-fighting in Washington, D.C. Abrahams, Marc, 'Scientist fighting crime and gravity', *Guardian*, Monday, 8 October 2012, http://www.theguardian.com/education/2012/oct/08/meditation-crime-prevention-research; see also Park, R. *Voodoo Science: The road from foolishness to fraud* (Oxford University Press, 2000, p. 30).

Mindfulness and the military Stanley, E. A., et al., 'Mindfulness-Based Mind Fitness Training: A Case Study of High-Stress Predeployment Military Cohort', *Cognitive and Behavioural Practice*, vol. 18 (2011), p. 566.

Neuroscience and meditation Desbordes, G., 'Neuroscience and Meditation', lecture, Massachusetts General Hospital & Boston University, 18 September 2012, http://isites.harvard.edu/fs/docs/icb.topic1117383.files/Neuroscience_Meditation_2012temp.pdf

Impacts of mindfulness on the brain Hölzel, Britta K., et al., 'Mindfulness practice leads to increases in regional brain gray matter density', *Psychiatry Research: Neuroimaging*, vol. 191 (2011), pp. 36–43.

Mindfulness and stress Williams, K. A., et al., 'Evaluation of a Wellness-based Mindfulness Stress Reduction Intervention:

A Controlled Trial', *American Journal of Health Promotion*, vol. 15, no. 6 (2001), pp. 422–32.

MBCT compared with other depression treatments Williams, M., et al., 'Mindfulness-Based Cognitive Therapy for Preventing Relapse in Recurrent Depression: A Randomized Dismantling Trial', *Journal of Consulting and Clinical Psychology*, vol. 82 (April 2014), pp. 275–86.

Mindfulness in schools trial Kuyken, W., et al., 'Effectiveness of the Mindfulness in Schools Programme: non-randomised controlled feasibility study', *British Journal of Psychiatry*, 203 (2013), pp. 126–31.

The Mindfulness in Schools Project (developer of the dot.be course) www.mindfulnessinschools.org

Mind wandering and creativity Baird, B., et al., 'Inspired by Distraction: Mind Wandering Facilitates Creative Incubation', *Psychological Science*, vol. 23 (2012), pp. 1117–22.

Mental rest and insight Kounios, John, 'The origins of insight in resting-state brain activity', *Neuropsychologia*, vol. 46 (2008), pp. 281–91.

A mind at rest and memory Tambini, A., et al. *Neuron*, vol. 65 (2010), pp. 280–90, doi: http://dx.doi.org/10.1016/j.neuron.2010.01.001.

Mindfulness vs mind-wandering Schooler, J. W., et al., 'The Middle Way: Finding the balance between mindfulness and mind-wandering', *Psychology of Learning and Motivation*, vol. 60 (2014), pp. 1–33.

A review of research on the impacts of different styles of meditation on emotion and attention Sedlmeier, Peter, et al., 'The psychological effects of meditation: A meta-analysis', *Psychological Bulletin*, vol. 138 (2012), pp. 1139–71.

Relaxation Response causes genomic changes Bhasin, M., et al., 'Relaxation Response Induces Temporal Transcriptome Changes in Energy Metabolism, Insulin Secretion and Inflammatory Pathways', *PLoS One*, 2013; 8(5): e62817.

CHAPTER TWO: EXERCISE YOUR MIND

Hatha yoga and anxiety Streeter, C., et al., 'Effects of Yoga Versus Walking on Mood, Anxiety, and Brain GABA Levels: A Randomized Controlled MRS Study', *Journal of Alternative and Complementary Medicine*, November 2010, 16(11): 1145–52, doi: 10.1089/acm.2010.0007.

Patanjali's 'spokes' (Ashtanga yoga) Sri Swami Satchindananda, *The Yoga Sutras of Patanjali*, new edition (Integral Yoga Publications, 2012).

Exercise, stress resistance and serotonin Greenwood, B. N. and Fleshner, M., 'Exercise, Stress Resistance and Central Serotonergic Systems', *Exercise and Sport Sciences Reviews*, vol. 39 (2011), pp. 140–9.

Exercise and mental abilities Aschwanden, Christie, 'Faster body, faster mind', *New Scientist*, issue 9902, 13 August 2014.

Physical stress levels from work are mediated by exercise Emeny, Rebecca, et al., 'Job strain associated CRP is mediated by leisure time physical activity: Results from the MONICA/KORA study', *Brain, Behavior, and Immunity*, vol. 26 (2012), pp. 1077–84.

Music can make exercise feel better Stork, Matthew J., et al., 'Music Enhances Performance and Perceived Enjoyment of Sprint Interval Exercise', *Medicine and Science in Sports and Exercise* (2014), doi: 10.1249/MSS.0000000000000494.

High-intensity exercise boosts brain cells Schmolesky, Matthew T. [env], Webb, David L. and Hansen, Rodney A., 2, 'The Effects of Aerobic Exercise Intensity and Duration on Levels of Brain-Derived Neurotrophic Factor in Healthy Men', *Journal of Sports Science and Medicine*, vol. 12 (September 2013), pp. 502–11.

The impacts of exercise on stress and mood (and exercise is 'Miracle-Gro' for the brain) Ratey, John J. and Hagerman, Eric, *Spark: How exercise will improve the performance of your brain* (Quercus, 2008).

Exercise helps the brain become more resilient to stress Schoenfeld, T., et al., 'Physical Exercise Prevents Stress-Induced Activation of Granule Neurons and Enhances Local Inhibitory Mechanisms in the Dentate Gyrus', *Journal of Neuroscience*, vol. 33, pp. 7770–7.

Exercise boosts mitochondria in the brain Steiner, J. L., et al., 'Exercise Training Increases Mitochondrial Biogenesis in the Brain', *Journal of Applied Physiology* (4 August 2011), doi: 10.1152/japplphysiol.00343.2011.

Exercise before you go into a stressful situation – it'll protect you Rejeski, W. J., et al., 'Acute exercise: Buffering psycho-social stress responses in women', *Health Psychology*, vol. 11 (1992), pp. 355–62.

Activity pyramid for adults http://extension.missouri.edu/p/n388.

Exercising outdoors has benefits over exercising indoors

Thompson Coon, J., et al., 'Does participating in physical activity in outdoor natural environments have a greater effect on physical and mental wellbeing than physical activity indoors? A systematic review', *Environmental Science and Technology*, vol. 45 (2011), pp. 1761–72, doi: 10.1021/es102947t.

CHAPTER THREE: NOURISH YOUR MIND

The Anatomy of Melancholy, Burton, R. (New York Review Books Classics, 2001).

The Food and Mood Project Survey, http://www.comfirst.org.uk/files/food_mood_survey_summary.pdf.

Gene variations and responses to caffeine Rogers, P. J., et al., 'Association of the Anxiogenic and Alerting Effects of Caffeine with *ADORA2A* and *ADORA1* Polymorphisms and Habitual Level of Caffeine Consumption', *Neuropsychopharmacology*, vol. 35 (2010), pp. 1973–83.

Low-fat dairy improves insulin resistance Rideout, T. C., et al., 'Consumption of low-fat dairy foods for six months improves insulin resistance without adversely affecting lipids or bodyweight in healthy adults: a randomized free-living cross-over study', *Nutrition Journal*, doi:10.1186/1475-2891-12-56.

Depression associated with lower omega-3s Frasure-Smith, N., et al., 'Major depression is associated with lower omega-3 fatty-acid levels in patients with recent acute coronary syndromes', *Biological Psychiatry*, vol. 55 (2004), pp. 891–6.

No clear evidence fish oils protect the brain (in older people) . . . Sydenham, E., et al. 'Omega 3 fatty acid for the prevention of cognitive decline and dementia', Cochrane Database of Systematic Reviews 2012, doi: 10.1002/14651858. CD005379.pub3.

. . . or prevent depression Bloch, M. H. and Hannestad, J., 'Omega-3 fatty acids for the treatment of depression: systematic review and meta-analysis', *Molecular Psychiatry*, vol. 17 (2012), pp. 1272–82, doi: 10.1038/mp.2011.

But is the mix of omega 3s important? Wenner Moyer, M., 'Fish Oil Supplement Research Remains Murky', *Scientific American*, 25 September, 2012.

B vitamin supplements don't help Malouf, M., et al., 'Folic acid with or without vitamin B12 for cognition and dementia', Cochrane Database of Systematic Reviews, 10.1002/14651858.CD004514.

Vitamin D Anglin, R. E. S., et al., 'Vitamin D deficiency and depression in adults: systematic review and meta-analysis', *British Journal of Psychiatry*, vol. 202 (2013), pp. 100–7.

Diet and brain cell production Strangl, D. and Thuret, S., 'Impact of diet on adult hippocampal neurogenesis', *Genes & Nutrition*, vol. 4 (2009), pp. 271–82.

A 'healthy diet' protects against depression many – but see Sanchez-Villegas, A., et al., 'Association of the Mediterranean dietary pattern with the incidence of depression', *Archives of General Psychiatry*, vol. 66 (2009), pp. 1090–8.

The Mediterranean Diet http://www.nhs.uk/livewell/good-food/pages/what-is-a-mediterranean-diet.aspx.

Fasting Young, E., 'Deprive yourself: the real benefits of fasting', *New Scientist*, issue 2891, 22 November 2012.

Low-carb diet in pregnancy makes babies fatter 'Mother's diet during pregnancy alters baby's DNA', BBC News, 18 April 2011, http://www.bbc.co.uk/news/health-13119545.

Pregnancy, diet and epigenetics http://www2.le.ac.uk/departments/genetics/vgec/schoolscolleges/epigenetics_ethics/case-studies/epigenetics-diet-and-pregnancy.

Diet and epigenetic changes McKay. J. A. and Mathers, J. C., 'Diet-induced epigenetic changes and their implications for health', *Acta Physiologica* (Oxf), June 2011, 202(2):103-18, doi: 10.1111/j1748-1716.2011.02278.x.

Nutritional genomics University California, Davis, http://nutrigenomics.ucdavis.edu/?page=information.

Effects of carbs and protein on levels of tryptophan Wurtman, R., et al., 'Effects of normal meals rich in carbohydrates or proteins on plasma tryptophan and tyrosine ratios1,2,3', *American Journal of Clinical Nutrition*, vol. 77 (2003), pp. 128–32.

Potential dangers of 5-HTP supplements Shaw, K. A., Turner, J., Del Mar, C., 'Tryptophan and 5-Hydroxytryptophan for depression', Cochrane Database of Systematic Reviews 2002, issue 1, art. no.: CD003198. DOI: 10.1002/14651858. CD003198; see more at http://summaries.cochrane.org/CD003198/DEPRESSN_tryptophan-and-5-hydroxytryptophan-for-depression#sthash.UHmyUmRQ.dpuf.

Gluten controversy Hamblin, J., 'This is your brain on gluten', *The Atlantic*, 20 December 2013 (http://www.theatlantic.com/health/archive/2013/12/this-is-your-brain-on-gluten/282550/).

FODMAPS and gluten 'The great gluten debate', Geddes, L., *New Scientist*, issue 2977, 9 July 2014.

Changing gut bacteria through diet changes brain function

Tillisch, K., et al., 'Consumption of fermented milk product with probiotic modulates brain activity', *Gastroenterology*, vol. 144 (June 2013), doi: 10.1053/j.gastro.2013.02.043. Epub 2013 Mar 6.

Gut microbes and mental health Bested, et al., 'Intestinal microbiota, probiotics and mental health: from Metchnikoff to modern advances: Part I – autointoxication revisited', *Gut Pathogens*, vol. 5 (2013), p. 5, doi:10.1186/1757-4749-5-5.

'Good bacteria' and anxiety Bercik, P., et al., 'The anxiolytic effect of Bifidobacterium longum NCC3001 involves vagal pathways for gut-brain communication', *Neurogastroenterology & Motility*, vol. 23 (2011), pp. 1132–9.

Prebiotics Roberfroid, M., et al., 'Prebiotic effects: metabolic and health benefits', *British Journal of Nutrition*, vol. 104 (2010), doi: 10.1017/S0007114510003363.

Drink eight glasses of water every day – really? Williams, C., 'Health myths: drink eight glasses of water per day', *New Scientist*, issue 2931, 26 August 2013.

Alcohol and anxiety Davies, M., 'The role of GABAA receptors in mediating the effects of alcohol in the central nervous system', *Journal of Psychiatry & Neuroscience*, July 2003; 28(4): 263–74.

CHAPTER FOUR: REST YOUR MIND

Light therapy for depression Terman, M., *Sleep Medicine Reviews*, vol. 11 (2007), pp. 497–507 (http://www.psychologytoday.com/files/attachments/111044/terman-2007-smr.pdf)

and Martiny, K., et al., 'A 9-Week Randomized Trial Comparing a Chronotherapeutic Intervention (Wake and Light Therapy) to Exercise in Major Depressive Disorder Patients Treated With Duloxetine', *Journal of Clinical Psychiatry*, vol. 73 (2012), pp. 1234–42.

Does light therapy work? The Carlat Psychiatry Report, Psych Central, http://pro.psychcentral.com/light-therapy-for-depression-does-it-work/002903.html#.

Circadian rhythms and depression Li, J. Z., et al., 'Circadian patterns of gene expression in the human brain and disruption in major depressive disorder', PNAS, vol. 110 (2013), pp. 9950–5.

Circadian rhythms and mood McClung, C. A., 'How Might Circadian Rhythms Control Mood? Let Me Count the Ways . . .', *Biological Psychiatry*, vol. 74 (2013). Pp. 242–9 and Terman, M. and Benedetti, F., 'Much Ado About . . . A Moody Clock', *Biological Psychiatry*, vol. 74 (2013), pp. 236–7.

Are you a lark, an owl or a hummingbird? Daily rhythm test, BBC, http://www.bbc.co.uk/science/humanbody/sleep/crt/.

Insomnia and anxiety Franzen, P. L., et al., 'Elevated amygdala activation during voluntary emotion regulation in primary insomnia', 27th Joint Conference of the American Academy of Sleep Medicine and The Sleep Research Society Baltimore, 1–5 June 2013.

Insomnia and memory, Drummond, S., et al., 'Neural Correlates of Working Memory Performance in Primary Insomnia', *Sleep*, http://dx.doi.org/10.5665/sleep.2952.

REM sleep and memory, Nishida, M., et al., 'REM Sleep, Prefrontal Theta, and the Consolidation of Human

Emotional Memory', *Cerebral Cortex*, vol. 19 (2009) pp. 1158–66.

Sleep loss and stress hormones Leproult, R., et al., 'Sleep loss results in an elevation of cortisol levels the next evening', *Sleep*, vol. 20 (1997), pp. 865–70.

Sleep problems in the UK, NHS, 2011, http://www.nhs.uk/News/2011/01January/Pages/sleep-problems-in-the-UK-highlighted.aspx.

Teenagers and school start time, Teensleep (study to investigate the effects of pushing back the school day), http://educationendowmentfoundation.org.uk/projects.

Sleep and the US military Young-McCaughan, S., 'The Role of Sleep in the Health and Resiliency of Military Personnel', www.dtic.mil/cgi-bin/GetTRDoc?AD=ADA582875.

Special Forces soldiers Haglund, M. E., Nestadt, P. S., Cooper, N. S., Southwick, S. M. and Charney, D. S., 'Psychobiological mechanisms of resilience: Relevance to prevention and treatment of stress-related psychopathology', *Development and Psychopathology*, 19:889–920, 2007.

Sleep stages Terman, M. and McMahan, I., Chronotherapy: Resetting Your Inner Clock to Boost Mood, Alertness, and Quality Sleep (Avery, 2012).

CHAPTER FIVE: RETUNE YOUR MIND

Silent reflection – or an electric shock? Wilson, T. D., et al., 'Just think: the challenges of the disengaged mind', *Science*, vol. 345 (2014), pp. 75–7.

'Cognitive Behavioural Therapy (CBT) – How it works',

NHS http://www.nhs.uk/Conditions/Cognitive-behavioural-therapy/Pages/How-does-it-work.aspx.

CBT for social anxiety disorder Mayo-Wilson, E., et al. 'Psychological and pharmacological interventions for social anxiety disorder in adults: a systematic review and network meta-analysis', *The Lancet Psychiatry*, vol. 1 (2014), pp. 368–76.

Stoicism and psychotherapy Robertson, D., *The Philosophy of Cognitive-Behavioural Therapy (CBT)* (Karnac Books, 2010).

Resilience and Dennis Charney's work Southwick, S. and Charney, D., *Resilience – The Science of Mastering Life's Greatest Challenges* (Cambridge University Press, 2012).

Positive psychology – work on optimism, motivation and character Seligman, M., *Flourish* (Nicholas Brealey Publishing, 2011).

James Stockdale Stockdale, J. B., *A Vietnam experience: Ten Years of Reflection* (Hoover Press, 1984)

Compassion training and altruism Weng, H. Y., et al., 'Compassion Training Alters Altruism and Neural Responses to Suffering', *Psychological Science*, vol. 24 (2013), pp. 1171–80.

Compassion meditation and emotion Lutz, A., et al., 'Regulation of the Neural Circuitry of Emotion by Compassion Meditation: Effects of Meditative Expertise', *PLoS One*, vol. 3 (2008), p. e1897.

Vagal tone and health, Porges, S. W. 'The polyvagal perspective', *Biological Psychiatry*, vol. 74 (2007), pp. 116–43.

Vagal tone – my feature for *New Scientist* Young, E., 'Vagus thinking: Meditate your way to better health', *New Scientist*, issue 2925, 18 July 2013.

Vagal tone, positive emotion and social connectedness Kok, B. and Fredrickson, B., 'Upward spirals of the heart: autonomic flexibility, as indexed by vagal tone, reciprocally and prospectively predicts positive emotions and social connectedness', *Biological Psychiatry*, vol. 85 (2010) pp. 432–6.

Loneliness and depression Cacioppo, J. T., 'Loneliness as a specific risk factor for depressive symptoms: Cross-sectional and longitudinal analyses', *Psychology and Aging*, vol. 21 (2006) pp. 140–51.

Social relationships and risk of death Holt-Lunstad, J., et al., 'Social Relationships and Mortality Risk: A Meta-anyalytic Review', *PLoS Medicine*, vol. 7 (2010), p. e1000316.

It's how lonely you feel; how to improve relationships Cacioppo, J. T. and Patrick, W., *Loneliness: Human Nature and the Need for Social Connection* (W. W. Norton, 2009).

We mistakenly think other people don't want to talk to us Epley, N. and Schroeder, J., 'Mistakenly Seeking Solitude', *Journal of Experimental Psychology*, vol. 143 (October 2014) pp. 1980–99.

CHAPTER SIX: TOUGHEN YOUR MIND

Ben Ainslie's best race Interview with G. Pawson, *Yachts & Yachting*, March 2012 (http://www.yachtsandyachting.co.uk/sailing-stars/ben-ainslies-best-race/).

'Are Alzheimer's and diabetes the same disease?' Griggs, J., *New Scientist*, issue 2945, 28 November 2013.

Willpower: Why Self-Control is the Secret to Success

Baumeister, R. and Tierney, J., *Willpower: Rediscovering Our Greatest Strength* (Penguin, 2012).

How to cultivate grit Duckworth, A., 'Can perseverance be taught', August 2013 – www.bigquestionsonline.com/print/227.

Angela Duckworth's work on grit Duckworth, A., et al., 'Grit: Perseverance and Passion for Long-Term Goals', *Journal of Personality and Social Psychology*, vol. 92 (2007), pp. 1087–101 and The Duckworth Lab http://sites.sas.upenn.edu/duckworth.

12-Item Grit Scale Duckworth, A., http://www.sas.upenn.edu/~duckwort/images/12-item%20Grit%20Scale.05312011.pdf.

Please God, don't let me die Brymer, E. and Schweitzer, R., 'Extreme sports are good for your health: A phenomenological understanding of fear and anxiety in extreme sport', *Journal of Health Psychology*, 18 (2013), 477–87, doi: 10.1177/1359105312446770. Highlighted by the British Psychological Society's Research Digest, 8 May 2013.

CHAPTER SEVEN: KEEP YOUR SENSES IN MIND

Beat influences walking pace Leman, M., et al., 'Activating and Relaxing Music Entrains the Speed of Beat Synchronized Walking', *PLoS One*, vol. 8, pe67932, doi: 10.1371/journal.pone.0067932.

Music and stress levels Labbé, E., et al., 'Coping with stress:

the effectiveness of different types of music', *Applied Psychophysiology and Biofeedback*, vol. 32 (2007), pp. 163–8.

Music can generate emotion Logeswaran, N. and Bhattacharya, J., 'Crossmodal transfer of emotion by music', *Neuroscience Letters*, vol. 455 (2009), pp. 129–33 and Kreutz, G., et al., 'Using music to induce emotions: Influences of musical preference and absorption', *Psychology of Music*, vol. 36 (2007), pp. 101–26.

Listening to music engages the brain's emotional regions Brown, S., 'Passive music listening spontaneously engages limbic and paralimbic systems', *Neuroreport*, vol. 15 (2004), pp. 2033–7.

The impact of lyrics Brattico, E., et al., 'A Functional MRI Study of Happy and Sad Emotions in Music with and without Lyrics', *Frontiers in Psychology*, vol. 2 (2011), doi: 10.3389/fpsyg.2011.00308.

Pleasurable music activates the reward centre Salimpoor, V. N., et al., 'Anatomically distinct dopamine release during anticipation and experience of peak emotion to music', *Nature Neuroscience*, vol. 14 (2011), pp. 257–62.

'Take two Joni Mitchells' 'Music as medicine has huge potential, study suggests', CBC News, 1 April 2013, http://www.cbc.ca/news/health/music-as-medicine-has-huge-potential-study-suggests-1.1359045.

Sad music can make you feel better Tartuffi, L., et al., 'The Paradox of Music-Evoked Sadness: An Online Survey', *PLoS One*, vol. 9, e110490.

Massage and immune function Rapaport, M., et al., 'A Preliminary Study of the Effects of a Single Session of

Swedish Massage on Hypothalamic – Pituitary – Adrenal and Immune Function in Normal Individuals', vol. 16 (2010), pp. 1079–88.

Touch relieves existential angst Koole, S. L., et al., 'Embodied Terror Management: Interpersonal Touch Alleviates Existential Concerns Among Individuals With Low Self-Esteem', *Psychological Science*, vol. 25 (2014), pp. 30–7.

Sex is good for the brain Glasper, E. R. and Gould, E., 'Sexual experience restores age-related decline in adult neurogenesis and hippocampal function', *Hippocampus*, vol. 23 (2013), pp. 303–12.

Dogs are great Vormbrock, J. K. and Grossberg, J. M., 'Cardiovascular effects of human-pet dog interactions', *Journal of Behavioral Medicine*, vol. 11 (1988), pp. 509–17.

Families who get a dog socialise more Paul, E. S. and Serpell, J. A., 'Obtaining a new pet dog: Effects on middle childhood children and their families', *Applied Animal Behaviour Science*, vol. 47 (1996), pp. 17–29.

Oxytocin and pets Beetz, A., et al., 'Psychosocial and Psychophysiological Effects of Human-Animal Interactions: The Possible Role of Oxytocin', *Frontiers in Psychology*, vol. 3 (2012), doi: 10.3389/fpsyg.2012.00234.

Décor, architecture and psychological wellbeing de Botton, A., *The Architecture of Happiness* (Penguin, 2007).

Chromotherapists believe colours can cure diseases Yousuf Azeemi, S. T. and Raza, M., 'A Critical Analysis of Chromotherapy and Its Scientific Evolution', *Evidence-Based Complementary and Alternative Medicine*, vol. 2 (2005), pp. 481–8, http://dx.doi.org/10.1093/ecam/neh137.

REFERENCES

Blue and red – their effects on mental tests Mehta, R. and Zhu, R., 'Blue or Red? Exploring the Effect of Color on Cognitive Task Performances', *Science*, vol. 323 (2009), pp. 1226–9.

Red makes women more attractive Elliot, A. J. and Niesta, D., 'Romantic red: Red enhances men's attraction to women', *Journal of Personality and Social Psychology*, vol. 95 (2008), pp. 1150–64.

Women are more likely to wear red when they're fertile Beall, A. T. and Tracy, J. L. 'Women Are More Likely to Wear Red or Pink at Peak Fertility', *Psychological Science*, vol. 24 (2013), pp. 1837–41.

The effect of red on performance Elliot, A., et al., 'Color and psychological functioning: The effect of red on performance attainment', *Journal of Experimental Psychology: General*, vol. 136, pp. 154–68.

The effect of red sports strips Hill, R. A. and Barton, R. A., 'Psychology: Red enhances human performance in contests', *Nature*, vol. 435 (2005), p. 293.

Green and creativity Lichtenfeld, S., et al., 'Fertile Green: Green Facilitates Creative Performance', *Personality and Social Psychology Bulletin*, vol. 38 (2012), pp. 784–97.

Matching mood to colour Carruthers, H., et al., 'The Manchester Color Wheel: development of a novel way of identifying color choice and its validation in healthy, anxious and depressed individuals', *BMC Medical Research Methodology*, vol. 10 (2010), p. 12.

Emotional states conveyed in human scent signals de Groot, J. H., et al., 'Chemosignals communicate human emotions', *Psychological Science*, vol. 23 (2012), pp. 1417–24.

Lavender's anti-anxiety effects Shuwald, A. M., et al., 'Lavender Oil – Potent Anxiolytic Properties via Modulating Voltage Dependent Calcium Channels', *PLoS One*, vol. 8 (2013), p. e59998, doi:10.1371/journal.pone.0059998.

More on lavender's biological actions Re, L., et al., 'Linalool modifies the nicotinic receptor-ion channel kinetics at the mouse neuromuscular junction', *Pharmacological Research*, vol. 42 (2000), pp. 177–82.

Lemon oil – anti-stress and anti-depressant effects (in rats) Komiya, M., et al., 'Lemon oil vapor causes an anti-stress effect via modulating the 5-HT and DA activities in mice', *Behavioural Brain Research*, vol. 172 (2006), pp. 240–9.

Vanillin and the rat brain Jinyong, X., et al., 'Vanillin-induced amelioration of depression-like behaviors in rats by modulating monoamine neurotransmitters in the brain', *Psychiatry Research*, 2014, doi:10.1016/j.psychres.2014.11.056.

Vanillin and mood Seubert, J., et al., 'Mood Induction with Olfactory Stimuli Reveals Differential Affective Responses in Males and Females', *Chemical Senses*, vol. 34 (2008), pp. 77–84.

Peppermint and alertness Moss, M., et al., 'Modulation of cognitive performance and mood by aromas of peppermint and ylang-ylang', *International Journal of Neuroscience*, vol. 118 (2008), pp. 59–77.

CHAPTER EIGHT: CHANGE YOUR MIND

Undiagnosed prediabetes Diabetes UK: Warning about the one in seventy people who have undiagnosed Type 2 diabetes: http://www.diabetes.org.uk/about_us/News_Landing_Page/warning-about-the-one-in-70-people-who-have-undiagnosed-diabetes/

INDEX

INDEX

yellow kite

books to help you live a good life

Join the conversation and tell
us how you live a #goodlife

🐦 @yellowkitebooks
📘 YellowKiteBooks
📌 Yellow Kite Books
📷 YellowKiteBooks